# The
# Core Knowledge™
# Series

## Resource Books for Children
## from Year 1 to Year 6

Lianne 5.1

# PRAISE FOR THE CORE KNOWLEDGE UK SERIES

'The Core Knowledge Sequence puts knowledge back into primary education. Rich in content, challenging and with clear progression and continuity, it offers an excellent framework to ensure that pupils leave primary school with solid foundations for future learning.'

– Peter Lawson, Head of Primary, Grindon Hall Christian School

'Our recent Core Knowledge lessons on the Arctic have provided our children with a wealth of understanding. The lessons give children the facts, then we are free to create an enjoyable and engaging learning experience. Core Knowledge fuels our pupils' desire to learn more about the world around them.'

– Emma Greaves, Reception Teacher, West London Free School Primary

'It is vital that children receive a solid body of knowledge when they are at primary school because it allows them to expand their comprehension and access a wider field of learning. The Core Knowledge approach does just that. I cannot recommend it enough.'

– Matthew Laban, Headteacher, Kingfisher Hall Primary Academy, London

'Creativity, the arts and design are crucial to the environment and life of every citizen. They should occupy a central place in the curriculum at both primary and secondary levels. The new series published by Civitas, giving examples of how the arts and creativity can play a part in the education of every child, is a real contribution to the teaching of these subjects in all our schools.'

– Sir Nicholas Serota, Director of Tate

'A strong foundation of knowledge gained in the earliest years of education is such an important asset for children, sparking their imagination and providing the cornerstone for their future learning. I welcome the aim of the Core Knowledge books to do just that and I am sure that they will be valued by many parents wishing to help their children to do well at school.'

– Munira Mirza, Deputy Mayor for Education and Culture of London

# What Your Year 5 Child Needs to Know

## PREPARING YOUR CHILD
## FOR A LIFETIME OF LEARNING

*Edited by* E. D. HIRSCH, JR

*General Editors for the Civitas UK edition:*
ROBERT WHELAN & TANYA LUBICZ-NAWROCKA

Original illustrations for this edition by MARK BEECH and GAIL McINTOSH

Published by

Civitas
55 Tufton Street
London SW1P 3QL

ISBN: 978-1-906837-27-3

Book design and layout by Luke Jefford (www.lukejefford.com)

Printed in Great Britain by Berforts Group Ltd, Stevenage, SG1 2BH

## Acknowledgements: US edition

This series has depended on the help, advice and encouragement of two thousand people. Some of those singled out here already know the depth of our gratitude; others may be surprised to find themselves thanked publicly for help they gave quietly and freely for the sake of the enterprise alone. To helpers named and unnamed we are deeply grateful.

*Editor-in-Chief of the Core Knowledge Series:* E. D. Hirsch, Jr

*Text Editors:* Souzanne A. Wright, Mathew Davis, Susan Tyler Hitchcock, John Holdren

*Editorial Assistance:* Skyler Breeden, Peter Locke, Kathleen E. Mason, James Miller, William Rowland, Charles Shields

*Art and Photo Research:* Matthew Davis, Susan Tyler Hitchcock, Peter Locke, Emily E. Reddick, Jeanne Siler

*Writers:* This revised edition involved a careful reconsideration and sometimes re-use of material in the first edition of this book, as well as others in the series. In that spirit, we acknowledge all of the writers and editors who contributed to either edition. Writers for the revised edition: Rebecca Beall Barnes (music), Kathryn Corrigan (language and literature), Victoria Crenson (science), Matthew Davis, Lisa Goff (art), Susan Tyler Hitchcock, Anne Isaacs (American history), Michael Marshall (language and literature), Deirdre McAfee (world history), Robert Watkins (science), Souzanne A. Wright (maths). Writers for the original edition: Nancy Bryson (science), Marie Hawthorne (science), John Hirsch (maths), John Holdren (history, language and literature), Pamela C. Johnson (history and geography), Blair Longwood Jones (literature), Bethanne H. Kelly (literature), Elaine Moran (visual arts), A. Brooke Russell (geography, science), Peter Ryan (music, language and literature),  Lindley Shutz (language and literature), Helen Storey (language and literature)

*Advisers on Subject Matter:* Marilyn Jager Adams, Karima-Diane Alavi, Richard Anderson, Linda Bevilacqua, Judith Birsh, Wayne Bishop, Louis A. Bloomfield, Cheryl Cannard, Holly DeSantis, Barbara Foorman, Paul Gagnon, David Geary, Andrew Gleason, Oleg Grabar, Charles F. Gritzner, Ted Hirsch, H. Wiley Hitchcock, Henry Holt, Blair Jones, Connie Juel, Eric Karell, Morton Keller, Joseph Kett, Charles Kimball, Mary Beth Klee, David Klein, Barbara Lachman, Karen Lang, Michael Lynch, Diana McGuiness, Sheelagh McGurn, Maurie McInnis, John F. Miller, Joseph C. Miller, Jean Osborn, Duana Osheim, Vikas Pershad, Robin Poynor, Margaret Redd, Bradly W. Reed, Donna Rehorn, Marion Roberts, Gilbert Roy, Nancy Royal, Mark Rush, Abdulaziz Sachedina, Gayle Sherwood, Janet Smith, Ralph Smith, Keith Stanovich, Paula Stanovich, Jeremy Stern, Nancy Strother, David

Summers, Nancy Summers, Marlene Thompson, James Trefil, Patricia Wattenmaker, Nancy Wayne, Christiana Whittington, Lois Williams, Dorothy Wong

*Advisers on Multiculturalism:* Minerva Allen, Barbara Carey, Frank de Varona, Mick Fedullo, Dorothy Fields, Elizabeth Fox-Genovese, Marcia Galli, Dan Garner, Henry Louis Gates, Cheryl Kulas, Joseph C. Miller, Gerry Raining Bird, Connie Rocha, Dorothy Small, Sharon Stewart-Peregoy, Sterling Stuckey, Marlene Walking Bear, Lucille Watahomigie, Ramona Wilson

*Advisers on Elementary Education:* Joseph Adelson, Isobel Beck, Paul Bell, Carl Bereiter, David Bjorklund, Constance Jones, Elizabeth LaFuze, J. P. Lutz, Sandra Scarr, Nancy Stein, Phyllis Wilkin, plus all the conferees at the March 1990 conference where the first draft of the curriculum was developed.

*Schools:* Special thanks to the schools – too many to list here – that have offered advice and suggestions for improving the Core Knowledge Sequence.

*Benefactors:* The Brown Foundation, The Challenge Foundation, Mrs. E. D. Hirsch, Sr, The Walton Family Foundation.

Our grateful acknowledgment to these persons does not imply that we have taken their (sometimes conflicting) advice in every case, or that each of them endorses all aspects of this project. Responsibility for final decisions must rest with the editors alone. Suggestions for improvements are very welcome, and we wish to thank in advance those who send advice for revising and improving this series.

## Acknowledgements: UK edition

*General Editors of the UK edition:* Robert Whelan & Tanya Lubicz-Nawrocka
*Contributing Editor of the UK edition:* Nigel Williams
*Editorial Assistant:* Catherine Green
*Author of British History:* Robert Peal
*Design and typesetting of the UK edition:* Luke Jefford
*Original illustrations for the UK edition:* Mark Beech and Gail McIntosh
*Maps:* Jo Moore, Ed Dovey, Paul Collicutt and Mark Otton
*Owl illustrations:* Mark Otton

Compiling the UK edition of a book that has already become an established classic in the United States has been both a privilege and a challenge. Our first thanks must go to E.D. Hirsch, Jr, Linda Bevilacqua and the team at the Core Knowledge Foundation for sharing with us the fruits of their labours over so many years. We fully share their view that all children deserve access to a first-class education, and we hope that the Civitas edition of the Core Knowledge texts will do as much for children in the UK as the US edition has done for thousands of children in the US and abroad.

Many people have helped us. We are especially grateful for the assistance given to the project by Anne Anderson in Visual Arts; Donald Kernohan and colleagues at Grindon Hall Christian School in Science; Andrew Phemister in British and European History and Geography; Sean Lang, Chris Gray, Margaret Lenton and Denis MacEoin in History; Chris Cull in Music; Peter Clarke in Mathematics; and Matthew Robinson in Language and Literature. Marilyn Brocklehurst of the Norfolk Children's Book Centre shared her passion for children's books and helped us to find titles for the suggested resources sections.

We are grateful to Gail McIntosh for permission to reproduce her excellent original illustrations from the US edition and for creating new illustrations for us; to Paul Collicutt for adding the dimension of colour to illustrations that were originally black and white and for creating new illustrations; and to all those generous authors, illustrators and copyright owners who have allowed us to reproduce material for this book because they share our passion for bringing to children the very best in words and images.

Thanks to our colleagues past and present at Civitas for their help, especially Emma Lennard, Curriculum Project Director; Annaliese Briggs for help with the UK Sequence; and Janet Russell for help with the text. Special thanks are due to Anastasia de Waal, Head of Family and Education at Civitas, for her help and guidance.

# A Note to Teachers

Throughout the book, we have addressed the suggested activities and explanations to 'parents', since you as teachers know your students and will have ideas about how to use the content of this book in relation to the lessons and activities you plan. To discuss using Core Knowledge UK materials in your school, please contact Civitas at 55 Tufton Street, London SW1P 3QL, 020 7799 6677.

*Email:* coreknowledge@civitas.org.uk

# Companion Website

There is a wealth of additional activities, readings and resources to supplement this book available on the Core Knowledge UK website. This includes a Teacher's Portal with teaching ideas and resources, curriculum planning documents and images from the book that are available for use by teachers and home educators. Please visit our website at:

www.coreknowledge.org.uk

# About the Editor

**E.D. Hirsch, Jr** is a professor at the University of Virginia and the author of *The Schools We Need* and the bestselling *Cultural Literacy* and *The Dictionary of Cultural Literacy*. He and his wife, Polly, live in Charlottesville, Virginia, where they raised their three children.

E. D. Hirsch, Jr receives no renumeration for editing the series nor any other renumeration from the Core Knowledge Foundation.

# Contents

## Language and Literature

## History and Geography

# Visual Arts

# Music

# Mathematics

# Science

# Foreword to the UK Edition of the Core Knowledge Series

This is the fifth in a series of books for parents who want to help their children do well at school. It describes what every child should aim to have learnt by the end of the school year. It is not a description of everything that could be known but rather a guide to the knowledge that children will need to advance to the next stage of their education. Nor is it primarily a textbook, although it could be used as such – along with other teaching resources – if schools wish.

The Core Knowledge series gives parents the tools to judge how effectively their children are being taught. And it provides teachers with clear aims that can be shared with parents, thereby enlisting them in the common cause of getting the best from every child.

Why publish a British version of a book originally designed for American children? For the last 50 years in both Britain and America there has been no consensus about how and what children should be taught. Sometimes knowledge was dismissed as mere 'rote learning', which was contrasted unfavourably with 'critical thinking skills'. Others argued that education should be 'child centred' not 'subject centred'. Professor Hirsch, who inspired the Core Knowledge series, was among the first to see that the retreat from knowledge was misguided. Above all, he showed that to compare 'knowledge' with 'thinking skills' was to make a false contrast. They are not mutually exclusive alternatives. Thinking skills can be 'knowledge-rich' or 'knowledge-lite'. The purpose of a good education is to teach children how to think clearly – to see through dubious reasoning, to avoid being conned, to learn how to question their own assumptions, to discover how to be objective or to argue a case with clarity. Knowledge does not get in the way of reasoning: it's what we reason with.

The Core Knowledge approach has six main strengths.

● It helps parents to bring out the best in their children. It provides a guide to what young people should be learning and helps parents decide on the school best suited to their child.

● It helps teachers. By providing clear expectations that are shared with parents, teachers are better able to benefit every child. Schools are always at their best when parents and teachers work together.

● It helps children to learn on their own initiative. The books are written in language suitable for each year group, so that children can read alone or with their parents.

● It provides more equal opportunities for everyone. Some children do not receive effective support at home, perhaps because some of us did not ourselves get the best education. A good school can do much to make up for lost ground and the Core Knowledge series is designed for this very task. The books describe what every child can learn if given the chance. What's more, many parents find that they learn as much as their children!

● It encourages social cohesion. Britain today has more cultures, ethnic groups and religions than 50 years ago. If we all share in a common stock of knowledge, social solidarity based on mutual respect for our legitimate differences is more likely.

● It strengthens democracy. A free and democratic society depends on the mass of people being well-informed. We often say that modern societies are 'knowledge-based'. It's true. People who do not share in the knowledge that is regularly used by television news programmes or in our newspapers are at risk of being misled.

We are keen to work with teachers who share our ideals and who hope to play a leading part in developing this new curriculum in Britain. In co-operation with teachers, we have been evolving lesson plans and teacher resource guides, which are available on our website at www.coreknowledge.org.uk.

*David G. Green*
Director of Civitas

# Introduction to the UK Edition of the Core Knowledge Series for Year 5

The concerns that led Professor Hirsch and others to set up the Core Knowledge Foundation in the USA in 1986 are shared by many in Britain. Civitas has acquired direct experience of the problem through its network of supplementary schools. Beginning with a group of children in the East End of London in 2005, Civitas now runs 22 supplementary schools for over 600 children in different parts of the UK. The children attend once a week, either on Saturdays or after school, for help with English and maths. The children are, for the most part, attending full-time schools in areas with higher-than-average indicators of social deprivation, where academic outcomes are not the best in the country. Some children join supplementary schools at the age of seven, eight or even older, unable to read properly and unable to handle simple addition and subtraction. Our approach in the Civitas Schools has been to employ dedicated teachers with high expectations and a commitment to providing solid learning foundations. Children are assessed annually and it has become quite usual to see them make two or three years of progress in their reading and maths ages over the course of one calendar year.

The concepts that Professor Hirsch mentions in his General Introduction such as 'critical thinking' and 'learning to learn' have been just as prevalent in the UK's schools, where the curriculum has become less knowledge-based and more focused on attaining 'skills', as if the two things can be separated. The acquisition of skills requires knowledge, and a knowledge-poor curriculum is one that condemns pupils – especially children from less advantaged backgrounds – to remain outside the mainstream of attainment and fulfilment. The Core Knowledge Foundation believes that all children should be able to unlock the library of the world's literature; to comprehend the world around them; to know where they stand (literally) on the globe; and to realise the heritage that the history of their country has bestowed on them.

Making a reality of this ideal has been the outstanding achievement of the Core Knowledge Foundation in the hundreds of schools across the USA where its curriculum is being taught, and it is why we so admire the work of Professor Hirsch and his colleagues at the Core Knowledge Foundation.

As Professor Hirsch explains in his General Introduction, the project operates within the overarching framework of the Core Knowledge Sequence, produced by dozens of educators over a gestational period of several years. To bring this sequence into the classroom or the home, the Sequence is fleshed out by a book for each year group. We at Civitas were honoured and delighted to be entrusted by the Core Knowledge Foundation with the task of adapting the books for teachers, parents and pupils in the UK. This has entailed some changes to reflect differences between our cultures. For example, Visual Arts looks at Hogarth's prints and Chippendale's chairs; our songs include British military airs like 'Heart of Oak' and Scottish ballads like the 'Skye Boat Song'; British musical nomenclature has been used in the Music chapter and metric rather than imperial measures take precedence in Science. We have revised the lists of resources to include books and educational materials readily available in the UK. However, for the most part, the US text has been left intact – because knowledge is universal!

We have adapted the Core Knowledge Sequence for the UK and it is freely available online at http://www.coreknowledge.org.uk/sequence.php. This will enable parents and teachers to understand how the grammar of each subject is unrolled over six years of primary school education. The UK Sequence follows the US Sequence very closely, with a few obvious changes. Maths has been slightly revised to reflect the demands of the National Curriculum; and British history and geography replace American. (American history and geography will be covered under World History and Geography.)

We share the view of the Core Knowledge Foundation that knowledge is best conveyed through subjects, and so we have followed their division of each book into chapters covering Language and Literature, History and Geography, Visual Arts, Music, Mathematics and Science. We will be producing volumes for each year group up to Year 6, and these will tie in with the UK version of the Core Knowledge Sequence.

In most states of the USA, children start their full-time education in Kindergarten when they are five rising six, whereas in the UK children of that age would be starting Year 1, having already spent a year in Reception. For this reason, the first book in Civitas Core Knowledge UK series, *What Your Year 1 Child Needs to Know*, represented, with small alterations, the text of *What Your Kindergartner Needs to Know*. The second book, *What Your Year 2 Child Needs to Know*, followed the text of the next book in the US series, *What Your First Grader Needs to Know*. This volume follows the text of *What Your Fourth Grader Needs To Know*, first published in the USA in 1992 and revised in 2004.

*Robert Whelan*
General Editor, Civitas Core Knowledge UK Project

# General Introduction to the Core Knowledge Series

## I. WHAT IS YOUR CHILD LEARNING IN SCHOOL?

A parent of identical twins sent me a letter in which she expressed concern that her children, who are in the same grade in the same school, are being taught completely different things. How can this be? Because they are in different classrooms; because the teachers in these classrooms have only the vaguest guidelines to follow; in short, because the school, like many in the United States, lacks a definite, specific curriculum.

Many parents would be surprised if they were to examine the curriculum of their child's elementary school. Ask to see your school's curriculum. Does it spell out, in clear and concrete terms, a core of specific content and skills all children at a particular grade level are expected to learn by the end of the school year?

Many curricula speak in general terms of vaguely defined skills, processes and attitudes, often in an abstract, pseudo-technical language that calls, for example, for children to 'analyse patterns and data', or 'investigate the structure and dynamics of living systems', or 'work cooperatively in a group'. Such vagueness evades the central question: what is your child learning in school? It places unreasonable demands upon teachers, and often results in years of schooling marred by repetitions and gaps. Yet another unit on dinosaurs or 'pioneer days'. *Charlotte's Web* for the third time. 'You've never heard of the Bill of Rights?' 'You've never been taught how to add two fractions with unlike denominators?'

When identical twins in two classrooms of the same school have few academic experiences in common, that is cause for concern. When teachers in that school do not know what children in other classrooms are learning in the same grade level, much less in earlier and later grades, they cannot reliably predict that children will come prepared with a shared core of knowledge and skills. For an elementary school to be successful, teachers need a common vision of what they want their students to know and be able to do. They need to have *clear, specific learning goals*, as well as the sense of mutual accountability that comes from shared commitment to helping all children achieve those goals. Lacking both specific goals and mutual accountability, too many schools exist in a state of curricular incoherence, one result of which is that they fall far short of developing the full potential of our children. To address this problem, I started the non-profit Core Knowledge Foundation in 1986. This book and its companion volumes in the Core Knowledge Series are designed to give parents, teachers – and through them, children – a guide to clearly defined learning goals in the form of a carefully sequenced body of knowledge, based upon the specific content guidelines developed by the Core Knowledge Foundation (see below, 'The Consensus Behind the Core Knowledge Sequence').

Core Knowledge is an attempt to define, in a coherent and sequential way, a body of widely used knowledge taken for granted by competent writers and speakers in the United States. Because this knowledge is taken for granted rather than being explained when it is used, it forms a necessary foundation for the higher-order reading, writing and thinking skills that children need for academic and vocational success. The universal attainment of such knowledge should be a central aim of curricula in our elementary schools, just as it is currently the aim in all world-class educational systems.

For reasons explained in the next section, making sure that all young children in the United States possess a core of shared knowledge is a necessary step in developing a first-rate educational system.

# II. WHY CORE KNOWLEDGE IS NEEDED

Learning builds on learning: children (and adults) gain new knowledge only by building on what they already know. It is essential to begin building solid foundations of knowledge in the early grades when children are most receptive because, for the vast majority of children, academic deficiencies from the first six grades can *permanently* impair the success of later learning. Poor performance of American students in middle and high school can be traced to shortcomings inherited from elementary schools that have not imparted to children the knowledge and skills they need for further learning.

All of the highest-achieving and most egalitarian elementary school systems in the world (such as those in Sweden, France and Japan) teach their children a specific core of knowledge in each of the first six grades, thus enabling all children to enter each new grade with a secure foundation for further learning. It is time American schools did so as well, for the following reasons:

## (1) Commonly shared knowledge makes schooling more effective.

We know that the one-on-one tutorial is the most effective form of schooling, in part because a parent or teacher can provide tailor-made instruction for the individual child. But in a non-tutorial situation – in, for example, a typical classroom with twenty-five or more students – the instructor cannot effectively impart new knowledge to all the students unless each one shares the background knowledge that the lesson is being built upon.

Consider this scenario: in third grade, Ms Franklin is about to begin a unit on early explorers – Columbus, Magellan and others. In her class she has some students who were in Mr Washington's second-grade class last year and some students who were in Ms Johnson's second-grade class. She also has a few students who have moved in from other towns. As Ms Franklin begins the unit on explorers, she asks the children to look at a globe and use their fingers to trace a route across the Atlantic Ocean from Europe to North America. The students who had Mr Washington look blankly at her: they didn't learn that last year. The students who had Ms Johnson, however, eagerly point to the proper places on the globe, while two of the students who came from other towns pipe up and say, 'Columbus and Magellan again? We did that last year.'

When all the students in a class *do* share the relevant background knowledge, a classroom can begin to approach the effectiveness of a tutorial. Even when some children in a class do not have elements of the knowledge they were supposed to acquire in previous grades, the existence of a specifically defined core makes it possible for the teacher or parent to identify and fill the gaps, thus giving all students a chance to fulfill their potential in later grades.

## (2) Commonly shared knowledge makes schooling more fair and democratic.

When all the children who enter a grade can be assumed to share some of the same building blocks of knowledge, and when the teacher knows exactly what those building blocks are, then all the students are empowered to learn. In our current system, children from disadvantaged backgrounds too often suffer from unmerited low expectations that translate into watered-down curricula. But if we specify the core of knowledge that all children should share, then we can guarantee equal access to that knowledge and compensate for the academic advantages some students are offered at home. In a Core Knowledge school, *all* children enjoy the benefits of important, challenging knowledge that will provide the foundation for successful later learning.

## (3) Commonly shared knowledge helps create cooperation and solidarity in our schools and nation.

Diversity is a hallmark and strength of our nation. American classrooms are usually made up of students from a variety of cultural backgrounds, and those different cultures should be honoured by all students. At the same time, education should create a school-based culture that is common and welcoming to all because it includes knowledge of many cultures and gives all students, no matter what their background, a common foundation for understanding our cultural diversity.

In the next section, I will describe the steps taken by the Core Knowledge Foundation to develop a model of the commonly shared knowledge our children need (which forms the basis for this series of books).

# III. THE CONSENSUS BEHIND THE CORE KNOWLEDGE SEQUENCE

The content in this and other volumes in the Core Knowledge Series is based on a document called the *Core Knowledge Sequence*, a grade-by-grade sequence of specific content guidelines in history, geography, mathematics, science, language arts and fine arts. The *Sequence* is not meant to outline the whole of the school curriculum; rather, it offers specific guidelines to knowledge that can reasonably be expected to make up about *half* of any school's curriculum, thus leaving ample room for local requirements and emphases. Teaching a common core of knowledge, such as that articulated in the *Core Knowledge Sequence*, is compatible with a variety of instructional methods and additional subject matters.

The *Core Knowledge Sequence* is the result of a long process of research and consensus building undertaken by the Core Knowledge Foundation. Here is how we achieved the consensus behind the *Core Knowledge Sequence*.

First we analysed the many reports issued by state departments of education and by professional organisations – such as the National Council of Teachers of Mathematics and the American Association for the Advancement of Science – that recommend general outcomes for elementary and secondary education. We also tabulated the knowledge and skills through grade six specified in the successful educational systems of several other countries, including France, Japan, Sweden and West Germany.

In addition, we formed an advisory board on multiculturalism that proposed a specific knowledge of diverse cultural traditions that American children should all share as part of their school-based common culture. We sent the resulting materials to three independent groups of teachers, scholars and scientists around the country, asking them to create a master list of the knowledge children should have by the end of grade six. About 150 teachers (including college professors, scientists and administrators) were involved in this initial step.

These items were amalgamated into a master plan, and further groups of teachers and specialists were asked to agree on a grade-by-grade sequence of the items. That sequence was then sent to some one hundred educators and specialists who participated in a national conference that was called to hammer out a working agreement on an appropriate core of knowledge for the first six grades.

This important meeting took place in March 1990. The conferees were elementary school teachers, curriculum specialists, scientists, science writers, officers of national organisations, representatives of ethnic groups, district superintendents and school principals from across the country. A total of twenty-four working groups decided on revisions in the *Core Knowledge Sequence*. The resulting provisional *Sequence* was further fine-tuned during a year of implementation at a pioneering school, Three Oaks Elementary in Lee County, Florida.

In only a few years, many more schools – urban and rural, rich and poor, public and private – joined in the effort to teach Core Knowledge. Based largely on suggestions from these schools, the *Core Knowledge Sequence* was revised in 1995: separate guidelines were added for kindergarten, and a few topics in other grades were added, omitted or moved from one grade to another, in order to create an even more coherent sequence for learning. Revised editions of the books in the Core Knowledge Series reflect the revisions in the *Sequence*. Based on the principle of learning from experience, the Core Knowledge Foundation continues to work with schools and advisors to 'fine-tune' the *Sequence*, and is also conducting research that will lead to the publication of guidelines for grades seven and eight, as well as for preschool. (*The Core Knowledge Sequence UK* can be downloaded from the Civitas Core Knowledge UK website www.coreknowledge.org.uk/sequence.php)

# IV. THE NATURE OF THIS SERIES

The books in this series are designed to give a convenient and engaging introduction to the knowledge specified in the *Core Knowledge Sequence*. These are resource books, addressed primarily to parents, but which we hope will be useful tools for both parents and teachers. These books are not intended to replace the local curriculum or school textbooks, but rather to serve as aids to help children gain some of the important knowledge they will need to make progress in school and be effective in society.

Although we have made these books as accessible and useful as we can, parents and teachers should understand that they are not the only means by which the *Core Knowledge Sequence* can be imparted. The books represent a single version of the possibilities inherent in the *Sequence*, and a first step in the Core Knowledge reform effort. We hope that publishers will be stimulated to offer educational software, games, alternative books and other imaginative vehicles based on the *Core Knowledge Sequence*.

These books are not textbooks or workbooks, though when appropriate they do suggest a variety of activities you can do with your child. In these books, we address your child directly, and occasionally ask questions for him or her to think about. The earliest books in the series are intended to be read aloud to children. Even as children become able to read the books on their own, we encourage parents to help their children read more actively by reading along with them and talking about what they are reading. You and your child can read the sections of this book in any order, depending on your child's interests or depending on the topics your child is studying in school, which this book may complement or reinforce. You can skip from section to section and re-read as much as your child likes.

We encourage you to think of this book as a guidebook that opens the way to many paths you and your child can explore. These paths may lead to the library, to many other good books and, if possible, to plays, museums, concerts and other opportunities for knowledge and enrichment. In short, this guidebook recommends places to visit and describes what is important in those places, but only you and your child can make the actual visit, travel the streets and climb the steps.

# V. WHAT YOU CAN DO TO HELP IMPROVE EDUCATION

The first step for parents and teachers who are committed to reform is to be sceptical about oversimplified slogans like 'critical thinking' and 'learning to learn'. Such slogans are everywhere and, unfortunately for our schools, their partial insights have been elevated to the level of universal truths. For example: 'What students learn is not important; rather, we must teach students to learn *how* to learn.' 'The child, not the academic subject, is the true focus of education.' 'Do not impose knowledge on children before they are developmentally ready to receive it.' 'Do not bog children down in mere facts, but rather, teach critical-thinking skills.' Who has not heard these sentiments, so admirable and humane, and – up to a point – so true? But these positive sentiments in favour of 'thinking skills' and 'higher understanding' have been turned into negative sentiments against the teaching of important knowledge. Those who have entered the teaching profession over the past 40 years have been taught to scorn important knowledge as 'mere facts', and to see the imparting of this knowledge as somehow injurious to children. Thus it has come about that many educators, armed with partially true slogans, have seemingly taken leave of common sense.

Many parents and teachers have come to the conclusion that elementary education must strike a better balance between the development of the 'whole child' and the more limited but fundamental duty of the school to ensure that all children master a core of knowledge and skills essential to their competence as learners in later grades. But these parents and teachers cannot act on their convictions without access to an agreed upon, concrete sequence of knowledge. Our main motivation in developing the *Core Knowledge Sequence* and this book series has been to give parents and teachers something concrete to work with.

It has been encouraging to see how many teachers, since the first volume in this series was published, have responded to the Core Knowledge reform effort.

Parents and teachers are urged to join in a grassroots effort to strengthen our elementary schools. The place to start is in your own school and district. Insist that your school clearly state the core of *specific* knowledge and skills that each child in a grade must learn. Whether your school's core corresponds exactly to the Core Knowledge model is less important than the existence of some core – which, we hope, will be as solid, coherent, and challenging as the *Core Knowledge Sequence* has proven to be. Inform members of your community about the need for such a specific curriculum, and help make sure that the people who are elected or appointed to your local school board are independent-minded people who will insist that our children have the benefit of a solid, specific, world-class curriculum in each grade.

Share the knowledge!

*E. D. Hirsch, Jr*
Charlottesville, Virginia

# Language and Literature

## Reading, Writing and Your Year 5 Child

This chapter presents poems, stories, brief discussions of grammar and writing and explanations of common sayings and phrases.

The best way to bring children into the spirit of poetry is to read it aloud to them and encourage them to speak it aloud so that they can experience the music in the words. Until children take pleasure in the sound of poetry, there is little reason to analyse it technically.

Most of the stories in this book are excerpts from longer works. If a child enjoys a particular story, he or she should be encouraged to read the full book. Most of these stories are available in child-friendly versions, if the young reader finds the original language of eighteenth- and nineteenth-century authors too challenging at this stage.

Parents and teachers can help to draw children into stories by asking questions about them. For example, you might ask:

'What do you think is going to happen next?'

'Why did one of the characters act as he did?'

'What might have happened if... ?'

You might also ask the child to retell the story. Don't be worried if children change events or characters: that is in the best tradition of storytelling and explains why there are so many versions of traditional stories.

You can also encourage children to write and illustrate their own stories. Some children may be interested in beginning to keep a journal or writing letters to friends or relatives, which are both good ways for children to cultivate their writing skills. Another way to build vocabulary and foster language skills is by playing word games such as Scrabble, Boggle or hangman, and doing crossword puzzles.

Standard written language has special characteristics that children need to learn, and in Year 5 children continue to learn about language as they write it: identifying parts of speech, using punctuation correctly and recognising sentence types. The treatment of grammar and language conventions in this book is an overview and the topics covered here are not intended to represent an all-encompassing literacy resource. Rather, they point students, teachers and parents towards further work that can be supported by available resources such as Irina Tyk's *Butterfly Grammar* and others included in the list of suggested resources on page 69.

In the classroom, grammar instruction is a part, but only a part, of an effective English language arts programme. Children should enjoy a rich diet of fiction, poetry, drama, biography and non-fiction. They should be involved in the writing process, inventing topics, discovering ideas in early drafts, revising towards 'publication' of polished final drafts – all with encouragement and guidance along the way. They should practise writing in many modes, including stories, poetry, journal entries, formal reports, dialogues and descriptions.

The collection of familiar sayings that concludes every Language and Literature chapter in the Core Knowledge UK series has been one of the most popular features of the books. These sayings have such common currency in our language that children will hear them repeatedly, without necessarily understanding what they are intended to convey. Parents and teachers are encouraged to explain the meaning of these sayings by using the explanation and example provided in each case, but then to encourage children to create their own examples.

# Poetry

## The Rhinoceros

### by Ogden Nash

The rhino is a homely beast,
For human eyes he's not a feast.
But you and I will never know
Why Nature chose to make him so.
Farewell, farewell, you old rhinoceros,
I'll stare at something less prepoceros.

# Monday's Child

Monday's child is fair of face,
Tuesday's child is full of grace,
Wednesday's child is full of woe,
Thursday's child has far to go,
Friday's child is loving and giving,
Saturday's child works hard for a living,
But the child that is born on the Sabbath day
Is fair and wise and good and gay.

# The Pobble Who Has No Toes

## by Edward Lear

The Pobble who has no toes
    Had once as many as we;
When they said, 'Some day you may lose them all';
    He replied 'Fish Fiddle de-dee!'
And his Aunt Jobiska made him drink
Lavender water tinged with pink;
For she said, 'The World in general knows
There's nothing so good for a Pobble's toes!'

The Pobble who has no toes
    Swam across the Bristol Channel;
But before he set out he wrapped his nose
    In a piece of scarlet flannel.
For his Aunt Jobiska said, 'No harm
Can come to his toes if his nose is warm;
And it's perfectly known that a Pobble's toes
Are safe – provided he minds his nose.'

The Pobble swam fast and well,
    And when boats or ships came near him
He tinkledy-binkledy-winkled a bell,
    So that all the world could hear him.
And all the Sailors and Admirals cried,
When they saw him nearing the further side,
'He has gone to fish for his Aunt Jobiska's
Runcible Cat with crimson whiskers!'

But before he touched the shore,
    The shore of the Bristol Channel,
A sea-green Porpoise carried away
    His wrapper of scarlet flannel.
And when he came to observe his feet,
Formerly garnished with toes so neat,
His face at once became forlorn
On perceiving that all his toes were gone.

And nobody ever knew,
   From that dark day to the present,
Whoso had taken the Pobble's toes,
   In a manner so far from pleasant.
Whether the shrimps, or crawfish grey,
Or crafty Mermaids stole them away –
Nobody knew; and nobody knows
How the Pobble was robbed of his twice five toes!

The Pobble who has no toes
   Was placed in a friendly Bark,
And they rowed him back, and carried him up
   To his Aunt Jobiska's Park.
And she made him a feast at his earnest wish
Of eggs and buttercups fried with fish;
And she said, 'It's a fact the whole world knows,
That Pobbles are happier without their toes.'

## Fog

### by Carl Sandburg

The fog comes
on little cat feet.

It sits looking
over harbour and city
on silent haunches
and then moves on.

## Dreams

### by Langston Hughes

Hold fast to dreams
For if dreams die
Life is a broken-winged bird
That cannot fly.

Hold fast to dreams
For when dreams go
Life is a barren field
Frozen with snow.

# A Tragic Story

## by William Makepeace Thackeray

There lived a sage in days of yore,

And he a handsome pigtail wore:

But wondered much, and sorrowed more,

   Because it hung behind him.

      He mused upon this curious case,

      And swore he'd change the pigtail's place,

      And have it hanging at his face,

         Not dangling there behind him.

           Says he, 'The mystery I've found –

           I'll turn me round,' – he turned him round;

              but still it hung behind him.

           Then round, and round, and out and in,

           All day the puzzled sage did spin;

           In vain – it mattered not a pin –

              The pigtail hung behind him.

           And right and left, and round about,

           And up and down, and in and out

           He turned; but still the pigtail stout

              Hung steadily behind him.

      And though his efforts never slack,

      And though he twist, and twirl, and tack,

      Alas! Still faithful to his back,

         The pigtail hangs behind him.

# Sky in the Pie

## by Roger McGough

Waiter! There's a sky in my pie,

Remove it at once if you please,

You can keep your incredible sunsets

I ordered mincemeat and cheese.

I can't stand nightingales singing
Or clouds all burnished with gold,
The whispering breeze is disturbing the peas
And making my chips go all cold.

I don't care if the chef is an artist
Whose canvases hang in the Tate,
I want two veg and puff pastry
Not the Universe heaped on my plate.

OK I'll try just a spoonful
I suppose I've got nothing to lose.
Mmm… the colours quite tickle the palette
With a blend of delicate hues.

The sun has a custardy flavour
And the clouds are as light as air,
And the wind a chewier texture,
(With a hint of cinnamon there?)

This sky is simply delicious
Why have I not tried it before?
I can chew my way through to Eternity
And still have room left for more.

Having acquired a taste for the Cosmos
I shall polish this sunset off soon,
I can't wait to tuck into the night sky.
Waiter! Please bring me the moon!

# The Lady of Shalott

## by Alfred, Lord Tennyson (abridged)

The Lady of Shalott *by John William Waterhouse*

The legend of King Arthur and his Knights of the Round Table has enthralled people for hundreds of years. We have read stories about King Arthur and his knights in other books in this series, and we will read 'Sir Gawain and the Green Knight' on page 22. In this extract from a lovely poem by Alfred, Lord Tennyson, we hear the sad story of the Lady of Shalott, who lives in a tower on an island where she spends her time weaving. She has been warned that, if she ever looks out of her window towards Camelot, something terrible will happen. So she sets up a mirror over her loom, where she can watch everything that is going by without actually looking out of the window. The she sees the handsome knight Sir Lancelot, reflected in her mirror…

There she weaves by night and day
A magic web with colours gay.
She has heard a whisper say,
A curse is on her if she stay
    To look down to Camelot.
She knows not what the curse may be,
And so she weaveth steadily,
And little other care hath she,
    The Lady of Shalott.

And moving through a mirror clear
That hangs before her all the year,
Shadows of the world appear.
There she sees the highway near
    Winding down to Camelot:
There the river eddy whirls,
And there the surly village-churls,
And the red cloaks of market girls,
    Pass onward from Shalott.

Sometimes a troop of damsels glad,
An abbot on an ambling pad,
Sometimes a curly shepherd-lad,
Or long-hair'd page in crimson clad,
    Goes by to tower'd Camelot;
And sometimes through the mirror blue
The knights come riding two and two:
She hath no loyal knight and true,
    The Lady of Shalott.

But in her web she still delights
To weave the mirror's magic sights,
For often thro' the silent nights
A funeral, with plumes and lights
    And music, went to Camelot:
Or when the moon was overhead,
Came two young lovers lately wed;
'I am half sick of shadows,' said
    The Lady of Shalott.

A bow-shot from her bower-eaves,
He rode between the barley sheaves,
The sun came dazzling thro' the leaves,
And flamed upon the brazen greaves
    Of bold Sir Lancelot.
A red-cross knight for ever kneel'd
To a lady in his shield,
That sparkled on the yellow field,
    Beside remote Shalott.

His broad clear brow in sunlight glow'd;
On burnish'd hooves his war-horse trode;
From underneath his helmet flow'd
His coal-black curls as on he rode,
    As he rode down to Camelot.
From the bank and from the river
He flashed into the crystal mirror,
'Tirra lirra,' by the river
    Sang Sir Lancelot.

She left the web, she left the loom,
She made three paces through the room,
She saw the water-lily bloom,
She saw the helmet and the plume,
   She look'd down to Camelot.
Out flew the web and floated wide;
The mirror crack'd from side to side;
'The curse is come upon me,' cried
   The Lady of Shalott.

In the stormy east-wind straining,
The pale yellow woods were waning,
The broad stream in his banks complaining,
Heavily the low sky raining
   Over tower'd Camelot;
Down she came and found a boat
Beneath a willow left afloat,
And round about the prow she wrote
   *The Lady of Shalott.*

And down the river's dim expanse –
Like some bold seer in a trance,
Seeing all his own mischance –
With a glassy countenance
   Did she look to Camelot.
And at the closing of the day
She loosed the chain, and down she lay;
The broad stream bore her far away,
   The Lady of Shalott.

Lying, robed in snowy white
That loosely flew to left and right –
The leaves upon her falling light –
Thro' the noises of the night,
   She floated down to Camelot:
And as the boat-head wound along
The willowy hills and fields among,
They heard her singing her last song,
   The Lady of Shalott.

Heard a carol, mournful, holy,
Chanted loudly, chanted lowly,
Till her blood was frozen slowly,
And her eyes were darkened wholly,
   Turn'd to tower'd Camelot.
For ere she reach'd upon the tide
The first house by the water-side,
Singing in her song she died,
   The Lady of Shalott.

Under tower and balcony,
By garden-wall and gallery,
A gleaming shape she floated by,
Dead-pale between the houses high,
   Silent into Camelot.
Out upon the wharfs they came,
Knight and burgher, lord and dame,
And round the prow they read her name,
   *The Lady of Shalott.*

Who is this? And what is here?

And in the lighted palace near

Died the sound of royal cheer;

And they crossed themselves for fear,

   All the knights at Camelot;

But Lancelot mused a little space;

He said, 'She has a lovely face;

God in his mercy lend her grace,

   The Lady of Shalott.'

---

## Lines and Stanzas

Poetry is made up of lines. Sometimes the lines of a poem are grouped into clusters called stanzas. In 'The Lady of Shalott', for example, each stanza contains nine lines. The first four lines of each stanza rhyme with each other, the fifth line rhymes with the ninth line, and the sixth, seventh and eighth lines rhyme.

---

# Stories and Myths

## The Fire on the Mountain

### An Ethiopian folk tale

People say that in the old days in the city of Addis Ababa there was a young man by the name of Arha. He had come as a boy from the country of Guragé, and in the city he became the servant of a rich merchant, Haptom Hasei.

This story takes place in Ethiopia. Read about African art, starting on page 163.

Haptom Hasei was so rich that he owned everything that money could buy, and often he was very bored because he had tired of everything he knew, and there was nothing new for him to do.

One cold night, when the damp wind was blowing across the plateau, Haptom called to Arha to bring wood for the fire. When Arha was finished, Haptom began to talk.

'How much cold can a man stand?' he said, speaking at first to himself. 'I wonder if it would be possible for a man to stand on the highest peak, Mount Sululta, where the coldest winds blow, through an entire night without blankets or clothing and yet not die?'

'I don't know,' Arha said. 'But wouldn't it be a foolish thing?'

'Perhaps, if he had nothing to gain by it, it would be a foolish thing to spend the night that way,' Haptom said. 'But I would be willing to bet that a man couldn't do it.'

'I am sure a courageous man could stand naked on Mount Sululta throughout an entire night and not die of it,' Arha said. 'But as for me, it isn't my affair since I've nothing to bet.'

'Well, I'll tell you what,' Haptom said. 'Since you are so sure it can be done, I'll make a bet with you anyway. If you can stand among the rocks on Mount Sululta for an entire night without food or water, or clothing or blankets or fire, and not die of it, then I will give you ten acres of good farm land for your own, with a house and cattle.'

Arha could hardly believe what he had heard.

'Do you really mean this?' he asked.

*'Since you are so sure it can be done, I'll make a bet with you.'*

'I am a man of my word,' Haptom replied.

'Then tomorrow night I will do it,' Arha said, 'and afterward, for all the years to come, I shall till my own soil.'

But he was very worried, because the wind swept bitterly across that peak. So in the morning Arha went to a wise old man from the Guragé tribe and told him of the bet he had made. The old man listened quietly and thoughtfully, and when Arha had finished he said:

'I will help you. Across the valley from Sululta is a high rock which can be seen in the daytime. Tomorrow night, as the sun goes down, I shall build a fire there, so that it can be seen from where you stand on the peak. All night long you must watch the light of my fire. Do not close your eyes or let the darkness creep upon you. As you watch my fire, think of its warmth and think of me, your friend, sitting there tending it for you. If you do this you will survive, no matter how bitter the night wind.'

Arha thanked the old man warmly and went back to Haptom's house with a light heart. He told Haptom he was ready, and in the afternoon Haptom sent him, under the watchful eyes of other servants, to the top of Mount Sululta. There, as night fell, Arha removed his clothes and stood in the damp, cold wind that swept across the plateau with the setting sun. Across the valley, several miles away, Arha saw the light of his friend's fire, which shone like a star in the blackness.

The wind turned colder and seemed to pass through his flesh and chill the marrow in his bones. The rock on which he stood felt like ice. Each hour the cold numbed him more, until he thought he would never be warm again, but he kept his eyes on the twinkling light across the valley, and he remembered that his old friend sat there tending a fire for him. Sometimes wisps of fog blotted out the light, and then he strained to see until the fog passed. He sneezed and coughed and shivered, and began to feel ill. Yet all night through he stood there, and only when the dawn came did he put on his clothes and go down the mountain back to Addis Ababa.

Haptom was very surprised to see Arha, and he questioned his servants thoroughly. 'Did he stay all night without food or drink or blankets or clothing?'

'Yes,' his servants said. 'He did all of these things.'

'Well, you are a strong fellow,' Haptom said to Arha. 'How did you manage to do it?'

*'He thought he would never be warm again, but he kept his eyes on the twinkling light across the valley.'*

'I simply watched the light of a fire on a distant hill,' Arha said. 'What! You watched a fire? Then you lose the bet, and you are still my servant, and you own no land!'

'But this fire was not close enough to warm me, it was far across the valley!'

'I won't give you the land,' Haptom said. 'You didn't fulfil the conditions. It was only the fire that saved you.'

Arha was very sad. He went again to his old friend of the Guragé tribe and told him what had happened.

'Take the matter to the judge,' the old man advised him.

Arha went to the judge and complained, and the judge sent for Haptom. When Haptom told his story, and the servants said once more that Arha had watched a distant fire across the valley, the judge said:

'No, you have lost, for Haptom Hasei's condition was that you must be without fire.'

Once more Arha went to his old friend with the sad news that he was doomed to the life of a servant, as though he had not gone through the ordeal on the mountaintop.

'Don't give up hope,' the old man said. 'More wisdom grows wild in the hills than in any city judge.'

He got up from where he sat and went to find a man named Hailu, in whose house he had been a servant when he was young. He explained to the good man about the bet between Haptom and Arha, and asked if something couldn't be done.

'Don't worry about it,' Hailu said after thinking for a while. 'I will take care of it for you.'

Some days later Hailu sent invitations to many people in the city to come to a feast at his house. Haptom was among them, and so was the judge who had ruled Arha had lost the bet.

When the day of the feast arrived, the guests came riding on mules with fine trappings, their servants strung out behind them on foot. Haptom came with 20 servants, one of whom held a silk umbrella over his head to shade him from the sun, and four drummers played music that signified the great Haptom was here.

The guests sat on soft rugs laid out for them and talked. From the kitchen came the odours of wonderful things to eat: roast goat, roast corn and durra, pancakes called injera and many tantalising sauces. The smell of the food only accentuated the hunger of the guests. Time passed. The food should have been served, but they did not see it, only smelled vapours that drifted from the kitchen. The evening came, and still no food was served. The guests began to whisper among themselves. It was very curious that the honourable Hailu had not had the food brought out. Still the smells came from the kitchen.

At last one of the guests spoke out for all the others:

'Hailu, why do you do this to us? Why do you invite us to a feast and then serve us nothing?'

'Why, can't you smell the food?' Hailu asked with surprise.

'Indeed we can, but smelling is not eating; there is no nourishment in it!'

'And is there warmth in a fire so distant it can hardly be seen?' Hailu asked. 'If Arha was warmed by the fire he watched while standing on Mount Sululta, then you have been fed by the smells coming from my kitchen.'

The people agreed with him; the judge now saw his mistake, and Haptom was shamed. He thanked Hailu for his advice and announced that Arha was then and there the owner of the land, the house and the cattle. Then Hailu ordered the food to be brought in, and the feast began.

# The Wonderful Chuang Brocade

### This folk tale is from a region in southern China called Chuang

For thousands of years the people of China have been famous for their rich art in silken brocades. The Chuang people of Kwangsi Province are especially well known for their beautiful designs and pictures. Some of them tell stories such as this one.

We learnt about China in Year 3.

In this province, at the foot of high peaks, in a thatched cottage, lived an old widow with her three sons: Lemo, Letui and Leju. The old mother was a most wonderful weaver of brocades, which merchants and folks bought from her to make vests, bedcovers and blankets. Her sons were woodcutters.

One day the old mother went to sell a fine brocade she had made. In the merchant's shop hung a painting of wondrous beauty. It showed a village with a rich, tall palace with colourful gardens around it. Beautiful flowers and ripe vegetables were everywhere; ducks, chickens and cows were all over. Never had she seen a more beautiful scene. Quickly she sold her brocade and bought the painting, forgetting the rice and other foods she needed.

At home she proudly showed the painting. 'How happy I would be to live in that palace with its gardens,' she said to her sons.

'That is a dream, *Ah-mee*,' spoke Lemo, the oldest son.

'Maybe we will live in such a place in our next life,' said Letui, her second son.

Then Leju, the youngest, said: '*Ah-mee*, you must weave a brocade just like the painting, and when you look at your work you will think you are living in the palace with those gardens.'

'You are right, son,' said the old mother, and she set to work at once.

Day in, day out and nights as well, she worked at the wooden loom with silk threads, and the scenes of the painting grew in beauty on the brocade.

She never stopped working. Her old eyes hurt from the smoke of the pine-oil lamps, but she did not stop. After one year, tears filled her eyes, but instead of stopping, she put her tears into the brocade and made of them a singing river and a shining pond full of fish. After two years, drops of blood fell from her eyes onto the brocade. Out of these she wove bright red flowers and a glowing sun.

So the old near-blind mother worked for three years until she finished putting the painting into the brocade. The sons were so proud of her work, they took it out of their dark hut and put it in front of the door where there was enough daylight to see and admire it. Everyone who saw it exclaimed, 'What a wonderful Chuang brocade!'

*Day in, day out, and nights as well, she worked at the wooden loom with silk threads, and the scenes of the painting grew in beauty on the brocade.*

All of a sudden a weird whirring wind came along and – *whisht!* – it picked up the brocade and carried it high, high up into the sky and the brocade disappeared.

The old mother fainted, everyone shouted... but the brocade was gone. The mother became very ill and no doctor could help her. She was forever crying for her brocade! Seeing this, Lemo said, 'Mother, stop grieving! I will find your beautiful brocade and bring it back to you.'

'Go, son, and may good fortune go with you,'

Lemo set out over mountains and across rivers. One day he came to a mountain pass, on one side of which stood a stone house. To the right was a stone horse, its mouth wide open, bent over an arbutus bush full of red berries.

At the door sat an old white-headed woman.

'Who are you and where are you going, young man?' she asked Lemo.

He told her the tale of his mother's beautiful brocade – how hard and long she had worked at it and how the wind had carried it away, and how very ill she had become.

'Young Lemo, I know all this. The winds of the mountains tell me many things. Your brocade is now in the Sun Mountain of the East with the beautiful fairies who live there. They saw the brocade and sent the wind for it. They are now copying your mother's beautiful work, and you can get it back only with the help of the stone horse. But the horse will help you only if you give him two of your teeth for the ones he is missing in his mouth so that he can eat the berries from the arbutus bush. Then he will take you far and wide to the Sun Mountain of the East.

'On the way you will come to a mountain of leaping flames through which you must pass. You must do it in silence and without fear. If you cry out even once, you will turn into charcoal.

'Then you will come to a sea full of jagged ice with knife-cutting cold winds tearing at you, but you must not cry out or even shiver with cold. If you do, you will be crushed by the wild tossing ice and buried in the icy water.

'If you go through these trials, you will get your mother's brocade.'

Lemo was silent. His face turned blue with fear and he hung his head and thought – for a long time. To lose his teeth and endure such terrible trials!

The old woman watched him. Then she said, 'Son, your face tells your thoughts. It says: it is too much! But you tried, so there is a little iron box full of gold nuggets. Go back home and live well.'

Lemo took the box and thanked her and left. But he was thinking hard. 'If I go home I must share the gold with all my family! There will be little for me... No! I will go to the city and live on my wealth.' So he turned his steps toward the big city.

The old mother waited and waited, pining for her beautiful brocade. 'If only I could see it before I die,' she cried continually.

Letui, her second son, said, 'Mother, I will bring you your brocade,' and he set off at once. He, too, came to the stone house with the old lady and her stone horse, and she told him just what she had told Lemo. Letui also thought and thought, and the old woman knew what was in his mind.

'Son,' she said, 'I can tell you think the trials are too much for you, but you started bravely, so here is a little iron box with gold nuggets. Go back and live happily.' But Letui thought as did Lemo, so instead of going home, he too turned towards the city.

At home the old mother waited, crying for her handiwork until her eyes gave out and she became completely blind!

Leju, the youngest son, said, 'Mother, I will go on the road to find your beautiful brocade and bring it back to you. You will be with kind neighbours who will take care of you while I am away.'

He bade her good cheer and went off. Like his brothers, he came to the stone house with the stone horse and the old woman. She told him how he could get the brocade only with the help of the horse, and of the dangers he must face.

Instead of thinking for a long time as his brothers had, Leju gave two of his teeth to the horse and mounted it. The horse ate the berries and then went off, swift as the wind. Horse and rider went through the burning mountain and the icy sea. But Leju sat firmly on the horse, thinking only of helping his mother, and so he reached the Sun Mountain and the palace where the lovely fairies were busy copying *Ah-mee's* masterpiece.

Leju spoke to them, telling them of his mother's sickness and blindness, and of how she continued to cry for her lost brocade. 'We will finish copying your mother's wonderful work by tomorrow morning,' said one of the maidens. 'Then you can take it back to your *Ah-mee.*' They gave him delicious fruits to eat, and he fell asleep. During the night the fairies hung a big glowing pearl on the rafter and wove by its light.

A maiden in a red dress finished first. She looked at her own work, and then at *Ah-mee's*. She sighed, 'I am afraid mine is not nearly as fine. I wish I could live in the beautiful place that is on her brocade.' So she began weaving her own image right near the fish pond that *Ah-mee* had woven.

Leju slept in the palace of the fairies, but the next morning, before the maidens arose, he took his mother's brocade, mounted the stone horse, and in a wink of time they were back at the stone house where the white-haired woman sat waiting for him.

'Leju, your mother is very ill,' she said. 'Hurry back. The sight of her brocade will bring her health.' Then she took the two teeth from the horse's mouth and put them back into Leju's. Next she put a pair of magic deerskin shoes on his feet and bade him good luck.

The shoes were like wings and took him swiftly to his home, where his mother was lying in bed, thin as a stick and barely alive.

'*Ah-mee*,' he shouted, 'I have brought you your brocade. Here!'

No sooner did she touch it than she began to feel well again. Her eyes opened wide and once again she could see! She got up and took her beloved work out into the open sunshine and then... a miracle happened! The embroidery of her brocade became a real place. Trees! Flowers! All were there before the rich palace, and by the fish pond stood the lovely maiden in her red dress.

Leju married the maiden, and the two lived happily all their lives.

One day two beggars came to their village. They were Lemo and Letui. They had spent all their gold, drinking, eating and making merry in the city, and now they were dressed in rags and begging for food. When they saw the beautiful garden where *Ah-mee*, Leju and his wife were walking and singing, they quietly slipped away, too ashamed to face their mother and brother.

*Horse and rider went through the burning mountain and the icy sea.*
*But Leju sat firm on the horse, thinking only of helping his mother.*

# Sir Gawain and the Green Knight

*The story of Sir Gawain is told in a poem written in the fourteenth century. We don't know the name of the poet, but he didn't use rhyme in most of his verses. Instead, he used alliteration, making several words in each line begin with the same letter or sound. You can see what the poem was like in the last part of this re-telling.*

Long ago, in the days when knights in armour served their ladies fair, the noblest of them all was King Arthur. At Camelot he held his court, where his knights of the Round Table were always ready to do his commands. They competed with each other to be the noblest and the bravest, fighting for right against wrong and defending the weak against the strong.

It was New Year's Day, and the knights and ladies of Camelot had all come to enjoy a banquet in the hall of Arthur's castle. There was plenty to eat, and all of the food was delicious. All were served with large portions and were enjoying their feast, but Arthur held back. He had developed a habit of not eating on New Year's Day until he had heard of some amazing adventure or some great deed of chivalry. On this particular day, his wish was granted in a very unusual way.

In the middle of the feast, the great doors of the hall burst open and in came the most frightening and gigantic knight on horseback, larger than any man who had ever been seen, with massive muscles, a thick head of hair and a bushy beard. He carried an enormous axe with a blade that glittered, it was so sharp. But the most astonishing thing about him was – he was completely green!

'Who is in charge of the noble company of knights?' he asked. 'I wish to speak with that man.'

'I am Arthur and I command these knights,' said the King. 'Will it please you to get down off your horse and join us in our feast?'

'No, Arthur,' replied the Green Knight, 'I will not stay here with you. I come only to offer you a challenge, a game such as people like to play in this season.'

'Nothing could please me more,' replied Arthur. 'What is your challenge?'

'It is this,' replied the giant. 'I hold here in my hand an axe. I will offer it to any man here, to give me a blow, as hard as he likes, in any part of my body. In one year to the day, that man must come to find me, and I will return the blow. That is all.'

The knights were silent. What a terrible challenge!

'Well, well, well,' said the green man. 'So this is the courage of the famous Round Table! Not one of you will play a little game with me.'

At that, Sir Gawain, the nephew of King Arthur , stood up. 'I will accept your challenge,' he said, 'although it is a foolish one. Never let it be said that the Round Table of Camelot refused such an invitation.'

Gawain left his place at the table and came down into the centre of the great hall. The Green Knight got down off his horse, gave Gawain his great glittering axe and bent down, exposing his neck. Gawain lifted the axe high in the air and brought it swiftly down on the green man's neck. With a thud, the giant's head hit the floor. Everyone gasped, but what happened next left them speechless. The Green Knight didn't stagger at all: he walked forwards on his strong legs, picked up his head and got back on his horse. He held his head to face the King and Gawain, and the lips started to talk.

'Be sure to keep your side of the bargain, Gawain. In a year to the day, you must come to me for a return blow. I am known as the Knight of the Green Chapel to all men. You will have no trouble in finding me – if you are brave enough to look!'

And with that, he pulled on the reins of his monstrous horse, turned it around and galloped out of the hall, with sparks flying from the horse's hooves.

There was a stunned silence, until King Arthur tried to cheer people up. 'Do not be afraid,' he said to Guinevere, 'this is just the sort of astonishing event that is perfect for a feast at New Year. I can eat my meal now, according to my custom. Hang up your axe,' he said to Gawain. 'It has hacked enough.' Gawain joined the others for the feast, and he ate as much as he could, but he couldn't help thinking about what he had to do in a year's time.

❧

The year passed and Christmas approached again. The knights and ladies of Camelot begged Gawain not to go on his search for the Green Knight. 'This is foolishness,' they said, 'to throw away the life of one of the noblest knights of the Round Table, and all for a game.'

But Gawain told them that he had to go. 'We have all promised to be brave and truthful. If I break my promise now, it will not only show me to be a coward and a liar, it will ruin the reputation of the Round Table.'

He put on his armour, mounted his horse, and set out in search of the Knight of the Green Chapel. Further and further he rode, he knew not where, until he found himself travelling through the forests of Wirral and into North Wales. The landscape was bleak, with very few people living there and many wild animals that threatened Gawain. The weather was bitterly cold, and Gawain had to sleep in the open air, still wearing his armour to stay warm. He asked everyone he met where he could find the Knight of the Green Chapel, but no one knew the name.

Then one day he saw through the trees the most beautiful castle, surrounded by a green park. He made his way to the gate and was welcomed by the lord of the castle, who was called Sir Bertilak. Gawain was given fine clothes to wear, instead of his armour, and he was led into a hall with a blazing fire, beside which he was served a delicious meal. The knights and ladies asked him who he was and he told them that he was Sir Gawain, nephew of King Arthur.

'How lucky we are!' the ladies and gentlemen said to each other. 'We have here with us the famous Sir Gawain, who will be able to tell us about the Round Table and the noble deeds of its knights.'

At that moment, the wife of Sir Bertilak entered the hall. She was beautiful and graceful, but she was accompanied by an old woman who looked very different, being short, ugly and covered in warts. Sir Gawain, who was courteous to all ladies, greeted them both with equal politeness. They took him to sit by the fireside between them while Gawain told them stories of the knights of the Round Table.

The feasting lasted for three days, at the end of which Gawain told Sir Bertilak that it was time for him to leave. Sir Bertilak asked Gawain why he wanted to leave the castle in such bitterly cold weather, so Gawain told him about the Green Knight and his challenge.

'Do you know, my lord, of the Green Chapel, where this giant lives? I must be there on New Year's Day, and that is only four days away.'

Sir Bertilak laughed. 'Now you will have to stay – you have no excuse for leaving at all! The Green Chapel is only two miles from here. My servant will guide you there on the morning of New Year's Day.'

Sir Gawain was delighted. 'In that case, my lord, I will gladly accept your offer and stay in your beautiful castle for four more days.'

'One thing more,' said Sir Bertilak. 'Let's make a bargain. You are tired and need to rest before you meet the Green Knight. Tomorrow, my men and I will go out hunting, while you rest here with my wife for company. At the end of the day, I will give you whatever I have caught during the day, and you must give me anything you have received here.'

Sir Gawain laughed. 'This is a strange request, which I gladly grant.' And so they made their bargain, and departed for their beds.

Before dawn the next day, Sir Bertilak and his knights were on their horses dressed in their finest hunting clothes. The huntsmen blew their horns and the bloodhounds bayed as they came out of their kennels, then everyone rode into the forest to hunt for deer.

Sir Gawain was fast asleep in his comfortable bed, until he heard the latch move on the door of his bedroom. He peeped over the sheets and saw that Lady Bertilak had come to visit him. He was so surprised that he pretended still to be asleep, but she just sat on the edge of his bed watching him. Eventually, he decided that it would be better to ask her what she wanted, so he pretended to wake up and greet her.

'Gracious lady,' he said, 'you do me too much honour to visit me in my room. Please allow me to get up and dress myself, so that I will be fit to see you.'

'Not at all, Gawain,' she replied. 'I have you at my mercy now and I'm going to tuck you in tightly. My husband is out hunting, and I have you all to myself, so now you can tell me all about the noble deeds of the knights of the Round Table, and the perfect respect with which they treat all ladies.'

'With pleasure, my lady,' said Gawain, and they spent the morning having a delightful conversation. Finally, as Lady Bertilak got up to leave, she said: 'Do you know, I wonder if you are Sir Gawain at all. I'm sure that he would not have treated a lady as you have treated me.'

Sir Gawain was shocked, fearing that he had said something rude without meaning it, but that was not what Lady Bertilak had in mind.

'Surely no knight of the Round Table, who knows how to behave with courtesy, could have passed so much time with a lady without asking for a kiss.'

Sir Gawain laughed. 'You put me to shame, my lady,' he said. 'Please grant your servant the honour of a kiss.'

And so Lady Bertilak bent down and kissed him. Then she left him to get dressed, while the servants prepared a delicious feast for the return of their master.

As evening fell, Sir Bertilak returned from the forest with the deer he and his huntsmen had killed that day. As he came into the hall, he said to Gawain: 'All of these animals that we have hunted and killed, I give to you. What do you have for me in return?'

Sir Gawain thought to himself: 'What have I been given today? Nothing – except a kiss from Lady Bertilak!' So he walked up to the lord of the castle and kissed him!

'Well,' said Sir Bertilak, 'I wonder where you got that present! But I won't ask, because that wasn't part of our bargain.'

They spent the evening feasting on the deer, and then went to bed. The next morning, Sir Bertilak was up early again, leading the hunt, while Sir Gawain lay snug in bed. Once again, he heard the latch on his door go up, and in came Lady Bertilak. She sat down on the edge of his bed and kissed him.

'Sir Gawain,' she said laughing, 'everyone knows that the knights of King Arthur's Round Table are the most faithful servants of their ladies fair. Please tell me some of the stories of true love that you know of from Camelot.'

So Gawain told her tales of brave knights rescuing damsels in distress and proving true to them even to death. Lady Bertilak was delighted by the romances and, at the end of the morning, she kissed Gawain again and left.

That evening, Sir Bertilak returned with an enormous boar that he and his huntsmen had killed. 'This is yours, Gawain,' he said. 'Now what do you have for me in return?' Sir Gawain surprised him again by giving him two kisses! 'You're doing well for yourself in my castle!' said Sir Bertilak, laughing. 'And you are an honest man, giving me everything you have received during the day. All honour to you, Gawain, and to the knights of the Round Table. Now let us feast and be merry!'

At the end of the evening, they all departed to bed. Sir Bertilak slept soundly after his hunting, but Gawain lay awake, thinking about the terrible trial that lay ahead of him. At last he dozed off, but he was troubled by dreams until he heard the latch on his bedroom door move, and there was Lady Bertilak sitting on the edge of his bed again. She bent down and kissed him.

'Good morning, Sir Gawain,' she greeted him. 'This is your last day with us, so we must make the most of it.' They spent the morning talking, with Gawain pretending to be cheerful when really he couldn't stop thinking about the Green Knight. Finally, Lady Bertilak got up to leave, kissed him, and then gave him a strange present: a green silk sash, to wear across his body underneath his armour. At first, Sir Gawain refused to accept it, but she insisted. 'This sash has magical powers,' she told him. 'Whoever wears it cannot be wounded or killed. Please wear it to keep yourself safe, but don't say anything about this to my husband.'

With that, she kissed him a third time and left. When Sir Bertilak returned from that day's hunting, he presented Gawain with a fox that he had killed. 'And what do you have for me today?' he asked. Gawain gave him three kisses, but he didn't give him the green sash. He knew that this was wrong because he was breaking the terms of their bargain, but he really didn't want to die the next day from the blow of the Green Knight's axe.

Gawain arose early the next day and put on his armour, taking care to wear the sash underneath everything else. He said farewell to Sir Bertilak, who told a young squire to ride with Gawain as far as the Green Chapel. The two of them rode for two miles to a place where the road went down into a valley.

'That path will take you to the Green Chapel,' said the squire, 'but if you value your life, you will not go there. Ride away – anywhere – and I promise I will say you did your duty.'

'That I cannot do,' replied Sir Gawain, 'for I would be a cowardly knight.' He rode down the path until he came to a cave overhung with moss. 'This must be the Green Chapel,' he thought, and he cried out: 'Here I am, Gawain, knight of the Round Table, and if anyone has any business with me, let him appear now.'

'Here I am!' boomed the Green Knight, appearing from the cave and looking even more frightening than before. He held a massive axe, its shining blade showing that it had just been sharpened. 'Now prepare to take the blow I promised you a year ago!'

Gawain bowed down to expose his neck and the Green Knight raised his axe. Just as he started to bring it down, Gawain glanced sideways at it and shrank away.

'What!' shouted the Green Knight, 'Is this the courage of the Round Table that we hear so much about?'

'I flinched once,' said Gawain, 'but I won't do so again. Do your worst.'

So the Green Knight raised the axe and brought it down swiftly, but stopped just before it reached Sir Gawain's neck.

'Why are you tormenting me?' asked Gawain. 'Just give me the blow and have done with it.'

'Very well, here it comes,' replied the Green Knight, and he brought down the axe with terrible force – but it only nicked Gawain's neck and drew a spot of blood. Gawain leapt back and drew his sword.

'That's enough, you've had your bargain, and now I can defend myself.'

The Green Knight leant on his axe. 'Don't be so angry, Gawain,' he said, 'I have treated you fairly. The first swing of my axe, which didn't harm you, was for the first day you spent in my castle, when you gave me the kiss my wife gave you. The second swing, which also did you no harm, was for the second day, when you gave me the two kisses. But the third swing, which grazed your neck, was for the third day, when you didn't give me the green sash my wife gave you. That was against our agreement. For you see, I am Bertilak, the lord of that castle. The elderly lady who is my wife's companion is Morgan La Faye, a sorceress, who wanted to see if the knights of the Round Table are really as brave as people say.

She turned me into the Green Knight and arranged for this little New Year's game. And now I invite you to return to my castle and celebrate the New Year with your friends there.'

But Sir Gawain was ashamed and would not go. He knew that he had not kept his promise to Sir Bertilak, because he wanted to save his life. He returned to Camelot, and told King Arthur, Guinevere and all the knights that he had disgraced himself, and that he would wear the green sash for the rest of his life as a reminder of his bad behaviour. King Arthur told him that he should not be so ashamed, because he had only failed in a small way, and that, however hard we try to be good, we all fail sometimes.

'If you are determined to wear the green sash,' said Arthur, 'then I will make a new rule. All knights of the Round Table must wear such a sash, clearly visible on their armour, to remind us all that we are only human, and we make mistakes. The important thing is to learn from your mistakes.'

So that is the story of Sir Gawain, whose green sash became the badge of the Round Table, and a reminder of how we must always try to be good, even if we fail sometimes.

*This is related in the writings of the most renowned romancers,*
*And ancient chronicles commonly confirm for us*
*That in Arthur's reign this report was recited.*
*Many a tale is told of him*
*Whose fame was free from spot*
*When noble knights and ladies fair*
*Kept court in Camelot.*

## Robinson Crusoe Saves Friday

### Adapted from *Robinson Crusoe* by Daniel Defoe

*The English writer Daniel Defoe wrote* Robinson Crusoe *(published in 1719) after hearing the story of a Scottish man who lived alone on a deserted island for almost five years. Defoe began with the factual story, imagined how such a character must have felt and added elements of danger and adventure to make a fictional story that readers would enjoy.*

*Robinson Crusoe was born in 1632 in York. He had always dreamed of seeing the world as a sailor. One day he ran away to sea against his parents' wishes. His first experience at sea was scary as there was a massive storm. However, Crusoe decided to go back to sea again and again. He lived through many other storms and adventures. On one trip his ship sank! On another trip, his ship was captured by pirates off the coast of Africa. When Crusoe was sailing in the Caribbean, his ship was wrecked and he was the only survivor. He lived alone on a desert island for many years. Let's read about what happened to Crusoe on that island.*

I, poor miserable Robinson Crusoe, was shipwrecked during a dreadful storm. Our ship sank and everyone else had drowned. I was almost dead and quite alone. I swam to the shore of an island which I called 'The Island of Despair'.

All the rest of the first day I spent thinking about everything that had gone wrong and all of the problems I had. I no longer had anywhere to live and didn't even have any clothes!

They had been torn to shreds and washed away when I was saving myself from the sinking ship.

I was very worried and I saw nothing but death before me. I was terrified that I would be devoured (eaten alive) by wild beasts or murdered by monstrous people. I was also scared of starving to death because I didn't know where I would find any food on this deserted island. I wrote down a list of all of my problems:

## EVIL

I am alone on an abandoned island, without any hope.

I am singled out and separated from all the world to be miserable.

I am completely on my own.

I have no clothes.

I have nothing to protect me from wild animals or violent people who may want to kill me.

I have no one to talk to.

## GOOD

But I am alive and have not drowned, as all my ship's company were.

But I am singled out, too, from all the ship's crew to be saved from the shipwreck and maybe can be saved from this island, too.

But I have not starved and have some food to eat that I have found on the island.

But it is so hot that, even if I had clothes, I could hardly wear them.

But I am on an island where I see no wild beasts to hurt me, as I have seen on the coast of Africa.

But my ship luckily sank close enough to the shore that I have been able to bring useful things like tools from the ship to the island so that I can look after myself as long as I live.

I could not tell what part of the world this might be. I knew it must be part of America and must be near the Spanish areas. But these areas are sometimes lived in by cannibals, people-eaters who violently murder and eat any human they capture. I was terrified just at the thought!

After two years of living alone on the island, one day I found a footprint in the sand on the beach. I was surprised and wondered whose it could be. After I had seen the footprint,

I walked about the whole island, wandering more to the west point of the island than I had ever done before. During all of these years I had never seen any human creature come near the island. I was curious, but I also felt dreadfully scared of falling into the hands of cannibals.

After checking about the island, I came back to my castle, as I called it, although it was a basic tent and campsite I had made for myself. It felt safe, but that night I still lay awake and wondered if I might be eaten before morning!

Finally, I fell into a deep sleep and I dreamt a strange dream. I dreamt that, as I was going out in the morning as usual from my castle, I saw two canoes and eleven wild-looking cannibals landing on the beach. With them was a prisoner, and they were planning to kill him. All of a sudden, the prisoner jumped away and ran for his life. I thought in my dream that he was running towards the trees near my castle to hide there. I called to him and told him I would hide him. In my dream I saved him from the cannibals. He became my companion and servant who would help me get food and supplies, and eventually escape from 'The Island of Despair'.

I awoke then and was thrilled at the idea of escaping from this island. But then I realised that this was just a dream. I felt disappointed, and I became very sad at the thought of spending more years alone on the island.

My dream didn't come true immediately, and I spent another year and a half continuing to live on the island like before. It was quite boring, though, with no one to talk to. Then one day I was surprised to see five canoes on the beach! I didn't see any people. Like in my dream, I felt excited but also scared. If there were five canoes, there must be about twenty or thirty people on the island. I didn't know whether they were kind or cruel, trustworthy or dangerous.

I waited in my castle all morning, feeling safe there but always on the lookout for the other people. I became impatient after a while, so I clambered up to the top of the hill. I saw them! There must have been at least thirty people. They had gathered wood and made a fire, and they had prepared meat to roast on it. I was mesmerised. I watched these strange people dancing around the fire and making ferocious and monstrous gestures. Now I was terrified! I thought they were cannibals.

While I watched, I noticed two miserable-looking prisoners who were dragged from the canoes. One was violently knocked down with a wooden club. The other victim was left standing by himself, waiting for when they wanted him. This poor prisoner wasn't tied up and saw that maybe he could become free. He made a run for it! He was fast and ran incredibly quickly along the beach, right towards me.

I was dreadfully frightened. I saw him running my way and was afraid that all thirty cannibals would run after him and see me. I felt calmer when I found there were only three cannibals who ran after the escaped prisoner. I felt even better when I saw that the escapee outran them easily.

There was a creek between them and my castle. Although it was high tide, the escapee plunged in, swam about thirty strokes, landed and ran again. When the three cannibals came after him and reached the creek, I saw that one didn't know how to swim so he couldn't cross the creek. However, I was horrified to see that the other two cannibals were fast swimmers and would catch up to the escapee. Like in my dream, I thought that now was the time to get myself a companion. I also felt it was my duty to save this poor man's life.

I immediately ran towards him as fast as I could. I called to the escaped prisoner who looked back at me. At first I think he was as frightened of me as he was of the cannibals. I beckoned with my hand to him, asking him to come towards me. I slowly walked towards the evil cannibals and I knocked one down. Then I saw that one of the other cannibals had a bow and arrow and was preparing to shoot at me! To protect myself, I shot at him first and killed him.

The poor escapee realised his enemies had been wounded or killed, but he was still so frightened that he stood stock still. I called 'Halloo' again to him, and I made signs for him to come towards me. I saw then that he stood trembling with fear, and that he was afraid of me because he thought I would kill him. I beckoned to him again to come to me. I smiled and encouraged him as much as I could to show him that I was friendly and not mean.

He came nearer and nearer, kneeling down every ten or twelve steps, to show he was grateful to me for saving his life. Then he kissed the ground and set my foot on his head.

I thought that this meant that he was swearing to be my slave forever. He then said a few words to me in a strange language I didn't know. Although I could not understand him, it was lovely to hear him speak. It was the first time in many years that I heard another person speak!

Then I carried the escapee to my tent on the far side of the island. I gave him bread and a bunch of raisins to eat, and some water because he was very thirsty after running during his grand escape.

He was a handsome fellow who was also very strong. I reckoned that he was about twenty-six years old. His hair was long and black, and his eyes seemed to sparkle. He kept making many gestures to show he was thankful to me for saving him. He also made all the signs imaginable to let me know he would serve me for as long as he lived. Although we didn't speak the same language, I understood him generally because of his gestures.

Later I began to speak to my new companion and teach him to speak in English. I let him know his name should be Friday, because that was the day I saved his life. I called him Friday for the rest of our lives.

*Robinson Crusoe and Friday had many other adventures together, which you can read about in Daniel Defoe's* Robinson Crusoe.

# A Voyage to Lilliput

## Adapted from *Gulliver's Travels* by Jonathan Swift

*After the appearance of* Robinson Crusoe *in 1719, stories about voyages, shipwrecks and distant islands became popular. Jonathan Swift's* Gulliver's Travels *(published in 1726) benefited from this popularity, but Swift's book was unlike any other travel book ever written. For one thing, it is written as if it is a work of non-fiction, whereas in reality it was the product of Jonathan Swift's amazing imagination! He describes miniature people and giants, talking horses and flying islands. In this extract, Gulliver describes Lilliput, where the people stand only six inches tall.*

My father had a small estate in Nottinghamshire; I was the third of five sons. He sent me to Emanuel College in Cambridge at fourteen years old, but he was unable to pay the fees, so I soon left Cambridge to be apprenticed to Mr James Bates, a successful surgeon in London. I became a doctor, and because I longed to see the world, I decided to be a ship's doctor.

Sir Francis Drake, whom we read about in Year 4, also travelled to the West Indies.

33

I sailed on voyages to the East and West Indies, then set out on a ship called the *Antelope* on a voyage to the South Sea. We set sail from Bristol on 4 May 1699, and at first all went well. However, we sailed into a terrible storm when we were north-west of Van Diemen's Land and the ship was wrecked. I escaped with some of my companions in a small boat, but the boat was drivenonto a rock and sank. My companions drowned, but I managed to swim until I came to land. I was so exhausted, I only just managed to struggle onto the beach, where I lay down and fell into a deep sleep.

I tried to get up but found that I couldn't move. My arms and legs were tied down, and even my thick hair was tied to the ground, so that I couldn't move my head. I could feel something – in fact lots of things – crawling over me, and soon I saw a tiny man, not six inches high, standing on my chin. I could feel a crowd of more little people following behind him, so I made a painful effort to free my left hand and some of my hair as I gave a great roar. They were so terrified that they ran away as fast as their little legs could carry them, but not before they had shot me with arrows, which felt like sharp pinpricks.

However, they soon returned, together with many more people whom I could hear but not see, as I could not turn my head. There was a sound of hammering and sawing that went on for about an hour, and some of the little creatures cut the cords that bound the left side of my head, so that I could turn it a little to the right. I saw that they had built a platform, almost as high as my head, and that a very important-looking man was standing on it. He made a long speech, of which I could not understand one word, but he sounded as if he was making both threats and promises to me, no doubt laying down conditions for untying me. I managed to wrench my arms up from the ground and point my finger towards my mouth to show that I was hungry, as I had eaten nothing since before the shipwreck. He understood what I meant, and gave orders for food to be brought to me.

A whole procession of cooks appeared, carrying sides of beef and legs of lamb, all beautifully cooked, but so small that each one was only a mouthful for me. When I indicated that I was thirsty, they brought me two of their largest barrels, each one full of wine. When I had finished eating and drinking, the important-looking man came and stood on my chest to make another speech. Although I couldn't understand what he was saying, he kept pointing towards the towers of a city that could be seen in the distance, as if he wanted to take me there. I tried to tell him that I wanted to be free from my ropes, but he shook his head. Then I fell into a deep sleep, as the wine they had given me contained a sleeping potion.

While I was asleep, the engineers brought a huge trolley on wheels which they used for transporting the great tree trunks that are used to build ships. They then used a very clever system of pulleys to raise my sleeping body, while the trolley was wheeled underneath me. It took fifteen hundred of the largest horses they could find, each one about four-and-a-half inches high, to pull me towards the city to see the Emperor of this country, which I later discovered was called Lilliput.

When I woke up, I found myself in the largest building in the city. This building had been a great temple, but it had not been used for many years. My ropes had been removed, but I was fastened by chains to my ankle, so that I could only walk for short distances within the temple. The Emperor came to see me and he tried to talk to me, but we could not understand each other. He instructed six of the wisest men in the kingdom to teach me their language, and he also set three hundred tailors to work to make me a new suit of clothes, as the clothes I was wearing had been ruined by the seawater.

As soon as I could speak a few words of Lilliputian, I asked the Emperor to grant me my freedom. He said that he could not do that immediately: it depended on how I behaved and whether or not the Lilliputians found me trustworthy. Gradually, they began to lose their fear of me when they found that I was gentle with them and let their children play in my hand. One day, the Emperor decided to review all the soldiers in his army, so he asked me to stand with my feet as far apart as possible while three thousand footsoldiers and three thousand soldiers on horseback marched through my legs. The Emperor was so pleased by this display that, a few days later, he granted me my freedom.

I soon found a way to repay the trust he had placed in me. To the north-east of Lilliput is another country, the island of Blefuscu, which is divided from Lilliput by a channel only

800 yards wide. Blefuscu and Lilliput were at war, and indeed they had been at war with each other so often, over many years, that people had almost forgotten what they were quarrelling about.

The people of Blefuscu had a great fleet, and the Emperor learnt from his spies that they were preparing to sail to Lilliput to invade his kingdom. I told the Emperor that I could help, if he would give me what I needed: strong ropes and bars of iron which I would use to capture the whole navy of Blefuscu. Their ropes were not much thicker than cotton thread, so I wound them together, three at a time, to make them stronger. Their iron bars were like knitting needles, so I twisted them together to make strong hooks. I then took off my jacket, shoes and stockings and waded into the sea.

I was able to walk most of the way, as the water was not much more than six feet deep, but there was a stretch of about thirty yards in the middle of the channel where I had to swim. As soon as I could feel the ground beneath my feet, I stood up and walked the last part of the journey to Blefuscu.

When the sailors in the ships saw me rising up out of the water on my way towards them, they were so terrified that they jumped out of their ships and swam to shore. I then fixed my iron hooks on the prows of their ships and used a penknife that I carried in my pocket to cut the chains holding the anchors. Each hook was attached to one of my strong threads, so as I began to wade back towards Lilliput, I was dragging the whole fleet behind me with the greatest ease.

When the people of Blefuscu saw what I was doing, they began to fire hundreds of arrows at me. The arrows were tiny, and only pricked me like pins, but I was afraid that one would hit my eye. Fortunately, I had a pair of glasses in one of my pockets, and these protected my eyes from the shower of arrows.

As I reached the middle of the channel, I was once again swimming, then for a long way I was able to walk with just my head above the level of the water. As I approached Lilliput, the Emperor and many thousands of his subjects were standing on the shore, trying to see what had happened. When they saw the fleet of Blefuscu approaching, they thought at first that they were being invaded, because they didn't see my head above the water. As I got closer to the land, I began to rise up out of the sea and the Lilliputians cheered. 'Long live the Emperor of Lilliput!' I cried, and they cheered even more. The Emperor was so delighted with me that he created me a nardac on the spot, which is the greatest title of honour he ever bestows on his subjects.

The Emperor knew that his kingdom was now safe from the threat of invasion, but that was not enough for him. He wanted me to make the people of Blefuscu his slaves. I told him that I could never be responsible for destroying the liberty of a brave nation, and he seemed to accept what I said, although I felt he was angry with me. The Emperor of Blefuscu came to Lilliput to make peace, which was drawn up on terms that were very good for the Lilliputians, but I knew in my heart that the Emperor would not forgive me for refusing to carry out his plan to destroy their country entirely.

*Shortly after this, Gulliver learns that the Emperor has decided to punish him for refusing to enslave the people of Blefuscu, so Gulliver escapes to Blefuscu, from where he is able to get back to England. He has many other adventures, visiting a land of giants and a land of talking horses. You can read about them all in* Gulliver's Travels *by Jonathan Swift.*

## Jim Hawkins in the Apple Barrel

### Adapted from the novel *Treasure Island* by Robert Louis Stevenson

*Jim Hawkins is the narrator of* Treasure Island, *which means that he tells us the story. He is a young boy and we see everything through his eyes, which makes it even more exciting. Jim helps his mother to run an inn, which stands in a lonely spot on the coast. One day an old sailor called* Billy Bones *arrives and decides to stay. He is fierce and frightening, and Jim soon realises that he is really a pirate! Billy Bones drinks too much and falls down dead. Because he has not paid his bill, Jim's mother searches his belongings to take the money that he owed her. But Jim and his mother find more than money: they discover a map of an island where treasure is buried!*

*Jim shows the map to Dr Livesey, the local magistrate, who shows it to Squire Trelawney, a rich man who lives nearby. Squire Trelawney says that he will pay for a ship to take them both to find the treasure, and that Jim can go along as the cabin boy. Unfortunately, Squire Trelawney can't keep a secret. He tells people in Bristol, where the ship, called the* Hispaniola, *is being fitted out, all about the treasure map. The Squire hires Captain Smollett to be the captain of the* Hispaniola, *and Smollett looks for sailors to be the crew. Some pirates, who know about the treasure map, decide to join his crew, and they are prepared to murder Dr Livesey, Squire Trelawney and all the honest men on board to get their hands on the treasure. The pirates are led by Long John Silver, hired as the ship's cook, who has a wooden leg and walks with a crutch. He seems to be kind and polite, but really he is ruthless and wicked.*

*One night, when young Jim Hawkins has finished his work, he decides to have an apple from the apple barrel on the deck. As the barrel is almost empty, he has to climb inside to reach the apples at the bottom. As he sits there eating his apple, the rocking of the ship lulls him to sleep. He is woken by two people talking who don't know he is in the barrel and can hear them. One of these people is Long John Silver. Let's find out what Jim heard...*

I climbed inside the apple barrel and managed to find a nice juicy red one to eat. I decided to have a rest and began to munch on my apple. As I sat there in the dark, listening to the sound of the waves crashing against the side of the *Hispaniola*, I started to doze off. This was the life; enough apples to keep my hunger at bay and the ship rocking me gently to sleep. Suddenly, thump! A great, heavy man sat down next to the barrel, which shook as he leant his shoulder against it. I was just about to jump out of the barrel when the man began to speak. It was Long John Silver's voice! I lay there, trembling and listening, afraid but curious. What was I about to overhear? He was talking to someone about pirates, particularly one really famous and wicked pirate called Flint – and worse than that, Long John Silver had actually sailed with him! So Long John Silver wasn't just our ship's cook – he was a pirate himself.

'Yes, I knew Captain Flint well enough. I sailed with him for years,' said Silver.

'Ah!' cried another voice, which I knew was that of one of the youngest sailors on board. 'He was the finest of them all, was Flint!'

'He was the terror of the high seas,' replied Silver. 'What he went after, he got. No ship, no crew and no captain was safe, once Flint had 'em in his sights. Once Flint and his men boarded a ship, it was time for everyone on that poor vessel to start saying their prayers, because they weren't long for this world. No mercy, he'd kill 'em all and get their treasure. What a man! Ain't no one ever come near him for plundering ships. Big ones, small ones, he'd get whatever was on board and burn the ship to ashes. You had to have a strong stomach to sail with Flint, but we all got rich. I saved two thousand pounds while I was sailing with him. A nice little fund to retire on. That ain't bad for a sailor and it's all safe in the bank, far away from thieving hands. Not all in the same bank mind you – a bit here, a bit there. Not too much in one place, in case anyone gets suspicious.'

'So you all got rich with Flint? That's the life for me!' said the young sailor. It was horrible to hear this young man being corrupted by the evil old pirate.

'No lad, not all,' said Long John. 'Because some of me shipmates weren't as careful as I was with their money. Most of Flint's men are on board with us now, and they sure needs the money. Poor as church mice, they are. I've seen some of 'em begging in the streets. Spent everything they ever got on drink and enjoying themselves as soon as they got to port. I likes to have a good time every now and then, but you has to think o' the future. Who's going to look after an old pirate when he can't sail the seven seas no more? No one – so make sure you've put something by. No good being rich just for a while when you're in port, I aims to be rich for the rest o' me life and live like the best of 'em – Dr Livesey, Squire Trelawney, Captain Smollett an' all. But this here little trip with Squire Trelawney should set us all up. We'll be rich men when we gets our hands on their treasure and then – then it's a life of luxury for old Long John Silver, my lad.
The *Hispaniola* is going to be my last ship.'

'And what happens to the Doctor, the Captain and the Squire then?' asked the young sailor.

'What do you think? They walk the plank. Ain't you never heard the saying, dead men tells no tales?'

My blood ran cold. This wicked man was planning to kill my friends and probably me, when all the time he was being as nice and polite as anything to us.

'Well, I tell you now,' replied the young sailor, 'I didn't much like the idea of what you was talking about till I had this talk with you, John; but I think I've changed my mind!'

'And a brave lad you are, and smart too, smart as paint. I see'd that when I set my eyes on you, and I'll talk to you like a man, not a boy,' answered Silver, slapping with the sailor so hard on his back that the barrel shook. 'A finer gentleman of fortune I never clapped me eyes on.'

'What's a gentleman of fortune?' asked the now thoroughly corrupted young sailor.

'Why a pirate, lad,' said Long John Silver. 'For you know, we don't always tell the truth exactly about what it is we do! Some folks seem mighty prejudiced against pirates, and to speak honest, it ain't the life for everyone. Gentlemen of fortune, they lives rough, and they risk hanging, but they eat and drink like strong men, and when a cruise is done, why, it's hundreds of pounds instead of hundreds of pennies in their pockets.'

Another pirate had by now joined Silver and his young companion. 'Now look'ee here, Long John,' said the other pirate, who was called Israel, 'here's what I want to know, how long are we a-going to wait before we attack? I've had about enough of that Cap'n Smollett; he's ordered me about long enough, by thunder! I want to go into that cabin, I do. I want to take their fine food and wines and enjoy some of that myself.'

'Israel,' said Silver, 'you're not the brainiest man in the crew, but listen to me; after all your ears are big enough! Now, here's what I say: you'll knuckle down, and you'll work hard, and you'll keep your mouth shut tight, and you'll wait till I give the word; d'ye hear that, my son?'

'Of course I do,' growled Israel. 'What I say is, when? When can we do it?'

'When! By the powers!' cried Silver. 'I'll tell you when. The last moment I can manage, and that's when. Cap'n Smollett is a good sailor, and Squire Trelawney has got the treasure map – I don't know where it is, do I? Neither do you. Well then, I let Trelawney find the treasure and get it aboard this ship. Then we'll see. If I was sure I could trust you all, I'd have Cap'n Smollett sail us half-way back home again before I struck a blow. Wait for now is all I say; but when the time comes, why, let her rip! You can have your fine food and your fines wines, Israel, there's only one thing I claim – I claim Squire Trelawney. I'll wring his head off his body with these hands! Hey old chap,' he said to the young sailor, 'you just jump up, like a sweet lad, and get me an apple, to wet my pipe like.'

I was absolutely terrified! If they discovered I was listening to their evil plan, they would throw me overboard for sure! I should have leapt out and run for it if I had found the strength, but my legs wouldn't move. I heard the man begin to get up, and then Israel stopped him.

'Oh, forget the apples! Let's have a swig of the rum.'

As the pirates each took swigs of the rum, a sort of brightness fell upon me in the barrel. I looked up and saw the moon had risen and was shining white on the sails. Almost at the same time the voice of the lookout shouted, 'Land ho!' We were in sight of the island where our map told us the treasure was buried.

Young Jim Hawkins now knows Long John Silver's evil plan. Will the pirates get away with it? What will Jim do next? And will they find the treasure? Read the rest of *Treasure Island* by Robert Louis Stevenson to find out.

# The Happy Prince

### Adapted from a story by Oscar Wilde that was published in 1888.

High above the city, on a tall column, stood the statue of the Happy Prince. He was covered all over with thin leaves of fine gold, for eyes he had two bright sapphires and a large red ruby glowed on his sword-hilt.

One night there flew over the city a little Swallow, on his way to Egypt. 'Where shall I rest?' he said. Then he saw the statue on the tall column. 'I will rest there,' he cried; 'it is a fine position with plenty of fresh air.' So he alighted just between the feet of the Happy Prince.

'I have a golden bedroom,' he said softly to himself as he looked round, and he prepared to go to sleep; but just as he was putting his head under his wing a large drop of water fell on him. 'What a curious thing!' he cried, 'there is not a single cloud in the sky, and yet it is raining.'

Then another drop fell.

'What is the use of a statue if it cannot keep the rain off?' he said; 'I must look for a good chimney-pot,' and he determined to fly away.

But before he had opened his wings, a third drop fell, and he looked up, and saw – Ah! What did he see?

The eyes of the Happy Prince were filled with tears, and tears were running down his golden cheeks. His face was so beautiful in the moonlight that the little Swallow was filled with pity.

'Who are you?' he said.

'I am the Happy Prince.'

'Why are you weeping then?' asked the Swallow.

'When I was alive and had a human heart,' answered the statue, 'I lived in the palace of Sans-Souci, where sorrow is not allowed to enter. In the daytime I played with my friends in the garden, and in the evening I led the dance in the Great Hall. Round the garden ran a very high wall, but I never cared to ask what lay beyond it, everything about me was

> Sans-Souci means No Worries.

so beautiful. My courtiers called me the Happy Prince, and happy indeed I was, if pleasure be happiness. But now that I am dead they have set me up here so high that I can see all the misery of my city, and though my heart is made of lead, I cannot choose but weep.'

'Far away,' continued the statue in a low musical voice, 'far away in a little street there is a poor house. One of the windows is open, and through it I can see a woman seated at a table. Her face is thin, and she has red hands, all pricked by the needle, for she is a seamstress. She is embroidering flowers on a satin gown for the loveliest of the Queen's maids-of-honour to wear at the next court ball. In a bed in the corner of the room her little boy is lying ill. He has a fever, and is asking for oranges. His mother has nothing to give him but river water, so he is crying. Swallow, Swallow, little Swallow, will you not bring her the ruby out of my sword-hilt? My feet are fastened to this pedestal and I cannot move.'

'I am waited for in Egypt,' said the Swallow. 'My friends are flying up and down the Nile, and talking to the large lotus-flowers.'

'Swallow, Swallow, little Swallow,' said the Prince, 'will you not stay with me for one night, and be my messenger? The boy is so thirsty, and the mother so worried.'

The Happy Prince looked so sad that the little Swallow was sorry. 'It is very cold here,' he said; 'but I will stay with you for one night, and be your messenger.'

'Thank you, little Swallow,' said the Prince.

So the Swallow picked out the great ruby from the Prince's sword, and flew away with it in his beak over the roofs of the town.

At last he came to the poor house and looked in. The boy was tossing feverishly on his bed, and the mother had fallen asleep, she was so tired. In he hopped, and laid the great ruby on the table beside the woman's thimble. Then he flew gently round the bed, fanning the boy's forehead with his wings. 'How cool I feel,' said the boy, 'I must be getting better.' He sank into a delicious slumber.

Then the Swallow flew back to the Happy Prince, and told him what he had done. 'It is curious,' he remarked, 'but I feel quite warm now, although it is so cold.'

'That is because you have done a good action,' said the Prince. And the little Swallow fell asleep.

When day broke he flew down to the river and had a bath. 'Tonight I go to Egypt,' said the Swallow, and he was in high spirits at the prospect. He visited all the public monuments, and sat a long time on top of the church steeple. When the moon rose he flew back to the Happy Prince. 'Have you any messages for Egypt?' he cried; 'I am just about to leave.'

'Swallow, Swallow, little Swallow,' said the Prince, 'will you not stay with me one night longer?'

'I am waited for in Egypt,' answered the Swallow. 'Tomorrow my friends will fly up to the beautiful waterfall. At noon the yellow lions come down to the water's edge to drink.

They have green eyes and their roar is louder than the roar of the waterfall.'

'Swallow, Swallow, little Swallow,' said the Prince, 'far away across the city I see a young man in an attic. He is leaning over a desk covered with papers, and in a glass by his side there is a bunch of withered violets. He is trying to finish a play for the Director of the Theatre, but he is too cold to write any more. His fire has gone out, and hunger has made him faint.'

'I will wait with you one night longer,' said the Swallow, who really had a good heart. 'Shall I take him another ruby?'

'Alas! I have no ruby now,' said the Prince; 'my eyes are all that I have left. They are made of rare sapphires, which were brought out of India a thousand years ago. Pluck out one of them and take it to him. He will sell it to the jeweller, and buy food and firewood, and finish his play.'

'Dear Prince,' said the Swallow, 'I cannot do that.' He began to weep.

'Swallow, Swallow, little Swallow,' said the Prince, 'do as I command you.'

So the Swallow plucked out the Prince's eye, and flew away to the student's attic room. It was easy enough to get in, as there was a hole in the roof. Through this he darted, and came into the room. The young man had his head buried in his hands, so he did not hear the flutter of the bird's wings, and when he looked up he found the beautiful sapphire lying on the withered violets.

'This is from some great admirer,' he cried. 'Now I can finish my play!'

The next day the Swallow flew down to the harbour. He sat on the mast of a large ship and watched the sailors hauling big chests out of the hold with ropes. When the moon rose he flew back to the Happy Prince.

'I am come to bid you goodbye,' he cried.

'Swallow, Swallow, little Swallow,' said the Prince, 'will you not stay with me one night longer?'

'It is winter,' answered the Swallow, 'and the snow will soon be here. In Egypt the sun is warm on the green palm trees, and the crocodiles lie in the mud and look lazily about them. Dear Prince, I must leave you, but I will never forget you, and next spring I will bring you back two beautiful jewels in place of those you have given away. The ruby shall be redder than a red rose, and the sapphire shall be as blue as the great sea.'

'In the square below,' said the Happy Prince, 'there stands a little match-girl. She has let her matches fall in the gutter, and they are all spoiled. Her father will be angry if she does not bring home some money, and she is crying. She has no shoes or stockings, and her little head is bare. Pluck out my other eye, and give it to her, and her father will not beat her.'

'I will stay with you one night longer,' said the Swallow, 'but I cannot pluck out your eye. You would be quite blind then.'

'Swallow, Swallow, little Swallow,' said the Prince, 'do as I command you.'

So he plucked out the Prince's other eye, and darted down with it. He swooped past the match-girl, and slipped the jewel into the palm of her hand. 'What a lovely bit of glass,' cried the little girl; and she ran home, laughing.

Do you remember reading Hans Christian Andersen's sad story of *The Little Match Girl* in Year 4?

Then the Swallow came back to the Prince. 'You are blind now,' he said, 'so I will stay with you always.'

'No, little Swallow,' said the poor Prince, 'you must go away to Egypt.'

'I will stay with you always,' said the Swallow, and he slept at the Prince's feet.

All the next day he sat on the Prince's shoulder, and told him stories of what he had seen in strange lands. He told him of the Sphinx, who is as old as the world itself and lives in the desert, and knows everything; of the merchants, who walk slowly by the side of their camels, and carry amber beads in their hands; and of the little people who sail over a big lake on large flat leaves, and are always at war with the butterflies.

'Dear little Swallow,' said the Prince, 'you tell me of strange things, but stranger than anything is the suffering of men and of women. Fly over my city, little Swallow, and tell me what you see there.'

So the Swallow flew over the great city, and saw the rich people having parties in their beautiful houses, while the beggars were sitting at the gates. He flew into dark lanes, and saw the white faces of starving children looking out hopelessly at the black streets. Then he flew back and told the Prince what he had seen.

'I am covered with fine gold,' said the Prince, 'you must take it off, leaf by leaf, and give it to my poor; the living always think that gold can make them happy.'

Leaf after leaf of the fine gold the Swallow picked off, till the Happy Prince looked quite dull and grey. Leaf after leaf of the fine gold he brought to the poor and the children's faces grew rosier, and they laughed and played games in the street. 'We have bread now!' they cried.

Then the snow came, and after the snow came the frost. The poor little Swallow grew colder and colder, but he would not leave the Prince. He tried to keep himself warm by flapping his wings, but at last he knew that he was going to die. He had just strength to fly up to the Prince's shoulder once more. 'Goodbye, dear Prince!' he murmured, 'will you let me kiss your hand?'

'I am glad that you are going to Egypt at last, little Swallow,' said the Prince, 'you have stayed too long here; but you must kiss me on the lips, for I love you.'

'It is not to Egypt that I am going,' said the Swallow. 'I am going to die.'

And he kissed the Happy Prince on the lips, and fell down dead at his feet.

At that moment a curious crack sounded inside the statue, as if something had broken. The fact is that the heart, which was made of lead, had snapped right in two.

Early the next morning the Mayor was walking in the square below in company with the Town Councillors. As they passed the column he looked up at the statue: 'Dear me! How shabby the Happy Prince looks!' he said. 'The ruby has fallen out of his sword, his eyes are gone, and he is golden no longer. There is actually a dead bird at his feet!' said the Mayor.

So they pulled down the statue of the Happy Prince and melted it down in a furnace.

'What a strange thing!' said the overseer of the workmen at the foundry. 'This broken lead heart will not melt in the furnace. We must throw it away.' So they threw it on a dust-heap where the dead Swallow was also lying.

'Bring me the two most precious things in the city,' said God to one of His Angels; and the Angel brought Him the leaden heart and the dead bird.

'You have rightly chosen,' said God, 'for in my garden of Paradise this little bird shall sing for evermore, and in my city of gold the Happy Prince shall praise me.'

# Learning about Language

## Parts of Speech

In English, there are eight parts of speech, which means there are eight possible jobs a word can do in a sentence. You know some of them from learning about language in Years 3 and 4. Here they are with examples of how each one can be used in sentences:

**Noun:** a word that names a person, place, animal, thing or idea

*I love **pizza** and **lemonade**.*

***Measles** is a terrible **disease**.*

47

**Adjective:** a word that modifies, intensifies or tells something about a noun

*It was a **dark** and **stormy** night.*

*My sister is really **intelligent**.*

**Pronoun:** a word that takes the place of a noun

***She** loved to play hide and seek, but **they** did not.*

**Verb:** a word that describes an action or a state of being

*We **caught** and **released** 17 fish.*

*I **am** an insomniac.*

**Adverb:** a word that adds to the meaning of a verb by telling how, or in what manner, the action occurred

*She reads **well**.*

*We ran **quickly** to the porch.*

**Conjunction:** a word that joins words, ideas or phrases in a sentence

*The lady bought a new hat **and** a new bag.*

*Since they pulled my teeth, I can **neither** eat **nor** sleep.*

**Preposition:** a word that tells you where one thing is in relation to another thing

*The horse galloped **over** the brow of the hill and **out** of sight.*

*I stored my suitcase **under** the bed.*

**Interjection:** a word expressing sudden emotion

*I like it, but, **good grief**, it was expensive!*

***Ouch!** That hurt.*

Words have jobs, just like people. And, they can change jobs just as we do. For example, you might think that the word 'run' is always a verb because it describes an action. But look at the way it is used in each of the following sentences.

*I **run** two miles a day.*

Here, **run** is a **verb**; it describes an action.

*My **run** lasts about 20 minutes.*

Here, **run** is a **noun**; it names a thing.

In order really to understand a sentence, you have to recognise the words and also understand what job each word is doing in the sentence.

## Complete Sentences

Every sentence must contain a verb. It tells us what the subject of the sentence is doing, and without it, you don't have a sentence! For example, is this a sentence?

*Gulliver the land of Lilliput.*

No, because we don't know how Gulliver and the land of Lilliput are supposed to be joined together. Is this a sentence?

*Gulliver **visited** the land of Lilliput.*

Yes it is. The verb links Gulliver – the subject of the sentence – with Lilliput – the place he visited.

Sometimes verbs are very small words, like 'is' and 'do', but they are still important! For example:

*No one **knows** where Neverland **is**.*

***Do** your homework before dinner.*

## Subject-Verb Agreement

Whenever you write sentences, make sure that your subject and your verb agree. We don't say 'he run' or 'they runs'. We say 'he runs' and 'they run'. A singular subject takes a singular verb, and a plural subject takes a plural verb. See if you can pick the right verb form for each of the following sentences:

*Pizzas **is** / **are** delicious.*

*My friends **live** / **lives** in the same street.*

*A flock of birds **was flying** / **were flying** around my swing.*

The last sentence is a little tricky. It might seem like there are many birds, so the subject must be plural. But really the subject of the sentence is flock, and there's only one flock. That's why we say: 'A flock of seagulls was flying overhead.' A noun which describes a group of people, animals or things is called a **collective noun**. Here are some examples:

A **herd** of cows

A **pride** of lions

A stamp **collection**

A football **team**

Collective nouns always take singular verbs:

*The **choir** is practising hard for the concert.*

*The older **class** enjoys cross-country runs.*

## Active and Passive Voice

Usually, we have sentences like the ones we saw above where the subject of a sentence is at the beginning and does the action of the verb. We say these sentences are in the *active voice*. However, sometimes we want to use the *passive voice* when we change the order to show that the subject is having the verb done to them. Here are some examples:

## Active voice

*Juan **is reading** a book.*

*The postman **delivered** the letters.*

*The ball **hit** Angelica.*

## Passive voice

*The book is **being read** by Juan.*

*The letters **were delivered** by the postman.*

*Angelica **was hit** by the ball.*

We get a different sense of the meaning of a sentence depending on whether it is in the active or the passive voice. Although most sentences in English are in the active voice, sometimes we want to use the passive voice because we don't know who or what 'did' the verb. Look at these sentences to see why.

| Active voice | Passive voice |
|---|---|
| Lily **took** a picture of the winner. | A picture **was taken** of the winner. |
| Jake **broke** the window with his football. | The window **was broken** by a football. |

Sometimes writers use the passive voice to provide some variety, but don't use passive verbs too often as it can become boring! We usually want be told clearly who is 'doing' the verb.

Here are some sentences with verbs in the active voice. Try turning them around to make them passive.

Jenny's mother **baked** a chocolate cake.

Maths **takes up** a lot of homework time.

Polar bears **inhabit** the Arctic.

Now try turning these passive verbs into active verbs.

Michael Morpurgo **was chosen** by most of the children as their favourite author.

The car **was driven** all the way to school by my father even though the petrol gauge was registering empty.

Fish **are eaten** by bears.

# Kinds of Sentences

There are different kinds of sentences. In Year 4, we learnt about the following kinds of sentences:

● A **declarative sentence** makes a statement and usually ends with a full stop.

● An **interrogative sentence** asks a question and ends with a question mark.

● An **imperative sentence** is an order or a command. It can end with a full stop or, when it is said with great emotion, with an exclamation mark.

In which category would you put the sentences below?

*Read chapter two.*

*It's hot today.*

*Go to your room!*

*Did you ask Mum?*

*The dog wagged its tail when Toni got home from school.*

Exclamatory sentences are sentences that are exclaimed, or shouted out, like 'Get out now!' or 'That's disgusting!' Both of these are complete sentences, but sometimes when we are very excited, we don't speak in complete sentences. Then we might make exclamatory statements like these:

*Yuck!*

*Yippee! The big jackpot!*

# Commas

Commas tell readers when to pause within a sentence and which groups of words to read together. Here are some situations in which we use commas:

**between the city and the county in an address**
   *Southampton, Hampshire*

**between items in a list** (but not when the word 'and' links the last two words in the list)
   *That man is mad, bad and dangerous to know.*

**to separate the words in a subordinate clause from the rest of the sentence**
   *I chose roses, even though they were very expensive at that time, to give to my mother on Mother's Day.*

**when you want to let the reader know that you are introducing another idea, without starting a new sentence**
   *I wrote the thank-you letter with my very best pen, but there were still a few blots on the paper.*

**after the words 'yes' and 'no'**
   *No, you may not stay up all night.*

**inside quotation marks, when writing dialogue**
   *'I'm so glad to see you,' said Pollyanna.*

# Colons and Semi-Colons

A *semi-colon*, like a comma, causes the reader to pause, but it causes a bit more of a break in the flow of the sentence. It links together clauses and ideas that belong together in the same sentence. This means that the words following the semi-colon should be on the same subject as the words before it. Semi-colons should not be used too often, but they can provide variety and give you another way of breaking up the sections of a sentence in a way that makes it clear to the reader which words belong together.

*He enjoyed his triumph; the regret came later.*

*Sit still while I tell you what I have just done; the explanation for my actions can wait.*

*We love to spend the summer holidays at the seaside; Cornwall, Devon and Guernsey have some of our favourite beaches.*

A *colon* introduces a list of things that are all related to the first part of the sentence, before the colon.

*In geography we learnt about the seven continents: Europe, Africa, Asia, North America, South America, Australia and Antarctica.*

*I have been to Stratford-upon-Avon to see several plays by Shakespeare:* A Midsummer Night's Dream, Hamlet *and* Othello.

*Before crossing the road, you should practise the Green Cross Code: look right, look left, look right again.*

Commas, semi-colons and colons all put a pause or break into a sentence, but they are not all of equal length. A comma gives you the shortest pause, then a semi-colon, then a colon.

We learnt in Music about the number of beats in a crotchet (one), a minim (two) and a semibreve (four). Commas, semi-colons and colons are a bit like that.

# Apostrophes

Apostrophes are used to show possession.

**Singular nouns** show possession by adding *'s*.

*My **brother's** bicycle is too big for him.*

*The **school's** intake was drawn from a wide area.*

Suppose the singular noun already ends in *s*? Then you still add *'s*.

We read the story of the Princess and the Pea in Year 2.

*The **princess's** bed was so uncomfortable that she couldn't sleep.*

*The ambulance took her to **St Thomas's** Hospital.*

*There were leaves on the **bus's** roof.*

Some people prefer not to add the *s* to the end of a word that ends in *s* when they are making it possessive. For example:

*King **Midas'** daughter turned to gold when he touched her.*

This is also correct! Possession in the singular can be indicated with or without the addition of *s* at the end of nouns ending in *s*.

**Plural nouns** usually end in *s*. To indicate possession, you just add an apostrophe.

*The **elephants'** tusks were made of ivory.*

*The candidates struggled with some of the **examiners'** questions.*

*Prince Charming was dazzled by the beauty of the **princesses'** ball gowns.*

Some nouns have plurals that do not end in *s*. We call them **irregular plurals**. Here are some of them.

| Singular | Plural |
| --- | --- |
| man | men |
| woman | women |
| child | children |
| tooth | teeth |
| mouse | mice |

To indicate possession, we just add *'s* in the usual way.

*The **men's** room is smaller than the **women's** room.*

*Mrs Danvers very nearly fell over the **children's** toys.*

Do you know the plural of goose? Or ox? Or sheep? (That's a tricky one!)

Apostrophes are also used in contractions to show that some letters have been left out. The contraction **that's** is short for **that is**. The apostrophe tells you the letter *i* has been left out. Similarly, the contraction **we're** is short for **we are**. **I'm** is short for **I am**. Which letters are missing from **don't, wouldn't** and **it's**?

> Do you remember the difference between **its** and **it's**?
>
> **It's** is short for **it is**, as in: 'It's a long way from home.'
>
> **Its** is a possessive pronoun, as in: 'The shirt had lost **its** buttons.'

## Speech Marks

Use speech marks when you want to distinguish somebody else's words from your own words. For instance, if you were writing a story about a head teacher giving advice to her students when they are leaving the school, you might use speech marks like this:

> *'You have all done well in your exams,' said Ms Philpot, addressing the final assembly, 'but you will find that you need to keep working hard in your next school if you want to build on that success.'*

Quotation marks are also used for titles of poems, songs, short stories and magazine articles.

> *We read 'Dreams', a poem by Langston Hughes.*

## Synonyms and Antonyms

A synonym is a word that means the same thing, or almost the same thing, as another word. *Quick* and *fast* are synonyms, and so are *costly* and *expensive*. Antonyms are words that are opposites. *Soft* and *hard* are antonyms. So are *good* and *evil*. See if you can match the words on the left with the synonyms and antonyms on the right.

| Synonyms | |
|---|---|
| bad | buccaneer |
| friend | evil |
| pirate | mate |
| try | spotless |
| clean | attempt |

| Antonyms | |
|---|---|
| victory | expensive |
| true | fail |
| succeed | shy |
| cheap | defeat |
| bold | false |

# Prefixes

Prefixes are groups of letters that are added to the front of words to make new words, with different meanings. In Year 4 we learnt a few prefixes, and we'll learn more now.

*im-* and *in-* mean not.

> Something that's **impossible** is not possible.
>
> Someone who's **inconsistent** is not consistent.

*non-* also means not.

> A **nonfiction** book is not fictional – that is, it's a true story.
>
> A **nonviolent** protest is not violent.

*mis-* means wrong, wrongly, bad or badly.

> If you **misspell** a word, you're spelling it incorrectly.
>
> If you **misbehave**, you behave badly.

*en-* means in or into.

> To **endanger** someone is to put that person in danger.
>
> To **entrap** someone is to draw the person into a trap.

*pre-* means before, or earlier.

> A **preview** lets you see or know about something in advance.
>
> A **prehistoric** event took place long ago, before people began recording history.

We learnt about prehistory in Year 1 when we learnt about the Ice Age.

# Suffixes

Suffixes are a lot like prefixes, but they are added to the end of a word.

*-y* is a suffix that can be used to make adjectives.

> Does anyone you know display greed? Then that person is **greedy**.

Are you ready to go to sleep? Then you must be **sleepy**, like Frère Jacques.

> We sang 'Frère Jacques' ('Brother John') in Year 2.

*-ly* and *-ily* are suffixes that are often used to make adverbs.

Take the adjective quick, add -ly and you get the adverb **quickly**.

In the same way, easy becomes **easily**.

*-ful* is a suffix meaning full of.

A **thoughtful** person is full of thoughts, and a **playful** baby is full of play.

*-able* or *-ible* is a suffix that means capable of or worthy of a specific action.

If a shirt is capable of being washed, we say it is **washable**.

If you can bend and flex your arms and legs well, we say you are **flexible**.

*-ment* is a suffix used to make verbs into nouns.

If everybody in the room agrees (verb), you have achieved **agreement** (noun).

If you amaze (verb) your parents, they are in a state of **amazement** (noun).

It's useful to know commonly used prefixes and suffixes because sometimes you can work out what a difficult word means by breaking it down into prefix, root and suffix. For example, you may never have read or heard the word 'misrule'. But if you break it into two parts – *mis-rule* – you can guess that it means to rule badly.

## Writing and Research

Once you've learnt how to write sentences, you can practise putting sentences together into paragraphs and longer works. In Year 4 we learnt about writing reports and formal letters. Here are some things you might try writing:

1. A letter to a friend or family member

2. A short story

**3.** A summary of what you did today

**4.** A description of an object or of a person

**5.** A poem

**6.** A report

To write a report, first choose a topic you'd like to learn more about. Then go to your school library or local library and ask the librarian to help you find information on your topic. (You can also find information by searching the Internet.) As you learn interesting facts or read quotations that you think you might want to use in your report, write them down, making a note of where you found them. Whenever you find something in a book, write down the title of the book, the author, where the book was published, by whom and when. Most of this information can be found in the first few pages of a book.

When you write your report, think of it as a set of paragraphs, each of which should have its own purpose. Before you start writing, you should have a good idea of what each paragraph is intended to accomplish. For instance, if you were writing a report on Australia, you might have an introduction about why you chose to write about Australia, a paragraph about the people who live there, another on the animals that can be found in the Outback and a third on Australia's Great Barrier Reef where beautiful sea creatures live. Your last paragraph should be your conclusion, in which you restate your point and finish up your report.

See what else you can find in Australia on page 99.

*Kangaroos live in Australia's Outback.*

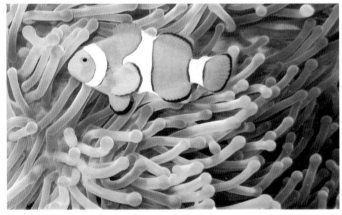

*Clownfish are just one example of the many different sea creatures you can find on the Great Barrier Reef.*

At the end of your report, you'll want to include a *bibliography*. A bibliography is a list of books and articles you used to write your report. Here's what some entries from a bibliography on Australia might look like:

Bodden, Valerie. *Great Barrier Reef.* London: Franklin Watts, 2011.

Moriarty, Aleta. *Australia.* Dunfermline: Franklin Watts, 2013.

Wojahn, Rebecca Hogue and Wojahn, Donald. *An Australian Outback Food Chain: A Who-Eats-What Adventure.* Minneapolis: Lerner Publishing, 2009.

Notice that the entries in a bibliography are listed alphabetically, by the author's last name. The titles of the books should also be italicised or underlined. Writing a report isn't easy, but, like other things in life, you can get good at it by practising.

# Familiar Sayings

*Every culture has some sayings and phrases that can be difficult to understand if you have never heard them before. In this section we introduce a handful of common English sayings and phrases and give examples of how they are used.*

## Beauty is only skin deep

*People use this saying to mean that you can't judge a person's character by how good he or she looks.*

'That new girl is very pretty,' Kim said.

'Yes, but I wonder if she's nice, too,' Carol said. 'After all, beauty is only skin deep.'

## Live and let live

*This saying means mind your own business and let other people live as they wish to live.*

'You need a haircut, Trevor.' Fatima put her hands on her hips. 'And look at those ugly shoes! You need to buy some new ones.'

'Listen, Fatima, I like the way my hair looks, and I think these are cool shoes,' Trevor said. 'I'm going to keep dressing the way I want to dress. As for you, you'd better learn to live and let live.'

## As the crow flies

*When a bird flies from place to place, it flies through the air and takes the most direct route. But when people walk or drive, they usually have to follow roads and often have to go further. When people give a distance 'as the crow flies', they mean the shortest distance between the two points, not the distance you would have to travel if you followed the roads.*

As Vishal and his mother drove along the river, they could see the beach on the opposite side. Vishal asked, 'How far is it to the beach?'

'It's only about a quarter of a mile as the crow flies,' his mother said. 'But we have to drive three miles north to the bridge and then three miles south once we cross the bridge.'

## The bigger they are, the harder they fall

*When a huge oak falls in the forest, it makes a tremendous crash. When a small sapling falls, you can barely hear it. When people use this saying, they mean that the larger or more powerful something is (it could be a person, a team, a country or something else), the bigger the shock will be when a setback occurs.*

'We'll never be able to beat United,' the captain told his manager. They're at the top of the Premier League and they haven't lost a game yet this season!'

'Never mind that,' said the manager. 'If we play our best game, we can beat them – the bigger they are, the harder they fall!'

## Bury the hatchet

*This phrase comes from Native American culture. When two nations declared war on each other, they were said to take up the hatchet. When they agreed to end their war, they were said to bury the hatchet. To bury the hatchet means to stop holding a grudge and make peace with someone else, to let bygones be bygones and forgive and forget.*

Colin could not forgive his sister for breaking his tennis racket. He kept up a sulky silence for days whenever he was around her. Finally, his sister said: 'Oh, Colin, can't we bury the hatchet? I hate it when you give me the silent treatment!'

## Birds of a feather flock together

*We use this saying to mean that similar people, or people who have similar interests, like to be with each other.*

'Those guys always eat lunch together,' Tina said, nodding towards a group of boys in the cafeteria.

'Yes,' said June. 'They're all in the cricket team and all they want to talk about is runs and wickets.'

Tina nodded. 'Birds of a feather flock together!'

## Blow hot and cold

*This phrase comes from one of* Aesop's Fables, *in which a man blows on his fingers to warm them up and then blows on his soup to cool it down. In both cases, the man is blowing air, but with a different effect. If a person says one thing and later says the opposite, we say that the person is blowing hot and cold.*

'Is Felicia going to try out for the swimming team this year?' Stacy asked.

Do you remember reading some of *Aesop's Fables* in Years 1 and 2?

'I don't know,' Tricia replied. 'Last week she was saying yes, but this week she's saying no. She's really blowing hot and cold.'

## Breaking the ice

*Before ice-breaking ships were invented, sailors who wanted to sail during the winter had to walk out onto frozen water and break up the ice before the boat could move forward. Nowadays people use the phrase 'breaking the ice' to refer to ending an awkward silence by beginning a conversation. People also use 'ice-breakers', which are usually fun and silly games, to help people to get to know each other in new groups.*

It was the first day of Guide camp. The four girls began to unpack their clothes and make up their beds in silence. None of the girls knew each other, and no one knew what to say. Finally, one of them broke the ice by saying: 'Hey, where's everybody from?'

## Bull in a china shop

*If a person is clumsy in a place where things can be upset or broken, or handles a delicate situation badly, we say the person is acting like a bull in a china shop.*

Kemar slammed the door behind him. A painting fell off the wall and his mother's crystal vase wobbled on the dining room table. 'I'm home!' he yelled, then tripped on the doormat and fell onto the floor.

'Honestly, Kemar,' his mother said as she helped him up, 'sometimes you're just like a bull in a china shop!'

## Don't count your chickens before they hatch

*Because not every egg in a nest hatches a baby chicken, people use this saying to mean that you may be disappointed if you count on having something before it is really yours.*

'I've got some really cool headphones to go with the iPod I'm getting for my birthday,' Elliot told Alex.

'How do you know you're getting an iPod for your birthday?' Alex replied. 'Don't count your chickens before they hatch.'

In Year 3 we learnt about the cycle of life and how chicks hatch from eggs.

## Don't put all your eggs in one basket

*Once upon a time a girl went to her family's henhouse to gather eggs for breakfast. Instead of taking only a few eggs, she packed all the eggs into her basket. On the way back to the house, she tripped and broke the eggs so there was nothing left for her family to eat that day. She then wished she hadn't put all her eggs in one basket. If someone tells you not to put all your eggs in one basket, the person is reminding you what can happen when you rely too heavily on one plan and don't think about what could go wrong.*

'Dan's older brother wants to go to Cambridge. He says he won't even apply to any other universities.'

'But what will he do if he doesn't get into Cambridge? Maybe he shouldn't put all his eggs in one basket.'

## Can't hold a candle to

*Before electricity, servants had to hold candles for their masters to light the way. When we say one person or thing can't hold a candle to another person or thing, we mean that the former is not nearly as good as the latter.*

'How's the frozen pizza?' the girls' mother asked.

'It's okay,' said Isabel. 'But it can't hold a candle to your homemade pizza!'

## Go to pot

*This phrase was originally used in the kitchen. All of the leftover scraps that weren't good for anything else went to pot. That is, they were thrown into a big pot to make a stew. Eventually, the meaning changed. Now when we say something has gone to pot, we mean it has not been taken care of and has gone bad or been ruined.*

'Have you checked the garden recently?' Dan asked.

'No,' Pete replied, 'not for a week or so.'

'You'd better get out there, or the weeds will take over and the whole thing will go to pot.'

## More haste, less speed

*This saying means that when you rush you don't do as good a job as when you are careful and take your time. When you make mistakes by rushing, it could take you longer in the end to finish things properly.*

It was Tony's night to do the dishes. He quickly rinsed all of the dinner plates, then ran the cutlery under the tap.

'What's your hurry?' his father asked.

'I told Karl I'd meet him at the park!'

'If you aren't more careful cleaning these dishes,' his father said, picking up a plate with spaghetti sauce on the rim, 'you'll have to do them again. Then you'll really be late. More haste, less speed.'

## Lightning never strikes twice in the same place

*We use this expression to mean that if something unfortunate has happened, the chances are that it probably won't happen again in exactly the same way.*

'Hey, Josie, don't stand there! Remember last month when a lightbulb fell and hit Mr Vasquez right on the head?'

'Yes, I remember. But what are the chances of that happening again? Lightning never strikes twice in the same place.'

## Half a loaf is better than none

*This means that having something is better than having nothing, even if it's not everything you want.*

Anna was looking forward to the school dance and had asked her mother to buy her a new dress and shoes to match. When her mother told her she could only afford the dress, Anna was disappointed, but her mother told her: 'You should be glad to have a new dress, Anna. Half a loaf is better than none.'

## Laugh, and the world laughs with you; cry, and you cry alone

*This saying means that when you are happy, people want to share your happiness, but when you are sad, people don't want to be with you.*

'Come on, Tom, cheer up!' Jo shook Tom's shoulder. 'Why are you in such a bad mood?'

'Oh, I don't know,' Tom said. 'Nobody likes me.'

'Well, what do you expect, with that big frown on your face?' Jo smiled. 'Laugh, and the world laughs with you; cry, and you cry alone!'

## Make ends meet

*When someone is having trouble making enough money to pay the bills, we say that person is struggling to make ends meet.*

'Where's your Dad?' Sarah asked.

'He's at work,' Elizabeth explained. 'He has to work overtime every night to pay the bills, and on weekends, too. He says he has to, just to make ends meet.'

## It never rains but it pours

*When people say this they mean that something that starts out bad can turn into a disaster, or that sometimes many bad things can happen all at once instead of being spread out over time.*

Keith limped into the kitchen and collapsed on a chair.

'What happened to you?' his brother asked.

Keith grimaced. 'What a rotten day! First I missed the bus and had to walk to school. When I got there, I was in trouble for being late. Then I messed up on my maths test, left my lunch at home this morning, twisted my ankle in gym class and now I think I'm getting a cold. It never rains but it pours!'

## Money burning a hole in your pocket

*Sometimes when you have some money, you are really tempted to spend it. You want to spend it so quickly that it seems like it's burning a hole in your pocket.*

'A lot of people on my paper round gave me tips for Christmas,' Luke said. 'I'm rich!'

'So why don't you open a savings account and start putting your money in the bank?' Julie asked. 'Otherwise, that money's just going to burn a hole in your pocket!'

## Once in a blue moon

*A blue moon is the second full moon in a calendar month. Blue moons are rare, so something that happens only once in a blue moon happens very rarely.*

'Lara,' Amira said excitedly, 'remember that skirt I liked? I just found it in the summer sale with 75 per cent off!'

'Wow! How often does that happen?' Lara replied.

'Once in a blue moon!' cried Amira.

> We learnt about the phases of the moon in Year 4.

## One picture is worth a thousand words

*Often a picture can explain something better than words.*

'Here's a picture of Rick after he won his diving medal.' Sonia showed Mrs Smith the photograph.

'Goodness!' Mrs Smith said. 'Doesn't he look proud!'

'Yes, he does,' Sonia said. 'Just look at his face. A picture is worth a thousand words!'

## Prevention is better than cure

*People use this saying to mean that it's better to anticipate a problem and try to prevent it than to wait until it gets really bad later on.*

'If you don't brush your teeth more often, you'll get cavities,' Rajen's sister said, 'and then you'll have to get fillings when you go to the dentist.'

'Yikes, I don't want that to happen!' Rajen said. 'I suppose you're right: prevention is better than cure.'

## Shipshape

*When a ship is ready to sail, with all its decks cleaned and equipment in good order, it is shipshape. We use this saying to describe anything that is in perfect order.*

Mrs Walters waved her hand around the messy classroom. The desks were littered with sheets of coloured paper, pots of paint, pans of water and paintbrushes. 'Pay attention!' she called out. 'Nobody goes to lunch until this room is shipshape.'

## Run-of-the-mill

*We use this saying to describe anything that is very ordinary.*

'How was your day, Carmen?' Mrs Morello asked.

'It was pretty run-of-the-mill,' Carmen replied. 'But I'm really looking forward to our field trip to the museum tomorrow.'

## Through thick and thin

*If you're riding a horse in the forest, it's harder to ride through thick woods (with lots of trees close together) than it is to ride through thin woods. But a determined rider will ride through thick and thin to get to his or her destination. We use this expression to describe someone who persists through good times and bad.*

'Maleek and I are best friends,' Dwayne explained. 'He's stuck with me through thick and thin.'

## Timbuktu

*Timbuktu is a famous town in Africa. When people use this term, however, they usually mean a place that seems exotic or very far away.*

When Julie's mother asked her to get a pint of milk from the shop, Julie said that first she would have to change her shoes. Then she wanted a different T-shirt, and finally started turning out her cupboard looking for a pair of sunglasses.

'For goodness sake, Julie,' said her mother, 'you're going to the corner shop, not Timbuktu!'

## Seeing is believing

*This saying means that you can't necessarily believe that something exists or is true unless you see the evidence for yourself.*

'You should have seen the fish I caught,' Eddie said. 'It was this big!' He spread his arms as wide apart as he could.

'Yeah, right,' said Mollie, shaking her head. She knew Eddie liked to exaggerate.

'I'm not kidding!' exclaimed Eddie. He ran into the house, then staggered out holding a gigantic fish. 'Wow!' said Mollie. 'Seeing is believing.'

## Make hay while the sun shines

*Farmers need dry weather to make hay, so they take advantage of sunny weather when it comes. This saying means that you should take advantage of good times when you have them, because they may not last forever.*

Daniel and Jonathan were watching a detective programme on TV when the advertisements came on. They were both surprised to see one of the most famous football players in the country advertising a new after-shave.

'Why does he even bother making ads?' asked Daniel. 'He makes millions just playing football.'

'But for how long?' replied Jonathan. 'He's just trying to make hay while the sun shines. Who's going to care what after-shave he wears in ten years' time?'

## You can lead a horse to water, but you can't make it drink.

*This saying means that you can show people what you want them to do, but you cannot force them to do it.*

Rachel disliked bowling. Her friends insisted that she come with them to the bowling alley, though, because they needed an extra person on their team.

'Who cares whether or not you hit a bunch of pins with a stupid ball,' Rachel thought to herself. When it was her turn to play, she crossed her arms over her chest and refused. She explained: 'Just because you got me to come with you doesn't mean I'm going to play. You can lead a horse to water, but you can't make it drink!'

# Suggested Resources

## Poetry

*Heard It in The Playground* by Allan Ahlberg (Puffin) 1991

*The Poetry Store* by Paul Cookson (Hodder Children's) 2005

*101 Poems for Children* chosen by Carol Ann Duffy (Macmillan) 2013

*Oxford Book of Story Poems* edited by Michael Harrison (OUP) 2006

*A Little, Aloud, for Children* edited by Angela Macmillan (David Fickling) 2012

*The Highwayman* by Alfred Noyes, illustrated by Charles Keeping (Oxford) 2013

*Classic Poetry* selected by Michael Rosen (Walker) 2009

## Stories

*Robin Hood and a World of Other Stories* by Geraldine McCaughrean (Orion) 2011

*Sir Gawain and the Green Knight,* retold by Michael Morpurgo, illustrated by Michael Foreman (Walker Books) 2005

*East of the Sun, West of the Moon* by Jackie Morris (Frances Lincoln) 2013

*The Wanderings of Odysseus: The story of the Odyssey* retold by Rosemary Sutcliff (Frances Lincoln) 2002

*Gulliver's Travels* by Jonathan Swift, retold by Martin Jenkins, illustrated by Chris Riddell (Walker Books) 2009

## Learning About Language

*Oxford Primary Grammar, Punctuation and Spelling Dictionary* (Oxford University Press) 2013

*Oxford Junior Illustrated Dictionary* (Oxford University Press) 2011

*Improve Your Grammar* by Rachel Bladon (Usborne) 2000

*Junior Dictionary and Thesaurus* by Cindy Leaney and Susan Purcell (Miles Kelly) 2011

*Perfect Pop-Up Punctuation Book* by Kate Petty and Jenny Maizels (Bodley Head) 2006

*You Can Do It! Grammar* by Andy Seed and Roger Hurn (Hodder Children's) 2011

*The Butterfly Grammar* by Irina Tyk (Civitas) 2008

## Mobile Apps

Grammaropolis (Grammaropolis LLC) app for iPhone and iPad [Practising parts of speech; free]

Mad Libs (Penguin) app for iPhone [Practising parts of speech]

# History and Geography

## Introduction

This chapter covers geography, world history and British history. Geography has been described as the study of what's where, why it's there and why we should care. It looks at how humans are challenged by, adapt to, utilise and change the natural environments in which they live. By Year 5, students should know the rudiments of world and British geography. They should be able to read and colour maps, and make simple maps of their own. They can be shown maps of their own town and county and be invited to study maps during field trips and family holidays. As their skills develop, they can be allowed to *navigate* on car journeys or to find their way around a city using a map. Our study of regions of the British Isles – that began in Year 4 with London, the South East, the South West and Northern Ireland – continues in Year 5 with the Midlands, Yorkshire and the East of England. This chapter also looks at Australia, New Zealand and the Pacific Islands. Students can learn more about geography from atlases, from books on other countries and by collecting stamps. There are excellent online resources such as *National Geographic for Kids*.

World history in Year 5 deals with the rise of Islam. British history covers the period from the reign of Queen Anne at the beginning of the eighteenth century through the American and French revolutions to the abolition of slavery at the beginning of the nineteenth century. Our approach to history is chronological and narrative: we have tried to show how the events of one era have led to those of the next. In the case of British history, it is particularly important for children to grasp the sequence of events that led to the birth of parliamentary democracy and the industrial revolution in Britain. These events were by no means inevitable or predestined, but were the result of struggles that linked generations across the centuries, as people learnt from the accumulated experience of their ancestors.

Topics in history can be linked to other chapters in this book. The feuds between the Lilliputians and the inhabitants of Blefuscu, depicted by Jonathan Swift in *Gulliver's*

*Travels*, reflected the politics of the time of Queen Anne and George I. The rococo style of art, developed in France in the eighteenth century, reflected aristocratic values that would soon be swept away by the French Revolution. In addition, the geography of New Zealand goes hand-in-hand with learning about geology in the Science chapter.

Parents and teachers are encouraged to build on the foundation provided here by discussing history with children; visiting historic houses, monuments and sites; visiting museums and galleries; and seeking out additional resources. There are many good books, DVDs and online resources suitable for Year 5 pupils, together with the many excellent television programmes on historical subjects.

# World Geography

## Maps

If you read *Treasure Island* earlier in this book, you already know how useful maps can be. In the story, the map tells Jim Hawkins and his friends where Treasure Island is and also where the treasure is buried. Maps can be useful in real life, too. But you have to know how to use them.

The map at the top of page 73 shows half the earth, as it might look from a spaceship in orbit. You may already know that the imaginary line that divides the globe around the middle is called the Equator. But what are those other lines running side-to-side, the ones parallel to the Equator? And what about the lines that run north and south on the map? What are they for?

Mapmakers draw imaginary lines and divide the world into sections in order to locate places accurately. The lines running parallel to the Equator are called parallels; they measure degrees of *latitude* north and south of the Equator. The lines that run from pole to pole are meridians; they measure degrees of *longitude* east and west of the *prime meridian*. You can remember the difference between meridians and parallels by remembering that parallels are parallel and meridians meet at the poles.

Can you see how the parallels and meridians intersect? Each point of intersection is a co-ordinate. Looking at the map, you can also see that each parallel and each meridian has its own number. We'll learn more about these numbers and about co-ordinates in a minute.

How does the map below it differ from the first map you looked at? The first map looks almost like a picture of a globe, but this one looks more like a globe cut open along a north-to-south seam through the Pacific Ocean and stretched flat. Stretching a map to fit a flat page is called a *projection*. Mapmakers do this to show the whole world on one map.

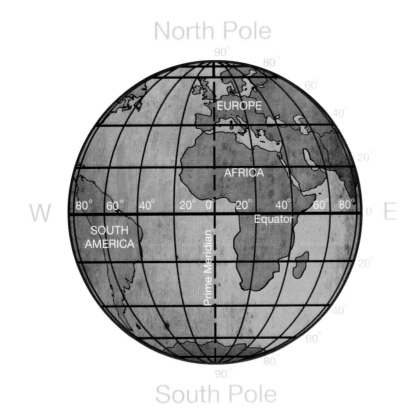

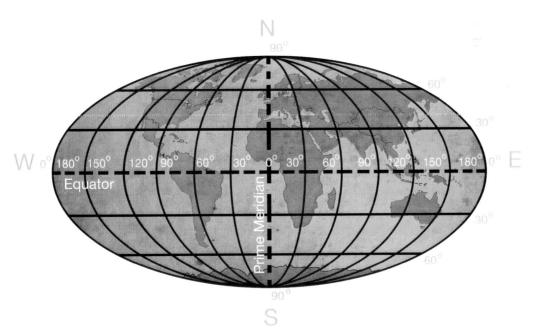

# Hemispheres

Mapmakers and people who use maps sometimes divide our earth into large sections shaped like half a grapefruit. These sections are called *hemispheres*. Hemisphere is a Greek word meaning half of a sphere. On the stretched-out map on page 73, you can see that the equator divides the globe into two hemispheres. Everything north of the equator is in the Northern Hemisphere; everything south of the equator is in the Southern Hemisphere.

The earth can also be divided into Eastern and Western Hemispheres. The meridian that divides these two hemispheres is the prime meridian, and it runs through Greenwich [GRENN-itch] just outside London. Years ago, when the system of longitude and latitude that we use today was set up, Greenwich was home to the Royal Observatory, where astronomers like Edmond Halley watched the stars. Mapmakers agreed to use this location for an imaginary line just as important as the Equator, but running from the North Pole to the South Pole. In England, it goes from Yorkshire to Sussex, then through France and Spain in Europe to Algeria, Mali, Burkina Faso, Togo and Ghana in Africa. As with all meridians, the ends are at the North and South Poles.

Can you find the prime meridian on the map? Look for the meridian that runs North and South through England and is marked 0°. The small, raised circle after the zero is a symbol that stands for *degree*. Degrees are the units we use to measure longitude and latitude.

Everything to the west of the prime meridian on the stretched-out map is in the Western Hemisphere, and everything to the east is called the Eastern Hemisphere. Find the Eastern and Western Hemispheres on the map and, if possible, on a globe.

*You can stand over the prime meridian in Greenwich, with one foot on either side.*

## Follow Your Finger

To look at the hemispheres in more detail you'll need a globe. First, find the prime meridian. With your finger, trace this line to the Equator. Do you see that the prime meridian is marked 0°?

Next trace your finger along the Equator moving west from the prime meridian. See how the degree numbers on the meridians go up as you go west? When you reach the 180th meridian (180°), you've gone exactly halfway around the world. The 180th meridian is the continuation of the prime meridian on the other side of the globe. The 180° line and the prime meridian (0°) divide the globe into the Eastern and Western Hemispheres.

Continue tracing your finger along the Equator to the west. What hemisphere are you crossing now? What happens to the longitude marks as you move back towards the prime meridian? Do the numbers keep getting larger or do they get smaller again?

Now try tracing your finger around some other meridians. What countries can you find that are on the same meridian? For example, you could start in Japan. Going north you find Russia. Go south and you reach Australia.

Now try tracing some other parallels. Do you notice how they are biggest near the Equator and smaller near the poles? What has the same latitude as Scotland? Travelling east, you would find Denmark, Sweden, Latvia and Russia. Or go west over the Atlantic to reach Canada.

## Co-ordinates

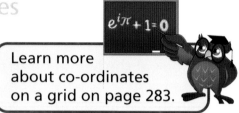

Learn more about co-ordinates on a grid on page 283.

Now that you know about the prime meridian and the Equator, you can find the co-ordinates for anywhere on the globe. Let's find the co-ordinates for Greece to see how it is done.

To begin with, you'll need to find Greece on the map on page 73 by looking for the Mediterranean Sea. Can you find Italy's boot? Greece is the peninsula sticking into the Mediterranean just east of Italy. You can see that a parallel and a meridian *intersect*, or cross, close to Greece. The parallel is marked 40° and the meridian is marked 20°.

So the co-ordinates of Greece are about 40° and 20°. When we write these co-ordinates we write 40° N, 20° E because Greece is 40° north of the Equator and 20° east of the prime meridian. 40° N tells you the latitude of Greece and 20° E tells you its longitude. Put the two together and you have its location.

Can you find 20° S, 20° E on the same map? What continent or ocean is this spot in? How about 20° S, 40° W?

## Map Scale

Have a look at the three maps that follow. Notice how each map focuses on a smaller area and shows more detail. The map of Europe shows more than 30 countries. The map of Italy shows only one country and the map of Venice shows only one city within that country. The map of Europe shows much more of the earth's surface than the country map and the country map shows much more than the city map.

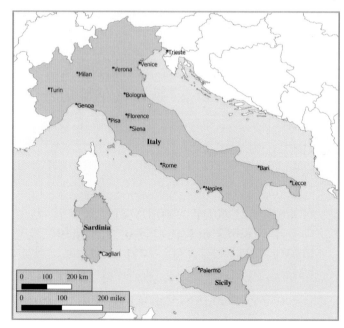

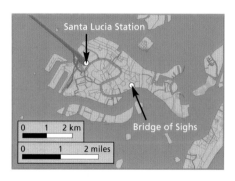

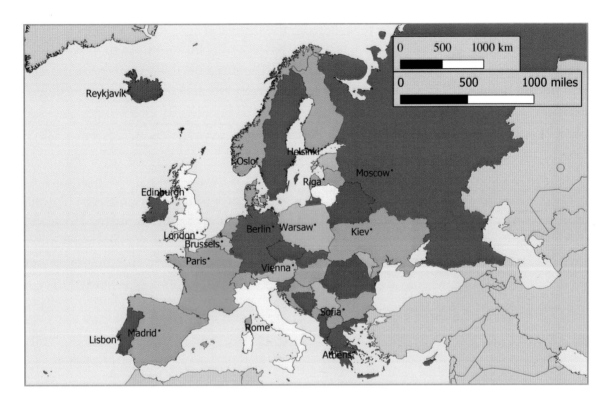

Each of these three maps is drawn to a different *scale*. Scale is the proportion between the distance on the map and the actual distance on the earth's surface. For instance, on one map a distance of one centimetre might represent one real kilometre; on another map one centimetre might represent one hundred kilometres.

To work out how much real distance is represented on a map, you'll need to find the map scale. The map scale looks like a ruler and is often located at the bottom of the map or in a corner. On the European map, the scale is in the top right corner. It tells you that the distance to the first mark represents 500 kilometres in real life. On the map of Italy, the first mark represents 100 kilometres but on the map of Venice it represents only 1 kilometre.

You can use the scale to measure distances from place to place. Get a ruler or a piece of string and use it to measure the distance from the Bridge of Sighs to the railway station. It should be about 14mm. Then place your ruler or string next to the scale for the city map to find out how many millimetres on the map represent one real kilometre: 7mm. So the distance between the Bridge and the station – as the crow flies – is about 2 km. A gondolier could take you between them (although it would be expensive) or you could walk.

Now look back at the map of Italy and measure the distance from Venice to Florence. You should find that this is also about 14mm. Does that mean it would be as easy to walk from Venice to Florence as it was to walk from the Bridge of Sighs to the railway station? Not so fast! You need to work out what that distance stands for on this map. If you place your ruler next to the scale, you'll see that 14 millimetres on this map represents 200 kilometres. If you tried to walk that far, you'd have very tired feet!

## Landscape as Sculpture – Reading a Relief Map

*A relief map of Wales*

The colours range from dark green at the same height as the sea (called *sea level*) through yellow to brown at 1,000 metres up. Rivers start high and flow downwards, as you know. They reach the sea at sea level. On the way, they pass between higher areas, so the river may be in a green strip but with yellow on either side. There are high mountains in south Wales but the highest (and brownest, on the map) are in the North West, an area called Snowdonia.

The map of Europe on page 77 is a political map. It shows political boundaries, like the boundaries between the countries. However, it does not tell you what the land itself looks like. You can't tell from this map whether Italy is full of mountains or is flat as a board. If you want to learn how flat or hilly a particular piece of land is, you need to consult a special kind of map, called a *relief map*. A relief map shows the higher and lower ground.

There are two main ways of showing heights on a map. For a large area, like a country, you can colour areas at different heights in different colours. Look at this map of Wales.

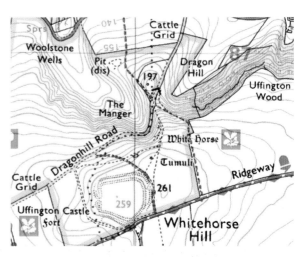

*A contour map*

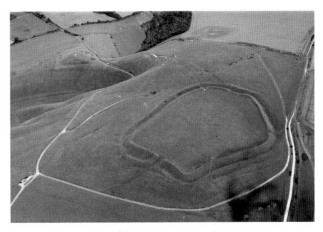

*Dragon Hill*                    *Uffington Castle*

For smaller areas, we use *contours*. You can draw a line around points on the map that are the same height. Draw more lines a few metres higher and lower. If the land is flat, there are very few contours. If you are climbing quickly, they are close together. If you walk along the line of a contour, you stay at the same height, going neither up nor down.

Look how the small, steep hill, Dragon Hill (197 metres high – can you see it marked on the map?) has close contours around it. Can you see the curvy road? It's a yellow line that follows the contour lines so it doesn't have to climb too steeply. When it does get steep, there is an arrow symbol across the road.

The larger hill of Uffington Castle (259 metres high – can you see it on the map?) is higher but flatter. There are more contour lines, but they are further apart. Around the top, can you see a ring of earthworks in the picture? They are marked on the map with rings of dots. Because they are about the same height, the brown contour line at 250 metres follows three sides. The east side is slightly higher but not by enough to need another contour line.

Below the road is a U-shaped dip called the Manger. The flat bottom has only a few contour lines, but the steep sides have many. Could you run up that hillside? What would you find at the top?

## Mountains of the World

One of the things a relief map can show you is where the tallest mountains are located. Look at the map on page 80. It shows some of the major mountain ranges of the world and some of the tallest peaks. A *peak* is the top of a mountain and a *range* is a group of connected mountains. Let's learn a little about these ranges and peaks.

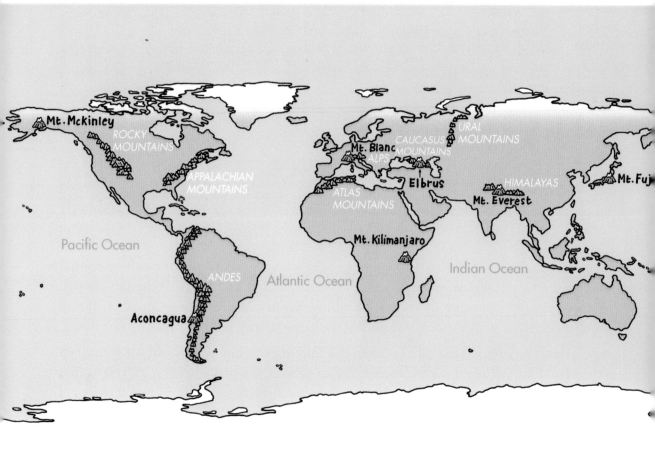

## The Alps

The Alps cover much of Switzerland and Austria, as well as parts of France and Italy. The highest peak in the Alps is Mont Blanc at 4,810 metres.

> In Year 4 we read in the Roman history section about the Carthaginian general Hannibal, who bravely marched his army of soldiers and elephants across the Alps to invade Italy.

In 1991 two hikers in the Alps came across a human body frozen in the snow. Tests revealed that the body was roughly 5,000 years old. Freezing temperatures had preserved the man's body so well that it was like an ice mummy. Scientists were able to determine how old the man was when he died, what he was wearing and even what he had eaten for his last meal. The iceman – nicknamed Ötzi – was about 40 when he died. He stood about five feet tall, wore a fur cap and leather shoes. He carried an axe as well as a bow and arrows. The iceman of the Alps has given scientists valuable new information about how people lived in pre-historic times.

*Archaeologists think Ötzi, the Iceman of the Alps, might have looked like this when he was alive, about 5,000 years ago.*

## The High Peaks of the Himalayas

Although the Alps are tall, they're not nearly as tall as the Himalayas, in Asia, where many peaks reach over 7,000 metres. This range includes the world's tallest mountain, Mount Everest, which rises 8,848 metres above sea level.

So why are some mountain ranges so much higher than others? A rule geographers have discovered about mountains is that 'young' mountains tend to be high mountains, while 'old' mountains tend to be lower. The

Learn more about geology and the Himalayas were formed on page 318.

Himalayas are quite young – for mountains, that is. They are only 50 million years old! They are six or seven times the height of the tallest mountains in Scotland, but those were once almost as big. Ice and water have worn them down over hundreds of millions of years.

Until 1953 no person had ever climbed to the top of Mount Everest. Freezing temperatures, ferocious winds, avalanches of snow and blizzards had stopped all who tried. Another obstacle was thin air. Human beings need oxygen to survive, but not all of the air in our atmosphere contains the same amount of oxygen. As you climb farther above sea level, the amount of oxygen in the air decreases – the air gets thinner. On top of Mount Everest the air is so thin that even the slightest movements can leave you gasping for breath.

*Edmund Hillary and Tenzing Norgay are all smiles after becoming the first to climb to the peak of Mount Everest.*

The first people to overcome all these obstacles and reach the peak were New Zealand mountaineer Edmund Hillary and his Tibetan guide Tenzing Norgay in May 1953.

## American Mountains

The Andes [AN-deez] in South America stretch nearly 4,500 miles from the southern tip of the continent to the Caribbean coast. The highest mountain in the Andes, Mount Aconcagua, rises 6,962 metres above sea level.

The Andes Mountains and the surrounding territory were the home of the ancient Inca people. The Incas built a famous city, Machu Picchu, on top of one of the mountains in the Andes.

*The ruins of Machu Picchu in the Andes*

The Appalachian Mountains extend nearly 1,800 miles up the eastern side of the United States of America. They include smaller mountain ranges with exotic names like the Blue Ridge Mountains of Virginia and the Great Smoky Mountains.

West of the Appalachians lie the Rocky Mountains. The Rockies stretch more than 3,000 miles, from New Mexico through the United States and Canada, and north to Alaska. Mount McKinley, in Alaska, is the highest mountain in North America at 6,194 metres.

*The worn peaks of the Blue Ridge Mountains in the Appalachians*

*The jagged peaks of the Rocky Mountains in Colorado*

The Rockies are much higher than the Appalachians – so much higher that the Appalachians look like hills in comparison. This is because the Appalachians are so much older than the Rockies, and have been worn down over millions of years by weathering and erosion. This is why the Appalachians look rounded, while the Rockies have more rugged and jagged peaks. Because of their height, the Rockies were a big barrier that settlers could not cross easily, but eventually paths like the Oregon Trail were created. These paths allowed settlers to cross the Rockies on their way to California and the West Coast.

African Mountains

The Atlas Mountains stretch for 1,500 miles along the north-western coast of Africa. These mountains are named after the god Atlas who, according to Greek mythology, had to support the sky on his shoulders through eternity. With an average height of 3,300 metres, the Atlas Mountains are tall enough to keep coastal rains from moving inland and watering the Sahara Desert.

*Mount Kilimanjaro*

The tallest mountain in Africa, at 5,895 metres, is Mount Kilimanjaro. This beautiful, towering peak is actually the remains of an ancient volcano. Even though it is close to the Equator, where temperatures are usually warm, Kilimanjaro is so high that it wears a cap of ice throughout the year.

# British Geography

## Let's Explore the East of England

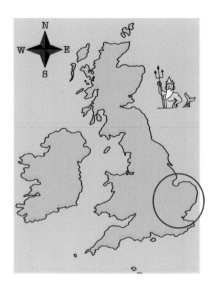

In Year 4 we learnt about London, the South East and the South West of England as well as Northern Ireland. Now we are going to explore the Eastern part of England.

Look at this map of England. Can you see the bulge of land that sticks out in the North Sea? This is East Anglia. A long time ago people called Angles came from north Germany to live in this area. That is why we now call this part of England 'East Anglia'. Further south is Essex, meaning the 'East Saxons', who came originally from a different region of Germany. If you look at a map of this area of England you will also see the counties of Norfolk, Suffolk, Bedfordshire and Hertfordshire.

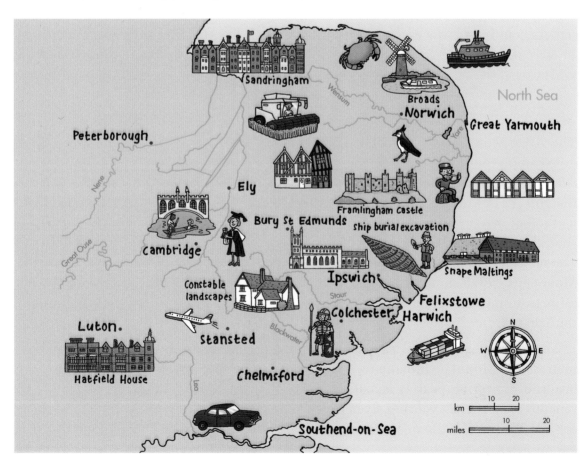

# What is the Weather Like in East Anglia?

*Suffolk farm, East Anglia*

When a cold wind blows from the east, East Anglia is the first area of land that the wind reaches. There aren't any hills to take the force of the wind, so sometimes it can be quite chilly. When a wet wind blows from the west, the rain falls on the hills before it reaches East Anglia. Therefore, it is quite dry and there is not as much rainfall as in other places in England. In the summer the weather can be warm and people like to visit the seaside. The long, warm summer days help farmers to grow wheat, barley and vegetables in enormous fields. You might have eaten cabbage, celery or lettuce that was grown in East Anglia. Wheat for your bread or cereal might have also been grown in East Anglia.

## Constable Country

John Constable, one of the greatest British painters, was inspired by the countryside on the border of Suffolk and Essex to create some beautiful paintings like *The Haywain* (1821). The cottage in the painting still exists. Can you find it on the map?

*Nowadays you can still see Willy Lott's cottage which is the one in Constable's painting.*

The Haywain

## Why are There Straight Rivers?

Can you spot any rivers on the map of East Anglia? A few hundred years ago, lots of the flat land in East Anglia was marshland. It is difficult to build or travel on marshland as you might sink! People decided to build rivers and ditches to drain the marsh water away. Ely is the name of a small town in East Anglia. The name Ely means 'Eel island'. Today it is a town on a hill, but it used to be an island in the marsh where people went out in boats to fish for eels. After the marsh water was drained away, people could build houses on the land and the town grew.

The rivers that people built to drain away the marshland are very straight. Can you see the difference between the straight, man-made rivers and the natural rivers that wind across the land? The straight rivers were built to carry the marsh water out to the sea. Because the land is flat, they also built windmills to push the water along. These rivers connect with lakes that are known as *broads*, and as most of these are in Norfolk, the area is known as the Norfolk Broads. Some people like to sail canal boats along the broads, which make a special habitat for wildlife and are home to kingfishers, otters and eels.

*Windmills in the Norfolk Broads push water along the canals.*

We learnt about different habitats in Year 2.

## What Do People Do in East Anglia?

As we have seen, there are lots of farms in East Anglia. There are also cities in the area, such as Cambridge. There is a famous university in Cambridge where you can study a

*Cambridge is a famous university city.*

*From Felixstowe, containers of goods travel around the world.*

range of subjects from Latin to engineering. People come from all over the world to study in Cambridge.

There are also many technology businesses in East Anglia where people use ideas from science to make things. On the coast, the busy container port of Felixstowe is part of a great system carrying goods around the world. Large metal boxes called containers are loaded from lorries or trains and stacked onto ships going to other ports in Europe, America and Asia.

## Did You Know?

In 1938 people found a ship-shaped hole in the ground in Suffolk! 1,400 years ago in Sutton Hoo, an Anglo-Saxon king died and was buried in a ship along with lots of treasure. The earth was piled up over the ship and became a mound. When people started digging in this mound, they found the treasure, although the ship had

*Excavation at Sutton Hoo*

rotted, just leaving an impression of what it had been like in the soil.

## Let's Explore the Midlands

Midlands means 'land in the middle', so we are talking about a region away from the sea in the centre of England. The Midlands are in the 'middle' of England. There is no coastline for you to look for, so you might need to look for place names, mountains or big rivers on your map to help you find it.

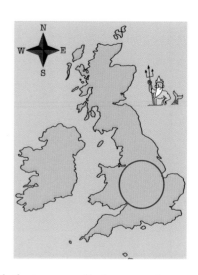

The biggest city in the Midlands is Birmingham. Millions of people live there and there are many shops and businesses. Land Rover cars are made in Solihull and Cadbury's chocolate is made in Bournville. There are lots of roads leading to Birmingham. Can you guess why the roads in this picture are called Spaghetti Junction?

*Spaghetti Junction*

*Canal boats carrying tourists and people on holiday often pass through Brindleyplace in Birmingham.*

There is a canal that runs all the way from London to Birmingham. This canal is the longest in Britain and is called the Grand Union Canal. A long time ago people used the canal to transport goods, but now it is used by people enjoying their holidays. Why do you think businesses no longer use the canal to transport goods?

The Midlands has many businesses because so many useful resources can be found there. Resources are anything you can use to make or do something. Iron and coal are found underground and people can dig them out to use them. This is called *mining*. In the Midlands, people have been mining for many years. Coal and iron are both very important for making things, which helped businesses to grow in the Midlands. Coal can be burned to make electricity which we use every day. There are not many mines left in England now, but there is one near Nottingham, in Edwinstowe.

Can you find the city of Derby on the map? Rolls-Royce makes engines for aeroplanes in a factory in Derby. Over 11,000 people work here, some on the aeroplane engines and some on submarines.

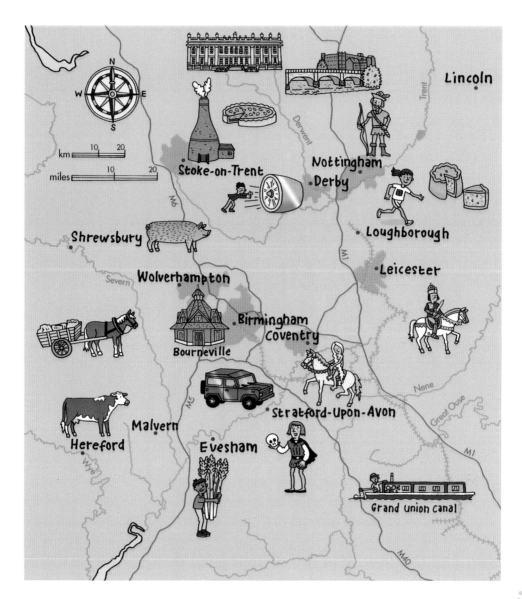

## What Can I Find in the Countryside?

Outside the cities of the Midlands, there is beautiful countryside. The river Wye flows past ancient, ruined castles, and the villages of the Cotswold hills are built from the local honey-coloured stone. The steep Malvern Hills were once volcanoes, but don't worry, they will not erupt again!

You can find out about volcanoes on page 313.

Can you spot Evesham on the map? In the summer you might find asparagus growing in the fields around Evesham. If you ever visit the area, you could even try some asparagus ice cream! The soil around Evesham is very *fertile* which means there are lots of nutrients in the soil to help vegetables to grow.

North-west of Evesham is the county of Shropshire. In the hills of Shropshire there is a farm that uses old fashioned ways of farming. Acton Scott Farm is set up in the same way a Victorian Farm would have been, many years ago. The farmers at Acton Scott don't use modern machines to do their work, but use horses instead of tractors. Which do you think would be easier? Famous breeds of farm animals, like Tamworth pigs and Hereford cattle, come from this area.

*This farmer is using horses to plough the land at Acton Scott Farm.*

Further north is a very hilly area called the Peak District. People like to go for walks or hikes in the beautiful countryside there. Dams have been built across several rivers to fill the valley up with water and form a *reservoir*, which is an artificial lake to store water, so that we will always have clean water to drink and wash in.

## Did You Know?

The Midlands have been host to many notable people and events. William Shakespeare, Britain's best-known writer, came from Stratford-upon-Avon, south of Birmingham. Robin Hood, so the story says, lived in Sherwood Forest, outside Nottingham. Almost a thousand years ago, Lady Godiva rode through Coventry with no clothes on as a protest against how heavily her husband, Leofric, was taxing the people. Leofric promised to abolish the taxes if she rode through the town naked. Out of respect for what Lady Godiva was doing for them, no one looked at her, except for one man who became known as Peeping Tom. According to legend, he was struck blind as a punishment. Leofric was as good as his word and let people off paying their taxes. The Wars of the Roses ended in the Midlands when Richard III died at the Battle of Bosworth Field in 1485.

We learnt about the Wars of the Roses and read about Robin Hood and his Merry Men in Year 3.

## Let's Explore Yorkshire and the Humber

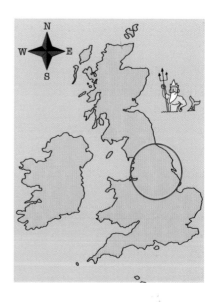

Yorkshire covers a very large area. It used to be the largest county in the United Kingdom, but it was divided up into four smaller counties: North Yorkshire, South Yorkshire, West Yorkshire and East Yorkshire. North Yorkshire is still the largest county in the UK. Like the other areas we have looked at, there are cities, towns, villages and countryside in Yorkshire. The county of Yorkshire is famous for its beautiful countryside, and also for tasty Yorkshire puddings! Have you ever eaten Yorkshire puddings?

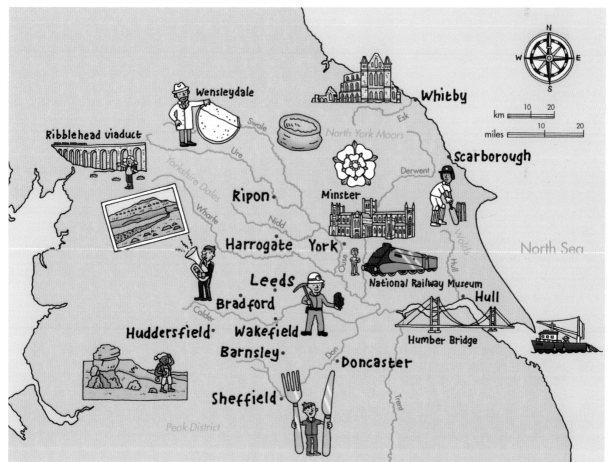

# What are the Yorkshire Dales?

In the UK there are special, protected areas called National Parks. The countryside in National Parks is especially beautiful, and there are laws to protect it and to make sure it cannot be spoiled.

The Yorkshire Dales National Park is a very special place because it has beautiful scenery, interesting wildlife and some very old villages. The word *dale* means valley. A valley is the low-lying land between mountains or hills. The Yorkshire Dales have high hills, steep valleys and fast-flowing rivers.

*Swaledale in the Yorkshire Dales National Park*

Farmers have grazed animals in the Yorkshire Dales for hundreds of years. A crumbly cheese is made in Wensleydale using milk from cows that graze on the Dales. Have you ever eaten any Wensleydale cheese? People visiting the Yorkshire Dales often go horse riding, rock climbing, mountain biking or hiking. There are lots of things to do in this big open space!

## Did You Know?

In Whitby, on the coast, there is an old ruined abbey. The author, Bram Stoker, set some scenes in his famous story *Dracula* there.

# What Can Be Found in the Cities?

Although Yorkshire is known for its beautiful countryside, there are also lots of important towns and cities too. When factories were built in Yorkshire, people came to live there and the towns and cities grew. Can you see Sheffield on the map? The city of Sheffield is famous for producing steel. Steel is a metal that doesn't stain easily, so is good for making cutlery.

*Have a look at your cutlery at home or in school; does it say it was made in Sheffield?*

In the city of York there is a big cathedral called York Minster. The word minster means an important church, and York is the home church of one of the Church of England's two archbishops. A long time ago, the cities of Leeds and Bradford grew rich making cloth and clothing. Now, the cities have many businesses, schools, hospitals and shopping centres. Like many other cities in Britain, they also have famous football teams!

*York Minster*

We learnt in Year 4 that the other archbishop is in Canterbury.

## What is a Viaduct?

The flat parts of the land in Yorkshire were ideal for building fast railway lines. The fastest ever steam locomotive was called *Mallard* and was built in Doncaster. It ran on the railway line between London and York. It is now in the museum there. But the hills caused a problem for the railway line. It is very difficult to make trains go uphill, so viaducts were built like this one at Ribblehead. A viaduct is a long bridge that is built very high up. It is much easier to make a train go across a viaduct than to go up and down each slope of a valley. So the viaduct needs to cross the valley from one side to the other, without sloping down or up. Viaducts are a very difficult thing for an engineer to build! Could you make a model of a viaduct?

*Ribblehead Viaduct connects either side of the valley so trains can cross easily.*

People who live in Yorkshire are very proud of their beautiful part of the country. They sometimes call it 'God's Own County', and they jokingly refer to 'On Ilkley Moor Baht 'At' as Yorkshire's national anthem!

Did you sing 'On Ilkley Moor Baht 'At' with us in Year 4?

## Questions for Geographers

Now you have explored the East Midlands, the Midlands and Yorkshire, see if you can answer these questions:

Why is East Anglia a good place to grow crops?

The Humber Bridge can save drivers a lot of time. How?

Why are there some very straight waterways in East Anglia?

Can you describe what a valley is?

What is mining?

What are the Yorkshire Dales?

Farmers grow asparagus in Evesham. Why?

Why did engineers build a viaduct at Ribblehead?

# World Geography

## Australia

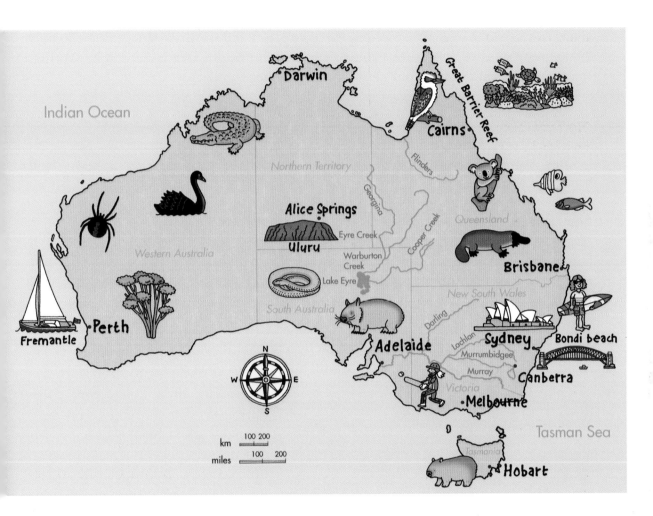

Australia is one of the largest countries on earth – so large that it's also a continent! Australia is called the land 'down under' because it is below the Equator. Most of the land in Australia is hot and dry desert, called the *outback*. In the south, where the temperatures are a little cooler, you will find cities such as Melbourne, Adelaide and Sydney. Can you find those cities on the map?

Australia is home to some amazing places and some very exotic animals. Let's find out more.

# Let's Visit the Outback

The Australian outback stretches for thousands of miles from east to west and from north to south. It is so hot and dry in the outback that there are not many people living there. Most of the people in Australia live in the coastal cities of the south, where the few major rivers reach the sea. The only well-known town far inland is Alice Springs, home to only 25,000 people. Alice Springs was able to grow up in this hot area because it has springs that provide it with water. That's how it got its name!

The Todd River in Alice Springs is called a 'dry river'. That is because there is very little water in it now. If it rains, the river can sometimes flow again. This is so unusual that, when it happens, people living in the town come out just to watch the river flow!

*Alice Springs is a remote town in the outback*

If you live in the outback, there might not be a school nearby. Some children have to watch their lessons on DVDs and be taught by a teacher through a computer or over the radio. Their teacher might be in a classroom hundreds of miles away.

*At sunset Uluru glows with an orange-red colour.*

Two hundred miles from Alice Springs is an enormous and very special rock. Uluru, which is also called Ayers Rock, is a massive piece of sandstone. If you walked all the way around the outside of Uluru, it would take over two hours! It would also be very hot, so you would need to walk very early in the morning, when the temperatures are cooler. In the light of a sunrise or sunset, Uluru looks as if it is a beautiful deep orange-red. The indigenous Australian people respect it as a sacred site.

# Let's Find Out About Australian Cities

Australia is a large *commonwealth* split into six *states*: Western Australia, Southern Australia, Queensland, New South Wales, Victoria and Tasmania. Tasmania is an island. Each state has its own state constitution and can make its own laws, in addition to the Australian government's laws. Australia also has several territories, the largest of which is called Northern Territory, but states have more power to govern themselves than territories.

*Perth is the only large city on the western side of Australia.*

The boundaries between the states and territories are mostly in the desert, so they follow the lines of meridians and parallels. The shape of Western Australia is either coastline or the meridian 129° east of Greenwich. The 26th parallel south of the Equator is the border between South Australia and the Northern Territory. The border between Queensland and New South Wales is more wiggly because it follows the line of hills and mountains, the Murray river and places where more people live.

Australia is a member of the Commonwealth of Nations, which is made up of more than 50 countries, most of which were once part of the British Empire. All of these countries are now independent and they control their own affairs, but their leaders like to meet together on a friendly basis to discuss things. The head of the Commonwealth is the Queen. Australia also has a special status as a *realm*, which means that the Queen is their head of state – in other words, Elizabeth II is the Queen of Australia.

The big cities of Adelaide, Melbourne, Sydney and Brisbane form an arc around the south-east coast. Perth is in the west and Darwin and Cairns are in the north. Canberra, the capital, is south of Sydney and about 90 miles inland, where dams were built on the Molongo River to create a large lake. The water from the lakes that were created makes it possible for people to live in this part of Australia.

On page 104 you can read about how the explorer Captain James Cook reached Australia in the eighteenth century. When he arrived, there were people living there already who became known as Aborigine

Learn about Charles Darwin, after whom the Australian city of Darwin was named, on page 336.

or Australian Aboriginal people. 'Aboriginal' comes from the Latin words *ab origine* meaning 'from the beginning'. The Australian Aboriginal people had been living there for so long – probably over 50,000 years – that, with the exception of people in some parts of Africa, they have been inhabiting the same land for longer than anyone else on earth.

*Cairns, on the north-east coast of Australia, enjoys a tropical climate.*

After the arrival of Captain Cook and his crew, the British government began to send convicted criminals to Australia. The prisons in Britain were getting too crowded, and so thousands of prisoners were sent in ships to establish a colony at Botany Bay. This was called *transportation*, and the convicts were made to do backbreaking farm work in the Australian sun with little food and severe punishments. In the middle of the nineteenth century, lots more people went to Australia in search of gold during a time called the *gold rush*. This is why many people living in Australia can trace their family tree back to Britain and Ireland. Cities like Melbourne and Sydney grew at this time when more people were moving to Australia. Today, the Sydney Opera House and Harbour Bridge are famous landmarks that people like to visit. In Melbourne there is a cricket ground that seats over 100,000 people and is even bigger than Wembley!

*The Sydney Opera House is a famous modern building that is an important part of the city's skyline, along with the Harbour Bridge.*

# Amazing Australian Animals

Australia is home to many animals that cannot be found anywhere else in the world. They *evolved* in Australia, but could not migrate anywhere else because the continent was surrounded by ocean. Some, like kangaroos, koalas and wombats are called *marsupials*. The name comes from an ancient Greek word for a pouch, because the mothers carry their young in a pouch on their tummies. The duck-billed platypus is a mammal, like cows, dogs and human beings, but the females lay eggs. (The platypus and the echidna are the only mammals that lay eggs.) All these animals might look cuddly but they can fight! Australia's snakes and spiders include some with strong and dangerous venom.

Learn more about evolution on page 333.

*Koalas are marsupials*

Off the Queensland coast, the Great Barrier Reef, formed from the minerals left by thousands of tiny corals, is home to many wonderful sea creatures, such as tropical fish, turtles and clams.

*The platypus is a very unusual mammal as it lays eggs.*

*You can find turtles on the Great Barrier Reef.*

# New Zealand

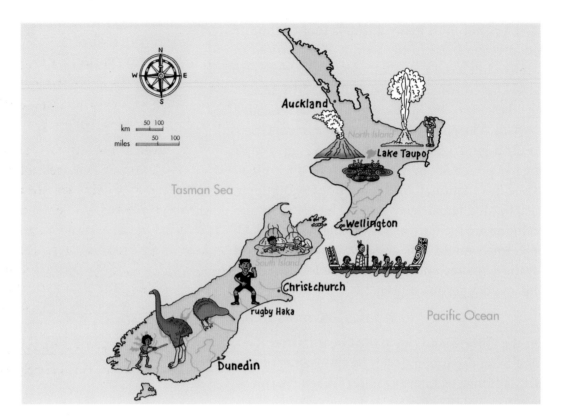

About two thousand kilometres east over the Tasman Sea from Sydney and Tasmania is the country of New Zealand. Like Australia, New Zealand is a member of the Commonwealth of Nations and, also like Australia, it is a realm, so Queen Elizabeth II is the head of state. New Zealand is made up of two islands, North Island and South Island. Lying on the edge of two tectonic plates, it is the site of several volcanoes, some of which around Taupo are still active. Earthquakes only rarely affect the cities but are very serious when they do. Buildings have to be strong enough to stay up when the earth feels a small tremor. Near some of the volcanoes, underground water is heated up until it bursts through the surface and forms a geyser. The water is hot enough to burn you, and forms hot pools of mud.

*The Pohuto Geyser in Rotorua erupts to a height of up to 30 metres on a regular basis, sometimes as often as 20 times a day.*

We learnt about a geyser called 'Old Faithful' in Year 2. Learn more about geysers and see a photo of Rotorua's hot springs on page 316.

Because New Zealand is so far out in the ocean, it was one of the last places where people came to live. The *Maori* people were the first there, arriving by canoe from the Polynesian Islands, probably around 700 years ago. Before New Zealand rugby matches, their national team, called the All Blacks, performs a traditional Maori war-dance called the *haka*.

*The All Blacks perform the haka before each rugby match.*

Before human beings arrived in New Zealand, birds were not in much danger of being caught and eaten, so bird species like the moa evolved *flightless*, meaning they had wings but could not fly. When people arrived and brought other *predators* (animals that eat other animals) like rats, these species were in danger, because they couldn't get away from their attackers. The moa, which was like a giant ostrich, is now extinct. Can you see it on the map? The other bird is a kiwi, which is also flightless but did not become extinct, probably because it is much smaller and can run away! It is the national symbol of New Zealand, and New Zealanders are sometimes called Kiwis!

*In 2011 many people died and buildings were destroyed in Christchurch, on the South Island, during an earthquake. This photograph shows the ruins of the cathedral.*

## The South Pacific

The Pacific Ocean is enormous. If you hold your globe in a certain way, the Pacific covers almost a hemisphere, with a thin ring of land around the edges.

There are no continents between Australia and America but there are some small islands dotted across the ocean. New Zealand is bigger than most other islands. Hawaii, which is a state of the United States of America, is a group of medium-sized islands north of the Equator. The other islands are small, especially in the south. These islands were formed either by volcanoes pushing molten rock up from under the sea or from coral reefs like the Great Barrier Reef.

*Fiji is known for its beautiful beaches and palm trees.*

They might look like the desert islands you've seen in stories, with palm trees and white sand, but they are often small and in danger from tropical storms. Earthquakes under the sea can cause *tsunamis*, which can send huge waves right across a small island. The word means 'harbour wave' in Japanese. See the Japanese print of *The Great Wave Off Kanagawa*, which shows a tsunami, on page 174.

Read more about earthquakes and tsunamis on page 311.

Melanesia, which means Black Islands in Greek, is a group of islands including New Guinea, Fiji, the Solomon Islands and many smaller islands. North of Melanesia are the tiny islands of Micronesia. To the east of both Melanesia and Micronesia is a large triangular area called Polynesia, which just means 'many islands' and includes Hawaii

and New Zealand. One of these Polynesian islands, Easter Island, is famous for its statues with giant heads, called *moai*. There are over 800 of them and they represent the spirits of the ancestors. They stand around the edge of the island, most of them looking inland. They are very heavy, weighing up to 80 tons, and the largest one is 10 metres high.

*Easter Island is known for its giant statues. We don't know how the islanders moved them around.*

# A great explorer:
## James Cook (1728-1779)

In Year 4, we read about Francis Drake. He sailed round the world, mostly in search of treasure. Two hundred years later, James Cook also went on several voyages around the world. He was looking to find new lands for his king and country, to make better maps and to make scientific discoveries.

James Cook was the son of a Yorkshire farm labourer who joined the Royal Navy in search of adventure. He became one of the most accomplished sailors in Britain and served in the Seven Years War in North America. When the war was over, he used his skills to survey, or measure, the new territories that Britain had won from the French in Canada. He became known as a man who was not only a very good sailor but a scientist as well. While he was working in Newfoundland, he witnessed an eclipse of the sun. His observations of this were very helpful to people who were making maps more accurate.

*James Cook*

We learnt in Year 4 how the Royal Society encouraged scientists to share and discuss their discoveries

Cook's first round-the-world voyage began in 1768. When he started, he thought he was only going to Tahiti on his ship *Endeavour* to make astronomical observations of the Sun, like the solar eclipse he had watched off Newfoundland in 1766. The Royal Society wanted to know how far away the Sun was. They hoped to calculate the distance by watching and timing the rare event of Venus passing across the face of the Sun. (Remember never to look at the Sun directly. Solar viewers are cheap and without one you can damage your eyesight.) Other expeditions were being sent to Norway and Hudson Bay, in Canada, to watch the same thing from other locations. If the timings of the event were different, it would be because people were looking from different places. If you cover your left eye and then your right, you will notice how what you see looks slightly different, because of the space between your eyes. Astronomer Edmond Halley worked out a method to use this information from different places to calculate the distance to the Sun.

Cook and his companions watched the journey that Venus made across the Sun in Tahiti. They then received orders not to sail home but to explore further, in search of the mysterious land of Terra Australis, or South Land, which people in Europe thought must lie on the other side of the globe. Cook reached New Zealand and made a map of its coast, sailing all the way around its two large islands. All the while he took notes of how the land could be used. For example, he chose one place as a good harbour for a settlement, and looked at the trees and plants to find good ones for building ships and making sails. The Maori who lived there had large canoes, sometimes carrying 100 people.

Next, Cook's expedition force sailed to the eastern coast of Australia, becoming the first Europeans to see it. Cook claimed the eastern part of Australia as British territory and named it New Wales (as there was already a New England in America). The word 'South' was added later, so we now know it as New South Wales.

> We first read about the great scientist Joseph Banks in Year 1.

Travelling with Cook was the botanist (plant scientist) called Joseph Banks, who had a good eye for animals, too. In the very first place they landed, Joseph Banks found so many different species of plants that Cook named the place Botany Bay in Banks's honour. In his journal, Banks recorded his observations of a strange animal that they had seen for the first time called – a kangaroo:

*Quadrupeds [four-footed mammals] we saw but few and were able to catch few of them that we did see. The largest was called by the natives Kangooroo. It is different from any European and indeed any animal I have heard or read of except the Gerbua of Egypt , which is not larger than a rat when this [the kangaroo] is as large as a midling [medium-sized] lamb; the largest we shot weighed 84 lb. It may however be easily known from all other animals by the singular property [unique habit] of running or rather hopping upon only its hinder legs carrying its fore bent close to its breast; in this manner however it hops so fast that in the rocky bad ground where it is commonly found it easily beat my grey hound, who though he was fairly started at [set to run after] several killed only one and that quite a young one.*

*This was one of the first illustrations of a kangaroo, made during the Cook expedition.*

Whenever they caught a kangaroo, the sailors ate it. They were hungry after all. They tried eating the plants they found. Some were good to eat and others made them very ill.

Cook arrived home in 1771 but didn't stay long. By 1772 he was off around the world again, still looking for that southern continent and not realising that he had already found it in Australia! He crossed the Antarctic Circle. (Can you find that on a globe?) No European before him had travelled that far south, where in midsummer the sun stays up all night but at midwinter it never comes up at all. He didn't reach Antarctica but discovered several other places, like New Caledonia in the Pacific Ocean and South Georgia in the southern Atlantic Ocean. He made detailed maps as he went. Always the scientist, he wrote about how few of his sailors died of a disease called scurvy. He thanked his supply of *sauerkraut* – shredded, pickled cabbage, containing some vitamin C – but it also helped that he frequently took on fresh food at the islands he visited. He was given a medal by the Royal Society for his work on scurvy.

A third voyage headed north, trying, as Francis Drake had tried before him, to find a northern sea passage from the Atlantic to the Pacific Ocean, which would avoid the stormy and dangerous trip around the tip of South America. Cook found the Bering Strait between America and Asia but the route was blocked by ice. Cook decided to spend the winter in Hawaii before trying to find the northern sea passage again the following year. Unfortunately, his life came to a sad end there in 1779 when an argument broke out with the islanders over a stolen boat. A Hawaiian chief was shot in a struggle and Cook and his men were chased to a beach. They scrambled to get back to their ship, but Cook stayed on the beach too long and was clubbed to death. There is a monument to Captain Cook in the grounds of his house in Buckinghamshire, but his most important memorial is the map of the South Atlantic, which he helped to draw for us.

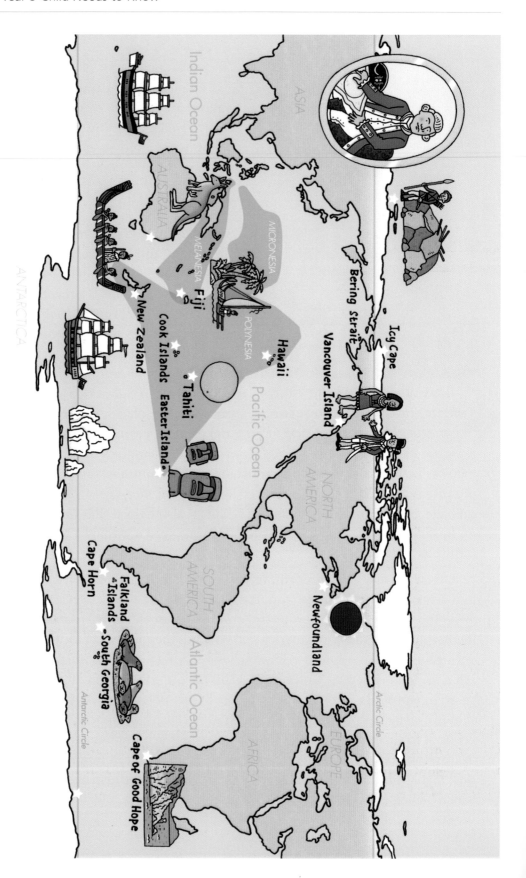

Can you spot where Captain Cook went to observe the eclipse of the sun in 1766? And the transit of Venus across the sun in 1769? (The tiny black dot is Venus!)

# World History

The Rise of Islam

The word *Islam* [IHS-lahm] means submission in the Arabic language, and for those who believe in the religion of Islam, it means submission to one God. Islam is a religion practised by more than a billion people around the world today and by almost three million people in the United Kingdom. We call these people Muslims.

Muslims follow the teachings of Muhammad [mu-HAMM-ad], who lived on the Arabian Peninsula during the medieval period, from 570 to 632. Muslims believe that about 1,400 years ago, in the city of Mecca [MEK-kah], Muhammad received the word of God, whom they name *Allah* [ah-LAH], the Arabic word for God.

The Prophet Muhammad

Muhammad was born in Mecca. Mecca was home to a holy building called the Ka'ba [KAH-bah]. In Muhammad's time, travellers who came to Mecca filled the Ka'ba with idols, or statues, of the many gods they worshipped. Local merchants wanted this practice to continue, because every traveller bringing an idol to the Ka'ba also spent money while visiting Mecca.

Muhammad was a trader himself. He loved his neighbours and his city, but he was uncomfortable with the way people were worshipping many gods and filling the Ka'ba with idols. To think over his concerns, he went alone into the mountains to meditate.

According to Islamic tradition, as Muhammad was meditating in a cave on Mount Hira, the Angel Gabriel appeared to him and ordered Muhammad to read some new religious verses which were the direct word of Allah. Muhammad

*The Ka'ba in Mecca is a holy site for Muslims*

began to read the verses, and continued to visit the cave for many years, during which he was given more and more verses to read.

Several years later, Muhammad is said to have undergone another miraculous experience. Muslims believe that Muhammad was taken up into the sky by angels. He travelled to Jerusalem, where he prayed with earlier prophets, including Abraham and Jesus. As he stood on a rock in the city of Jerusalem, he *ascended* (or went up) into heaven and received God's instruction to tell people to pray five times a day. Muslims later built a large shrine called the Dome of the Rock in Jerusalem to commemorate this great event.

See the Dome of the Rock on page 161.

## Trouble in Mecca

Muhammad began telling people in Mecca about his experiences and the ideas that were coming to him. At the time, the people of Mecca followed various religions. There were some Jews and Christians who believed in a single God, but there were many others who worshipped many gods. Muhammad's insistence that there was only one God upset some of these people, and they tried to stop him from spreading his message. But Muhammad continued sharing his ideas. Gradually, more people came to believe that he was a true prophet.

Muhammad taught that every action or thought should be guided by the will of God. He urged Muslims to see themselves as God's creatures, placed on earth to serve God and humanity. He told his followers that God judges people's actions when they die. If they have done good things in life, they will be rewarded; if they have done evil, they will be punished.

At first, Islam was just a local religion with a few followers, but as Islamic ideas spread, Muhammad and his followers came into conflict with the powerful merchants in Mecca. These traders made a living by welcoming visitors to Mecca and trading with them. They thought these visitors might not come to Mecca anymore if they heard that Muhammad was preaching that there was only one God. Finally, they forced Muhammad to leave the city. In 622, he and his followers moved north to a city that is now called Medina.

Muhammad's journey to Medina is called the *Hijra* [hidj-ra]. It is a very important event in the history of Islam – so important that it is the starting point for the Muslim calendar. Muslims will describe an event by saying how many years after the Hijra it happened, in the same way that Christians will refer to events happening after the birth of Jesus.

The Hijra also led to the construction of the first mosque [MOSK], or Muslim place of worship. The night he arrived in Medina, Muhammad began to build a rough structure, now considered the first mosque of Islam.

There are mosques all over the world. Mosques have minarets [min-ah-RETS], or towers from which a holy man calls the faithful to prayer five times a day. Before entering a mosque, Muslims must remove their shoes and wash at a special fountain. They sit on rugs laid down on the mosque floor in a room designed to face toward Mecca. When the prayer leader arrives, the faithful stand, raise their hands together above their heads and follow a series of prayer movements. They end by kneeling and lowering their heads to the ground.

*These are minarets of the Mosque and Khanqah of Emir Shaykhu, which are important places of worship Egypt.*

## Muhammad's Return

In Medina, Muhammad continued to hear messages from Allah. Muhammad expected all people in Medina, no matter what their religion, to live in peace and harmony. Some of the Jews in Medina refused to accept Muhammad as the leader of the city. Soldiers of Mecca were trying to attack Medina and take it over, and these Jews in Medina had been helping the armies from Mecca. That made it even harder for Muhammad and the Jews to agree. Finally, in 630, Muhammad himself led an army in a raid on Mecca. His goal was to rid the city of people who worshipped many gods.

Muhammad and his men took Mecca without much fighting. Muhammad removed all the idols from the Ka'ba and dedicated the temple to the worship of the one God of Islam.

Two years after restoring the Ka'ba to the worship of one God, Muhammad delivered his last sermon. He asked his followers to obey God and treat each other with justice and kindness. After giving this sermon, Muhammad felt that his life was complete. He returned to Medina and died at the age of 63.

## The Qur'an

While Muhammad was alive, many of his followers committed to memory the verses he had received from Gabriel. After Muhammad died, his followers wrote down these verses, which Muslims believe are the exact words spoken by Allah. They are still studied today, written down in a book called the Qur'an [kohr-AN].

The Qur'an is the holy book of the Islamic religion. Its title means 'the recitation', and it recalls the instruction given to Muhammad by Gabriel to repeat Allah's words. The Qur'an is written in Arabic. Muslims prefer to study it in its original language, even if they do not speak Arabic. Because Muslims believe that the Qur'an contains the actual words of God, learning to read and recite those words is an act of worship.

*This girl is reading the Qur'an.*

110

See a decorated prayer from the Qur'an on page 162.

Some of the important words of Islam can be spelt in different ways. Qur'an is sometimes spelt Koran, Mecca is also spelt Makkah, and Ka'ba is sometimes written as Kaaba. Muslim is sometimes spelt as Moslem and Muhammad as Mohammed.

## The Five Pillars of Islam

Devoted Muslims compare their religion to a building that is supported by five pillars. The Five Pillars of Islam are five rules that form the central philosophy of the Islamic faith.

### The First Pillar: *Shahada* [sha-HA-dah] in Arabic

As a statement of their faith, Muslims say: 'There is no God but Allah and Muhammad is his Prophet.' This simple statement is the basis of all Muslim belief. It is the first thing whispered into a child's ear when he or she is born and the last thing a Muslim hopes to speak at the moment of death.

*Friday is a special day of worship for Muslims. These Muslim people are praying at Imam Mosque in Iran.*

### The Second Pillar: *Salat* [sah-LAHT] in Arabic

*Salat* means prayer. Muslims recite prayers at dawn, midday, afternoon, evening and night. At each of these five times of day, they stop what they are doing to bow down in worship in the direction of Mecca.

### The Third Pillar: *Sawm* [sowm] in Arabic

*Sawm* means fasting, or going without food and drink. Muslims fast during daylight hours throughout the holy month that they call *Ramadan* [rah-mah-DAHN]. Muslims believe fasting brings spiritual rewards. When the fast is over, at the end of Ramadan, Muslims celebrate with a festival.

### The Fourth Pillar: *Zakat* [ZACK-at] in Arabic

Through *zakat*, or giving to others, Muslims share and show kindness in a practical way to those less fortunate.

*Zakat is one of the most important aspects of Muslim worship. This group of poor people is waiting patiently outside a hotel for the benefactor to deliver zakat: a free meal in this case!*

### The Fifth Pillar: *Hajj* [hadj] in Arabic

The *Hajj* is a word for the pilgrimage, or religious journey, to Mecca. All healthy Muslims are expected to make a pilgrimage to Mecca at least once in their lives. Today, about three million Muslims go to Mecca every year.

## Spreading the Word of Islam

After Muhammad's death, Muslims began conquering other lands, taking over territories so that they could govern them according to the rules of their religion. One by one, the great cities of the ancient Middle East – Damascus in Syria, Antioch in Turkey, Tyre in Lebanon and Jerusalem in today's Israel – were taken over by Muslims. Islamic armies and settlers pushed east and reached India and China after many years. Others pushed west through Egypt and across North Africa. In 711, Muslims crossed the Mediterranean Sea and moved into what is now Spain. Seeking to expand their influence, they began marching over the Pyrenees mountains to France, but in 732 French soldiers met and stopped them near Poitiers.

It's hard to imagine a world without 1, 2 or 3. But do you remember that the Romans used other numerals? They wrote I for 1, V for 5 and X for 10. In our daily life, we use *Arabic numerals*, used by Muslim scholars from the Arab world, who may have learned them from scholars in India. Muslims introduced these symbols to Europeans. Nowadays, the whole world uses Arabic numerals.

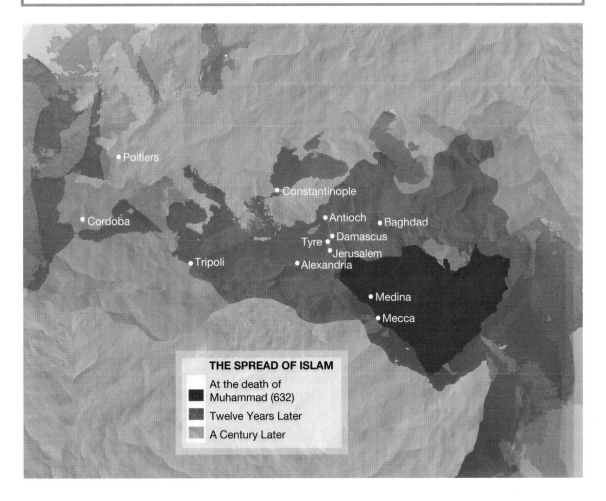

THE SPREAD OF ISLAM

At the death of Muhammad (632)

Twelve Years Later

A Century Later

Muslims lived in Spain for the next seven centuries. They built strong forts, beautiful mosques and graceful palaces, like the Alhambra (see page 159). They developed irrigation systems to grow their crops better and brought plants to Spain from all over the world: cherries, apples, pears, almonds, sugar cane and bananas.

The Angel Gabriel urged Muhammad to read, and reading and learning have been important in the Islamic religion ever since. Spain's city of Córdoba became a great centre of Muslim learning and culture. Muslim scholars studied the Qur'an along with other works of science and philosophy from many cultures, including ancient Greece. The Muslim philosopher Avicenna (in Arabic, *Ibn Sina*), who lived in the country of Persia (today's Iran) from 980 to 1037, wrote medical books that influenced doctors for generations.

*The Great Mosque of Córdoba in Spain later became a cathedral. This mosque-cathedral is an example of Islamic architecture in Western Europe.*

## The Crusades

Three different religions considered Palestine, the land that included Jerusalem, a Holy Land. It was the home of King David, an ancient leader of the Jewish people, and the place where the ancient Jewish king Solomon had built his temple. Therefore, the Jews considered Jerusalem a holy city. Since Christians believed that Jesus was crucified, buried and resurrected in Jerusalem, they also considered it a holy city in their religion.

Muhammad had visited the city as well and, according to Islamic belief, rose up into the heavens during that visit. Therefore, Muslims considered Jerusalem a very important holy city in their religion.

Muslims took over Jerusalem as early as the seventh century. There they lived peacefully with those of other religions until about 1000 A.D., when their leader encouraged his people to destroy the Holy Sepulchre [SEPP-uhl-ker], considered by Christians to be the tomb of Jesus. In 1095 the Pope, leader of the Western Christian church, declared that Christians should go to war to reclaim the city of Jerusalem and the important Christian monuments in it. He called for a *Crusade*, a war to win the Holy Land for Christianity.

Christians from all over Europe armed themselves and started on the long journey east. To capture Jerusalem in 1099, Christian soldiers had to fight many fierce battles. Over the next 200 years, many passionate Christians travelled to the Holy Land. Some entered Jerusalem peacefully, but some attacked. This long series of conflicts over the Holy Land and the city of Jerusalem is called the Crusades.

*Saladin's expert fighting won him the city of Jerusalem in 1187, and Christian Crusaders bowed down to him. However, Richard I later tried to take it back during Third Crusade.*

We learnt about the Crusades in Year 3.

The word *crusade* comes from the Latin word for cross. The Christian soldiers fighting in these wars were called Crusaders. The Muslims called these wars the *Frankish* invasions. Frankish is another word for French, but the Muslims used it to refer to all Western Europeans, whom they saw as invading their territory.

One of the most famous meetings during the Crusades took place in 1192, when King Richard I of England (called Richard the Lionheart) met Saladin of Egypt, a mighty Muslim leader. Richard won his name 'lionheart' because of his bravery and eagerness to fight. He joined with the King of France to lead a Crusade to the Holy Land. It is known as the Third Crusade.

Saladin had become the most powerful Muslim of his time by conquering territory in North Africa. In 1187, he had captured Jerusalem. As Richard's small army approached the city, Saladin's troops surprised them outside the city gates. Even after his horse was killed beneath him, Richard the Lionheart kept fighting. Saladin, admiring Richard's courage, sent him more horses. Saladin had such respect for Richard the Lionheart that, even though he won the war, he agreed not to destroy things sacred to Christians and agreed to let Christians make safe pilgrimages to Jerusalem.

The Crusades involved long and bloody battles and cost many lives, but they also opened up communication between Europe and the Middle East. More trade and travel happened between these two parts of the world than ever before, and the geography, culture and learning of the Middle East became more widely known.

*The Third Crusade*

# British History

## Why was Great Britain Created?

### The Last Stuart

Do you remember studying the Glorious Revolution? It was called 'glorious' because in 1688 parliament peacefully chose a new king and queen, without any of the terrible fighting that had taken place during the English Civil War earlier in the century. James II had been removed as King because he was a Catholic who was trying to make England a Catholic country again, so his Protestant daughter Mary II and her Dutch husband William III staged a peaceful invasion of England and took the throne. There were battles in Scotland and Ireland, where many people did not accept the new King and Queen, but most people in England welcomed the new arrangement.

*King William III*

Mary died six years later, but William carried on as king until 1702 when his horse tripped over a molehill and he was thrown to the ground. He broke his collarbone, caught pneumonia and died. William and Mary had been unable to have children, so the crown passed to Mary's sister Anne. Queen Anne was the last monarch of the House of Stuart.

Anne was desperate to have a son who could succeed her as king, but although she became pregnant eighteen times, none of her children survived long enough. Despite her troubles, Anne was a wise and important queen. It was during her reign that England won a great victory over her old enemy France, and the nation of Great Britain was created.

*Queen Anne*

## The Creation of 'Great Britain'

Parliament was very worried about Queen Anne's lack of children. Her half-brother, the former James II who had been removed from the throne and was now called James Stuart, believed that he was the rightful king of England. The kings of France and Spain thought James Stuart should be king of England too. However, he was a Catholic. So the year before Anne became queen, Parliament searched Europe for her nearest living Protestant relative who could succeed her. In Germany they found a lady called Sophia of Hanover, who was the grand-daughter of James I. Parliament passed a law in 1701 called the Act of Settlement. It declared that when Anne died, the English crown would pass to her distant German cousin Sophia.

Most people in England were happy with this settlement, but the Scottish people were not. Since 1603 the same monarch ruled Scotland and England but they had remained different countries. The Scots were furious that they were not consulted about Sophia succeeding Queen Anne, and many Scots liked the idea of being ruled by James Stuart. So, in 1703 the Scottish Parliament declared that when Queen Anne died, they would choose their own monarch.

*Queen Anne is presented with the Act of Union.*

The English were very worried about this development. They knew that if James Stuart became King of Scotland, he could raise an army to invade England and take back the throne that many claimed was rightfully his. The English proposed that Scotland and England should become one country, sharing one monarch and one Parliament based in Westminster. At first the Scots disliked this idea. However, the Scottish leaders were slowly won round with the help of some very generous bribes! On the 1 May 1707, the Act of Union was passed.

In Year 1 we saw how the flags of England and Scotland were put together to create the Union Flag. The Irish flag (St Patrick's cross) was added to it later, making it the Union Jack that we know today.

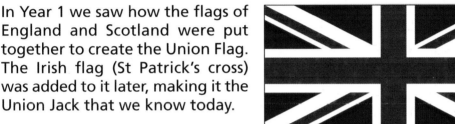

*Union Jack*

*St George's Cross*

*St Andrew's Cross*

*St Patrick's Cross*

*Union Flag of England and Scotland*

The first article of the Act of Union declared that the two kingdoms of England and Scotland would become one kingdom. The United Kingdom of Great Britain had been created. The Act also described the flag that this new country would use, combining the diagonal white cross of St Andrew (patron saint of Scotland), and the red cross of St George (patron saint of England).

Queen Anne was thrilled, and led a grand procession to St Paul's Cathedral. She declared that the Scottish and the English must now 'have hearts disposed to become one people'.

*Queen Anne's Heraldic badge included the English rose and the Scottish thistle.*

## John Churchill

It may seem boastful that this new country was called 'Great' Britain, but this was not the intention. The 'Great' was meant to distinguish it from the area of North-West France known as Brittany. However, it would prove to be a fitting description. The one hundred years after the Act of Union saw Britain grow from being an unstable, unimportant island off continental Europe to become the most powerful nation in the world. The first step was taken by a soldier called John Churchill, the Duke of Marlborough, who many say is the greatest military leader Britain has ever produced.

*John Churchill was an extremely successful British military leader.*

*The Duke of Marlborough is signing the dispatch at Blenheim.*

During the reign of Queen Anne, the French King Louis XIV controlled much of Europe. He wanted his grandson Phillip to be king of Spain, but the Dutch, the English and the Germans did not want the power of Louis XIV to grow even greater. This caused the War of Spanish Succession. The Duke of Marlborough led an army of soldiers from several countries, who called themselves the allies because they were allied, or united, against Louis XIV. They won a famous victory at a German village named Blenheim in 1704. The French army was camping outside the village, so Marlborough's army marched through the night and surprised them by attacking at 8 A.M. In the battle, 20,000 French troops were killed, compared with 12,000 allies. The people of England were overjoyed by the news of Marlborough's victory.

*Blenheim Palace*

The Duke of Marlborough became a great national hero and was given land near Oxford to build himself a magnificent house. He called it Blenheim Palace. Nearly two hundred years later, a descendant of John Churchill, the first Duke of Marlborough, was born in that palace. He was named Winston Churchill. He was not the Duke of Marlborough, but he became a very important Prime Minister who led Britain and her allies to victory in the Second World War.

## Monarchs of the House of Hanover

George I reigned for 13 years from 1714 to 1727

George II reigned for 33 years from 1727 to 1760

George III reigned for 60 years from 1760 to 1820

George IV reigned for 10 years from 1820 to 1830

William IV reigned for 7 years from 1830 to 1837

# How Did Parliamentary Government Develop?

*George I*

## George I

Queen Anne died in 1714. Sophia of Hanover was supposed to become queen, but she had died one month earlier. Instead, the crown passed to her son Georg Ludwig, the Elector of Hanover. This was called the *Hanoverian Succession*.

Georg Ludwig arrived in London on 18 September and was crowned George I of Great Britain. For many people, it was a strange sight. There were 57 other descendants of James I with a better claim to the throne than him, but they were all Catholics. So, he was plucked from ruling the small German state of Hanover to become the King of Great Britain. He had only visited England once in his life and spoke no English. He took little interest in England, and spent a lot of time going back to visit Hanover.

James Stuart, who had been James II, was dead by this time, but his son, also called James Stuart, still believed he should be king, and many people in England secretly agreed. They called themselves *Jacobites* (a name taken from *Jacobus*, the Latin word for 'James') and planned an uprising against George I. In the north of Scotland, in an area known as the Highlands, the fierce 'clan' warriors were some of the most dedicated Jacobites. Led by an Englishman called the Earl of Mar, they organised an army to rebel against George I and put James Stuart on the throne. James Stuart arrived from France, but he did not seem like he would make a good king. He was shy, unfriendly and a bad soldier. The Jacobite uprising, known as 'The Fifteen' because it took place in 1715, was a failure. James Stuart quickly gave up and went to live in Italy, but the Jacobites kept on plotting for many years to get a Stuart back on the throne.

## The First Prime Minister?

George I spent a lot of time in Hanover, which was his home. He was not so interested in what was going on in Britain and, as a result, he relied on his ministers, who were normally members of parliament, to make the decisions. From now on, the monarch reigned but ministers ruled. This suited parliament very well.

Robert Walpole was a farmer from Norfolk and a member of parliament. He loved drinking and eating and he also loved money and power: he wanted to become the most powerful politician in Britain. Walpole was not an honest man: he would bribe other politicians to get his way, but he was good at his job. He became Chancellor of the Exchequer and First Lord of the Treasury, as he had a reputation for being very good at managing money. He knew how to get members of parliament to do what he wanted, often by bribing them or by giving positions to his friends and relatives, and he could get parliament to agree to any laws he wanted to pass. As a result, people began referring to him as the prime minister, even though there was no such job at the time. 'Prime' means 'first', and from this time on, whoever was the most important politician in the government would be referred to as the prime minister.

*Robert Walpole is talking to the Speaker of the House of Commons.*

Walpole was popular with George I and with his son, George II, who gave him a house: number 10 Downing Street, near to parliament. Walpole recommended that the house should be used by whoever was First Lord of the Treasury, instead of belonging to him personally. The Prime Minister lives at number 10 Downing Street to this day, and on the front door are painted the words 'First Lord of the Treasury'.

*George II*

## George II

In 1727 King George I died and his son became King George II. At first, George II did not like Robert Walpole because he thought he had become too powerful. However, Walpole had become good friends with George II's wife, Queen Caroline, and promised that parliament would give the King more money if he could keep his job. George II had to agree.

Walpole's main ambition as Prime Minister was to keep Britain out of any foreign wars, as they were very expensive and meant that taxes had to go up. He was successful for nearly twenty years, and Britain grew wealthier as her foreign trade flourished. This was a happy period in Britain's history, but Walpole's peace could not last forever and, in 1739, war with Spain broke out. However, his achievements had a lasting impact. Walpole strengthened parliamentary government, which meant that the King had to share power with his ministers in Parliament. In 1755 George II complained: 'Ministers are the kings in this country, I am nothing there.'

## How Were the Stuarts Finally Defeated?

*'Bonnie Prince Charlie'*

### Bonnie Prince Charlie

By 1745, the British army was busy fighting the French in the War of Austrian Succession. The Jacobites took this opportunity to stage one last rebellion. In the wild moors of the Scottish Highlands, the dream that a Stuart might once again rule Scotland and England lived on. The Highlands were ruled by ancient 'clans', each led by a clan 'chief'. The clansmen were mostly poor farmers, but they were also fierce warriors.

The Jacobites found a new hope in James Stuart's eldest son, Charles Edward Stuart. He was likeable, he inspired people and he was a good soldier. He was also very good looking, so his Highland supporters named him 'Bonnie Prince Charlie'. Prince Charlie landed in Scotland in July 1745 and the Highland clans rushed to welcome him. The Highlanders wore Scottish tartan and caps with white cockades and armed themselves with traditional Scottish swords called claymores. With these soldiers, Prince Charlie won a series of victories in Scotland, and by November his 6,000 men were marching south towards London. With most of his army fighting in Europe, King George II was terrified. He even loaded a boat on the Thames with treasure ready to escape to Hanover.

For years, Jacobites had held secret meetings across Britain where they toasted their 'rightful' king and plotted rebellion. Prince Charlie expected that, when he invaded, all of these secret Jacobites would rush to his support. In reality, most of them were not brave enough to commit treason and stayed at home. Prince Charlie marched as far south as Derby, but his soldiers grew disappointed and missed the Highlands. They turned around and marched all the way back to Scotland.

## The Battle of Culloden

By now, George II had raised an army, led by his son the Duke of Cumberland, and put a price of £30,000 on the head of Prince Charlie. Cumberland's red-coated soldiers shadowed the retreating Jacobites to the Highlands of Scotland, where they met for a final battle on Culloden Moor in April 1746. Cumberland tore apart the Jacobite army with his cannons and cavalry, and they were easily defeated.

*The Battle of Culloden*

Bonnie Prince Charlie escaped from the battlefield, and for weeks he hid in the moors of Scotland. A beautiful young woman named Flora MacDonald found him and planned his escape. She disguised him as her Irish maid and, under the name Betty Burke, he took a boat to the Isle of Skye and from there to France.

Bonnie Prince Charlie spent the rest of his life in Italy, where he died on 30 January 1788. The Hanoverians were now safely established as Britain's new royal family as there were no more Stuarts who could take back the throne.

You can sing the Skye Boat Song on page 197.

# How Did Britain Gain an Empire?

## Global Trade

Do you remember studying the exploration of the 'New World' during the 1500s and 1600s? In the years that followed, European merchants began to trade with these far-off lands. In order to improve their trade, European countries would take over territories in the New World. They built forts and towns for merchants and soldiers to live in, and these territories became known as colonies. By 1750, Britain had established colonies in West Africa, North America, South America, the Caribbean and India.

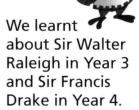

We learnt about Sir Walter Raleigh in Year 3 and Sir Francis Drake in Year 4.

*Canadian bearskin has been used to make these bearskin hats worn by the Queen's Guard.*

British merchants would exchange British-made goods for new exotic luxuries. From Canada they would buy beaver and bear skins; from America tobacco and cotton; from the Caribbean sugar; from South Asia spices such as pepper, ginger and cinnamon; from China tea and cups to drink it from which they decided to call 'china'; and from Africa they would buy slaves – you will read about the slave trade later in this chapter.

During the peace of the early eighteenth century, Britain's overseas trade flourished. Ports such as Liverpool, Glasgow and Bristol became very rich, and beautiful houses were built for the wealthy merchants and their families. However, such trade was not easy. European nations would argue over who could trade where, so small wars constantly broke out and profits were lost. Britain decided that to continue their profitable global trade they would have to rule the seas.

*Teacups and saucers like these were imported to Britain from China.*

## The Seven Years War

In 1756, the French invaded a British colony off the coast of Spain called Minorca. A member of parliament called William Pitt was very angry. He was a good speaker and was loved by the British people. He made passionate speeches in Parliament calling for war with France, and the King was forced to make Pitt Prime Minister.

*British ships in the Seven Years War fought battles around the world, including this one near Havana, Cuba.*

Pitt took Britain into a new war against France that lasted until 1763, so it was called the Seven Years War. Although the Seven Years War was between nations in Europe, the battles were fought in trading colonies all around the world. There were conflicts in Africa, India, North America, South America and the Philippine Islands.

## Canada

One of the most important victories of the war was won in Canada. By 1756, Britain ruled thirteen colonies along the eastern shore of North America. However, France controlled the land to the north, south and west of these colonies. The British were worried that the French would close in on their colonies and take control of the whole continent. So, Pitt chose a flamboyant and ruthless General called James Wolfe to take Canada from the French.

The centre of French rule in Canada was a well-defended city called Quebec. It was situated on the St Lawrence River, on top of a sheer cliff called the Heights of Abraham. The St Lawrence River was full of rocks and shallow sand, but Wolfe carefully sailed 8,000 soldiers up the river to an island outside the city where they landed. The Heights of Abraham looked impossibly steep, but Wolfe found a narrow pathway up the cliffs. At the dead of night, he sent the Highland Fusiliers, who were well used to such mountainous terrain, up the pathway for a surprise attack on the French. A fierce battle ensued. Wolfe was shot twice but carried on fighting. On the third shot, he hit the ground and died. The British kept fighting and won the Battle of Quebec. The enormous North American territory of New France now became part of the British Empire.

*This famous painting shows the death of General Wolfe.*

## India

In 1600, the British formed the East India Company so that wealthy merchants could trade for goods such as tea, cotton and silk. By 1750, the Company had a series of coastal trading

*An artist shows a British officer riding in an Indian procession.*

colonies in Madras, Calcutta, Surat and Bombay. The British merchants were very respectful of the Indian people: they adopted their food and dress, married Indian women and learned about their customs and habits.

However, by the time of the Seven Years War, the mighty Mughal Empire which had ruled India was crumbling, and India was breaking up into smaller states run by princes. One Prince, called the Nawab of Bengal, disliked the growing British power in Calcutta. He allied with the French, and together they captured Fort William – the British trading post in Calcutta. A fiercely ambitious British soldier named Robert Clive, who was stationed in Madras, took action. In 1757 he marched a small army of 3,200 soldiers to Bengal to face the Nawab's 40,000 soldiers at the Battle of Plassey. The Nawab's army were crushed by Clive's artillery.

After the Battle of Plassey, increasing numbers of British troops were sent to India to support the East India Company. British officials became more involved in the government of India, and expanded their power throughout the former Mughal Empire.

## Rule Britannia

The British sometimes described 1759 as the 'year of miracles'. By the end of the war, Britain had gained territories in Canada, North America, West Africa, the Philippines and India. The British Empire was born. The Empire would last for two hundred years, but its legacy has been a source of disagreement. Did the Empire help foreign countries progress, or did it cause great human suffering? This is something you will consider next year.

William Pitt became a national hero for leading his nation through the Seven Years War. The Union Jack flag could be seen flying in celebration of each military victory and British people began to celebrate 'Britannia' – a female figure used to represent the growing Empire. In 1740, there was the first ever performance of the song 'Rule Britannia', with the words: 'Rule, Britannia! rule the waves: Britons never will be slaves.' The British refused to be slaves, but they did not see a problem with forcing millions of people in other countries to be ruled by them.

*You can see this statue of Britannia in Plymouth.*

'Rule Britannia' is sung every year at the Last Night of the Proms, together with 'Land of Hope and Glory' that we read about in Year 4.

## Life as a British Seaman

During the eighteenth century, the Royal Navy grew into the most effective fighting force in the world. In 1700, it contained 270 warships but by 1805 there were 950. To provide all these warships with their crews, Parliament sent 'press gangs' around Britain to carry out *impressment*. Impressment meant forcing men to serve in the Royal Navy and it was extremely unpopular.

The life of a Royal Navy sailor was very hard. Trapped at sea for months on end, they would have to live on a diet of salt meat, stale water and hard biscuits full of maggots and weevils. Many sailors died of a disease called scurvy. It would cause your gums to bleed and rot, and your teeth to fall out. The disease was caused by a lack of vitamin C, so British sailors were made to eat lemons and limes to prevent it. As a result, they were nicknamed 'limeys'.

Punishments were fierce. The most infamous was flogging with the cat-o'-nine-tails. This was a whip made up of nine knotted cords designed to cut the skin and inflict terrible pain. The punishment would be delivered for something as small as falling asleep on duty, and the whole crew would gather on deck to watch. Some sailors found their treatment unbearable, and would occasionally mutiny, or refuse to follow their officers' orders and take control of the ship.

Nevertheless, for many young men, joining the navy was a chance to see the world and make a large amount of money. Sailors who rose to the rank of 'able seamen' were extremely proud of their profession. They would wear colourful clothing, extravagant hairstyles, gold jewellery and – having learnt the art from the Polynesian societies of the South Pacific – tattoos. After months at sea, they would land at a port, drink lots of rum and have enormous celebrations. It was a hard life, but one full of adventure and excitement.

*The HMS Victory was Admiral Nelson's ship at the Battle of Trafalgar.*

131

# How Did America Gain Independence from the British Empire?

## The Thirteen Colonies

When the British arrived in North America, they brought diseases such as smallpox and measles that wiped out much of the Native American population. The land was easily occupied by British settlers. The first English colony was established in 1607 and named Jamestown, after James I. By 1770, there were thirteen British colonies in North America with a population of around two million settlers.

*These men show what it might have been like to live in Williamsburg, Virginia during the eighteenth century.*

The names of these colonies, which are now parts of the United States of America, often reveal their British connection: Virginia (after Elizabeth I, known as the Virgin Queen); Georgia (after George II); Carolina (after Charles II, whose name in Latin was Carolus); and Maryland (after Henrietta Maria, the Queen of Charles I). The American colonists were British subjects, who lived by the laws of the Parliament and shared British rights and freedoms. However, the Seven Years War would break this relationship.

## Taxation without Representation

Fighting the Seven Years War had cost a huge amount of money, and the British national debt rose to £140 million. In 1760, George III became King. Unlike George I and II, he spoke English as a first language and claimed: 'I glory in the name of Briton.' However, he was stubborn and not very clever, and frequently argued with his minsters. It was decided that the American colonists should help with the national debt by paying more taxes. The war, the government claimed, was fought to protect the colonies from the French, so why should the colonies not now pay for some of the cost?

This decision made the colonists extremely angry. They believed that parliament could not force American colonists to pay taxes because the colonies were not represented by members of parliament in London. Colonists protested, held meetings and cried out:

*Paul Revere engraved and printed this image of the Boston Massacre.*

*The Boston Tea Party*

'No taxation without representation.' The British were worried and sent the army to Boston, Massachusetts, in 1768.

Boston is a city in the North East of America. In March 1770, a group of Bostonians started taunting British troops. The troops shot into the crowd and killed five colonists. The event was named the Boston Massacre and news of it spread throughout America.

Three years later, there was even more protest in Boston. The British declared that Americans could only buy tea from the East India Company, which charged a very high price. In angry resistance, a group called the Sons of Liberty dressed up as Native Americans, boarded the merchants' ships in Boston harbour and dumped all of the 342 crates of tea overboard. The sea turned black with tea.

King George III and his parliament were furious, and passed even more laws limiting the rights and freedoms of the American colonists. Colonists called the new laws the Intolerable Acts, because they could not tolerate or put up with them.

## Declaration of Independence

The American colonists pleaded with George III to give them the same rights and privileges as those people who lived in Britain, but he would not change his mind. They began to realise that if they wanted to be free, they would have to break away from British rule. Representatives from all of the thirteen colonies met in a city called Philadelphia. They chose a shy but highly educated lawyer from Virginia called Thomas Jefferson to write a letter to King George III announcing that America was to break away from British rule.

*Benjamin Franklin, John Adams, Thomas Jefferson and others drew up the Declaration of Independence in 1776.*

It was signed on the 4 July 1776, and called the Declaration of Independence.

The Declaration stated:

*We hold these truths to be self-evident, that all men are created equal, that they are endowed by their Creator with certain unalienable rights, that among these are life, liberty, and the pursuit of happiness.*

Americans see the signing of this document on 4 July as the birth of their country and celebrate it as Independence Day every year.

## American War of Independence

King George III was not willing to let go of these profitable colonies, so a war was fought for nearly eight years between Britain and the American colonists. It was much like a civil war, and many in Britain opposed it because they felt they were fighting their own fellow-countrymen.

*During Paul Revere's ride, he let everyone know 'the redcoats are coming!'*

The war began when British soldiers planned to raid a store of guns and ammunition in a town called Lexington. An American spy called Paul Revere learnt about these plans and rode through the night telling every town he passed 'the redcoats are coming!' (Soldiers in the British army wore bright red uniforms and were known as redcoats as a result.) When the British arrived in Lexington, colonial militiamen were ready to meet them. They were not trained soldiers like the British troops but volunteers with little or no experience of warfare. As the British redcoats marched towards the militiamen, a shot was fired. A poet called Ralph Waldo Emerson wrote that this was 'the shot heard round the world'.

The American leaders chose a man named George Washington to take command of their army. He had fought for the British during the Seven Years War; he was an intelligent general and an inspiring leader. The Americans had only 15,000 volunteer soldiers, compared with the British army of 30,000 professional soldiers. However, motivated by their thirst for freedom, they won many battles.

In 1778, the French entered the war on the side of the Americans because they wanted to get revenge on the British. With the help of the French army and navy, the Americans were able to win the war.

Lord North, the British Prime Minister, found it extremely difficult to carry on the war on the other side of the Atlantic – news would take three months to reach him and his orders would take another three months to reach the army. In 1781, General Washington surrounded the British army at Yorktown in Virginia and the British army surrendered.

*George Washington crossing the River Delaware*

A small and unprepared nation of disunited colonies had beaten the mightiest nation on earth. When Lord North heard the news, he cried: 'Oh God, it's all over.' A peace treaty between America and Britain was signed in 1783, and the United States of America was born. General George Washington was chosen to be their first President.

# What was the Effect of the French Revolution on Britain?

In 1774 Louis XVI became the King of France. He lived in the magnificent Palace of Versailles with his wife, Queen Marie Antoinette. She spent lots of money on jewellery and parties, and seemed to care little for the poor people of France. When she was told that they were starving, with no bread to eat, she was reported to have said: 'Let them eat cake!'

*King Louis XVI lived a life of luxury.*

Although France was rich and powerful, the ordinary peasants lived in poverty, doing backbreaking labour and paying taxes to the church and the nobles. What made it worse was the fact that ordinary people were the *only* people paying tax. The wealthy aristocrats didn't pay any! Nor did the church-leaders, many of whom were also very wealthy. The king had the power to imprison anyone he liked without a trial. Many thought he was a *tyrant*, someone who uses their power cruelly. Such an unfair society could not last forever.

Supporting the American War of Independence had left France with a large national debt, so Louis XVI had to raise taxes. The common people of France could not tolerate this. They wanted all people to share equal rights, and for the nobles and the church to lose their privileges. On 14 July 1789 the people of Paris stormed a prison called the Bastille and released its prisoners. This act showed that they no longer obeyed the King, and revolution in France had begun. The French people still celebrate Bastille Day every year on 14 July.

The people of Paris imprisoned Louis XVI, Marie Antoinette and their children. One of the leaders of the revolution was a man called Maximilien Robespierre, a very strict and serious lawyer who made long speeches about virtue and reason. Robespierre was willing to do anything to make the revolution succeed and he sentenced anyone

*Marie Antoinette was sentenced to death and was taken to be beheaded.*

who opposed the revolution to death. During a period called the Reign of Terror many thousands of people were sent to the guillotine to have their heads cut off.

Louis refused to meet the demands of the people and 1793 he and his wife Marie Antoinette were sentenced to death. Dressed as common people, with their hair roughly cut, they were taken to the guillotine and beheaded. France was now a republic – a nation ruled without a monarch.

## War in Europe

At first, the people of Britain celebrated the French Revolution. They saw it as similar to their own uprising against Charles I in the previous century. Some British politicians even thought the endless war between France and Britain would now end. This was not the case, because in 1793 France declared war on Britain.

Since the King had been killed, France had no clear leader. So a truly extraordinary man rose through the French army to lead the nation. His name was Napoleon Bonaparte. He was from a small island near Italy called Corsica, and at the age of ten he was sent to a military academy in France. He did not make friends easily and was teased for being short and having a strange accent. However, he spent all of his time studying and planning his path to greatness.

*Napoleon Bonaparte crossing the Alps*

At seventeen he became an officer in the army; at twenty-six, he was commanding the French army in Italy; and aged twenty-nine he seized power in Paris and put himself in charge of the entire country. In 1804 he made himself 'Emperor' of France.

Napoleon was one of the greatest military commanders the world has ever seen, and his armies conquered the ancient kingdoms of Europe. He soon controlled much of Europe and divided it up between members of his family.

## The Battle of Trafalgar

Napoleon's next target was Great Britain, and by 1805 he had 200,000 soldiers stationed on the French coast. He called them the Army of England. If Napoleon could defeat the British

*Joseph Turner's painting* The Battle of Trafalgar *shows HMS* Victory, *Admiral Nelson's ship, capturing the French ship* Redoubtable. *The flags on the mainmast of the* Victory *spell out 'duty', the last word of Nelson's message 'England expects that every man will do his duty'. On the left, we can just see the prow of another English ship, the* Temeraire. *We looked at Turner's painting of this ship in Year 4.*

*The death of Horatio Nelson*

navy and gain control of the English Channel, he could invade and conquer Great Britain. The British people were terrified, and parents told their children of the evil 'bogeyman' (a nickname for Bonaparte) who would come and eat them during the night if they misbehaved.

The job of stopping Napoleon's invasion was given to a forty-seven year old admiral in the Royal Navy called Horatio Nelson. Nelson was a brave and accomplished sailor who had already lost his right eye and his right arm fighting the French. He found the French navy off the Spanish coast at Cape Trafalgar and prepared to attack. A signal was raised on his ship the HMS *Victory* that read: 'England expects that every man will do his duty'. Nelson divided his fleet of 27 ships in two and sailed them in parallel lines straight at the 33 French vessels. This was a brilliant move, and 22 of the French ships were destroyed.

Towards the end of the battle, Nelson was shot through the shoulder. Nelson declared to Thomas Hardy, Captain of the *Victory*: 'Hardy, I do believe they have done it at last… my backbone is shot through.' He was taken below deck, where he died four hours later. He had saved Britain from invasion, and a new square in London was named after the Battle of Trafalgar. Nelson's statue was placed on a column in the middle of Trafalgar Square. Have you seen it?

## The Battle of Waterloo

The threat of invasion was over, but the British continued to fight Napoleon's armies for another ten years. Napoleon invaded Spain and made his brother Joseph the king. The British army was sent to Spain to help the people to fight back. The campaign was led by an experienced general called the Duke of Wellington. Together with the Spanish, Wellington pushed Napoleon's forces back to France. In 1814, Napoleon was finally defeated and ordered to spend the rest of his life living alone on a small Mediterranean island called Elba.

Only one year later, Napoleon escaped from Elba and returned to a hero's welcome in France. He made himself Emperor once more, and raised another great army. The British, Dutch and Germans allied (joined together) to defeat Napoleon, and Wellington was sent into battle with an army of 68,000 men. The two greatest military commanders of the age, Napoleon and Wellington, met on 18 June 1815 on a battlefield called Waterloo, which is now in Belgium. It was a fierce battle that lasted all day, with no clear winner. However, late in the afternoon the Prussian allies arrived and tipped the balance of the battle. Napoleon was defeated. He was imprisoned on the island

*Wellington thanks the Prussian General Blucher*

of St Helena in the middle of the Atlantic Ocean, and died there seven years later. The Duke of Wellington went on to be Britain's Prime Minster in 1829-30 and again in 1834.

# Why was Slavery Abolished?

## The Slave Trade

Have you ever wondered why there are so many people of African descent living in America and the Caribbean? Most of them are descended from African people who were taken from their homes, shipped across the Atlantic Ocean and forced to work as slaves. From the first slaving voyage of 1562 to the abolition of the slave trade (a law ending it) by Britain in 1807, an estimated 3.5 million Africans were sold into slavery by British merchants.

British colonists built enormous farms called 'plantations' in the Americas, where they grew sugar, tobacco and cotton. The plantation owners realised that, if they used slave labour, they could save a lot of money, which is why they imported people from Africa.

*Slaves worked on many plantations to harvest and process cotton, which would then be made into fabric for clothes.*

## The Atlantic Passage

Slavery is a terrible thing, but unfortunately it has been practised in many countries, almost since the start of human societies. Britain was not alone in using slaves as cheap labour: other European and Arabic nations were involved with the slave trade. Merchants paid African tribes to capture members of rival tribes and bring them to colonies on the coast where they would be kept in large trading forts called *barracoons*. From here, the slaves would be loaded onto British merchant ships to make the Atlantic passage – the long boat trip carrying the slaves across the Atlantic.

The conditions on these ships were so bad it is hard to imagine them. Hundreds of slaves would be crammed side-by-side onto wooden bunk beds and chained by the feet. Here they would have to live for the entire crossing, sometimes up to three months, unable to move. Disease spread like wildfire and one in ten would die before making it to America. Once a day the slaves would be taken above board (onto the deck) and made to dance, in order to keep them exercised. Some would jump overboard, preferring to drown than to experience any more suffering. A slave ship was so foul that sailors said it could be smelt before it could be seen.

*Slaves were crammed into every spare space on the ship during the Atlantic Passage.*

## Life as a Slave

Those slaves who survived the Atlantic Passage and landed in the Americas would be auctioned off to plantation owners. Depending on their age, gender, health and behaviour, a slave could cost between £5 and £80. Often, the slave would have the name of their new owner burnt onto their skin with hot iron; this was called *branding.*

Slaves would be made to farm sugar, cotton, coffee and ginger; sometimes they cut down trees or looked after livestock. They worked for six days a week and would never have a holiday. They were separated from their friends and family and not allowed to practise their own religion, speak their own language or even get married.

Any disobedience was cruelly punished. Slaves would be beaten or whipped for not working hard enough. More serious punishments included wearing iron neck collars, having their ear nailed to a post or having parts of their body chopped off. On a plantation slaves usually didn't live long because of this treatment, living on average for eight miserable years.

## Abolition

During the 1780s a small group of people began to campaign for the abolition of slavery (to have it made illegal). One of them was a student at the University of Cambridge called Thomas Clarkson. He was from a religious family and he believed that slavery was evil. He dedicated his life to abolishing slavery, beginning in 1787 when he formed the Committee for the Abolition of the African Slave Trade. As its members wanted to see slavery abolished, they called themselves *abolitionists*.

*Thomas Clarkson addressed many audiences, including this Anti-Slavery Society Convention in 1840.*

The abolitionists collected information about the cruelty of slavery, including whips, handcuffs, shackles, branding irons and diagrams of slave ships. They travelled around Britain making passionate speeches, explaining its cruelty. Clarkson persuaded 300,000 British people to boycott sugar grown on slave plantations. He also persuaded 400,000 people to sign a petition demanding the end of slavery. He travelled a total of 35,000 miles making speeches across Great Britain and was nearly drowned by angry slave traders whilst visiting Liverpool.

There were also African abolitionists, such as the freed slave named Olaudah Equiano. Equiano was a slave in Virginia who saved enough money to buy his freedom and travelled to England. In 1787, he published his autobiography, which includes descriptions of the brutal cruelty of slavery. It was a popular book that helped the abolitionist cause. Equiano died before slavery was abolished, but the fight continued. A Member of Parliament called William Wilberforce, who was an evangelical Christian, joined the campaign. He lobbied Parliament for eighteen years for the abolition of the slave trade.

*Olaudah Equiano*

In 1807, the abolitionists finally achieved their aim. Wilberforce's bill for the abolition of the slave trade passed through Parliament and became law. Other countries continued the slave trade for many years, but Britain had become the first country in history to make slavery illegal. In 1833 Wilberforce died, and one month later slavery was abolished throughout the entire British Empire. It had taken nearly fifty years for Clarkson's campaign to conquer this evil, but finally it was achieved.

## What was Life Like in Georgian Britain?

In 1709, Daniel Defoe divided the population of England into seven groups, from highest to lowest in money and power. They were:

1. The great
2. The rich
3. The middle sort
4. The working trades
5. The country people

6. The poor
7. The miserable

Read part of Daniel Defoe's story of Robinson Crusoe on page 29.

143

## The Aristocracy

By the 'great', Defoe meant the aristocracy. This was a class of extremely rich landowners. They led privileged lives, spending half of the year in their large country houses, and the other half of the year in London attending Parliament. Those most powerful held aristocratic titles such as Duke, Marquis, Earl and Viscount. As members of the House of Lords, they had an automatic place in Parliament.

*This cartoon pokes fun at 'Macaronis'*

The aristocracy certainly knew how to enjoy themselves. Horse racing, playing cards, hunting and golf were all popular during this period. During the 1700s, aristocratic fashions became extraordinary. Women wore enormous towering white wigs and powdered faces. Fashionable men were called 'Macaronis' because they copied Italian styles and wore elaborate clothing and powdered wigs. Another popular, but potentially deadly, pastime was duelling. If a gentleman felt he had been insulted, he would call the culprit out for a duel. The duellists would stand at a set distance from each other and each had one shot with a pistol.

## The Middling Sort

By 1770 there were 9,400 British merchant ships bringing £13.2 million of goods into the country, and exporting £14.3 million worth of goods. This wealth from trade caused the growth of a new class of people. They were not from landowning, aristocratic families, but they were not poor. Due to the fact that they were between these two groups, they were called the 'middling sort'. They were merchants, doctors, lawyers, bankers and writers. They lived in grand terraced houses, which can still be seen in the fashionable cities of the Georgian period such as Bath, Cheltenham and Leamington Spa.

*Many families of the 'middling sort' lived along the Royal Crescent in Bath.*

The middling sort would have enough money to buy fine food, and to decorate their houses with new comforts such as wallpaper and curtains. Often, they were ambitious and intelligent. They spent money on books and formed societies for sharing new ideas in philosophy, religion, technology and economics.

The 'middling sort' of people had enough money to buy Thomas Chippendale's chairs, like those on page 155.

## The Poor

The great majority of Britain's population were poor farmers and labourers. Craftsmen such as silversmiths and tailors would live comfortably, but most of them led hard lives. The worst poverty was to be found in cities such as London. A famous writer called Henry Fielding described the streets of London as: 'oppressed with hunger, cold, nakedness and filth… They starve and freeze and rot amongst themselves; but they beg and steal and rob amongst their betters… There is not a street that does not swarm all day with beggars, and all night with thieves.'

Alcohol was cheap and many of the poor drank themselves to death with a newly popular drink called gin. It was said that by the 1730s in London, there was one gin shop for every 11 people. When Parliament tried to limit the amount of gin people drank with

*This print of 'Gin Lane' comes from an engraving by William Hogarth.*

See other engravings by William Hogarth and learn about printmaking on page 171.

the 1751 Gin Act, there were angry riots in the street. However, the poor could do very little to change their condition. Only the rich and powerful were allowed to vote in elections, and if the poor stood up for themselves they could be ruthlessly punished. Even petty theft could result in a public hanging.

## Women

Men dominated Georgian Britain. Women could not have careers in politics, trade or professional jobs, and another two centuries would have to pass before they were granted the right to vote. Married women were not even allowed to own personal property. As soon as they married, everything they had became the property of their husbands. However there were some small improvements.

*Mary Wollstonecraft*

A brave, freethinking lady named Mary Wollstonecraft was one of the first women to propose that they should enjoy equal rights to men. She wrote these ideas down in a book called *Vindication of the Rights of Women*. Wollstonecraft's daughter, Mary Shelley, was also extremely clever and wrote the novel *Frankenstein*. Many Georgian women were successful writers. Women wrote most of the great novels of that time. Jane Austen's novels such as *Pride and Prejudice* are still widely read today.

## Criminals

The most famous criminals in Georgian Britain were highwaymen, armed robbers on horseback who attacked wealthy travellers at night on dark, deserted roads. The people of Britain came to dread the sound of galloping hooves and pistol shots, followed by the infamous cry: 'Your money or your life!' The best-known highwayman was Dick Turpin, who was hanged at York in 1739.

The highwaymen of the sea were pirates, who would regularly rob merchant ships of their cargoes on the high seas. The most famous eighteenth-century pirate was called Blackbeard, but his real name was probably Edward Teach. He captured a French ship, renamed it the *Queen Anne's Revenge*, and terrorised the Atlantic, capturing over 40 vessels. He wore a large crimson coat stuffed with swords, pistols and knives. To make himself even more terrifying, he wove burning wicks laced with gunpowder into his hair. The Royal Navy sent Captain Robert Maynard to find Blackbeard, and in 1718 Blackbeard was ambushed and killed. His head was cut off and hung from the mast of Maynard's ship.

*Captain Maynard ambushed Pirate Blackbeard and eventually killed him.*

# Suggested Resources

## Geography

*Discover Countries: New Zealand* by Jane Bingham (Wayland) 2012

*Understanding World Maps* by Jack Gillett (Wayland) 2012

*Geography Now: Mountains* by Jen Green (Wayland) 2012

*Starting Geography: Maps* by Sally Hewitt (Franklin Watts) 2009

*Australia in Our World* by Aleta Moriarty (Franklin Watts) 2010

*Explorer Travel Guides: Mountains* by Chris Oxlade (Raintree) 2013

*Mapping (Investigate Geography)* by Louise Spilsbury (Heinemann) 2010

*Discover Countries: Australia* by Chris Ward (Wayland) 2013

## Online resources

*Mapzone,* at the Ordnance Survey, http://mapzone.ordnancesurvey.co.uk/mapzone/ especially the sections on 'Understanding Scale' and 'Relief and Contour'

*Captain James Cook* at the Royal Museums Greenwich: www.rmg.co.uk/captain-cook

## British History

*The Usborne History of Britain* (Usborne Internet-linked Reference) by Ruth Brocklehurst (Usborne) 2008

*The Georgians* by Ruth Brocklehurst (Usborne) 2008

*Bonnie Prince Charlie and All That* by Allan Burnett (Birlinn) 2006

*The Story of Britain* by Patrick Dillon (Walker) 2010

*A Little History of the World* by E. H. Gombrich (Yale) 1935; 2008

*The Georgians: 1714-1837* by David Haycock (Kingfisher) 2007

*The Ultimate Kings and Queens Sticker Book* by Bridget Hopkinson, illustrated by Catherine Goldsmith (Dorling Kindersley) 1999

*Great Tales From English History: Cheddar Man to DNA* by Robert Lacey (Abacus) 2007

*Africa and the Slave Trade* by Dan Lyndon (Franklin Watts) 2013

*Britannia: 100 Great Stories From British History* by Geraldine McCaughrean (Orion Children's) 2004

*Our Island Story* by H.E. Marshall (Civitas/Galore Park) 1905; 2005

*Kings and Queens* by Tony Robinson (Red Fox) 2001

*Britain's Kings and Queens* by Michael St John Parker, revised by Brenda and Brian Williams (Pitkin Guides) 2011

## DVDs

*Amazing Grace* (Momentum Pictures Home Entertainment) 2007. (About William Wilberforce and the anti-slavery campaign.)

*Bonnie Prince Charlie* (DD Video) 1948; 2003

*A Tale of Two Cities* (ITV Studios Home Entertainment) 1958; 2007

## Places to Visit

Blenheim Palace in Woodstock (built for John Churchill, first Duke of Marlborough) http://www.blenheimpalace.com/

Geffrye Museum in London (domestic interiors covering 400 years) http://www.geffrye-museum.org.uk/

Kensington Palace in London (state rooms of Mary II, Queen Anne, George II) http://www.hrp.org.uk/KensingtonPalace/

HMS Victory in Portsmouth (Nelson's flagship) http://www.hms-victory.com/

# Visual Arts

## Introduction

This chapter complements the history and geography chapters by discussing examples of Islamic art, as well as rococo art which represented aristocratic values that were overturned by the French Revolution. Parents and teachers can build on the brief treatment offered here by exposing children to additional books and pictures and by taking them to visit museums and interesting buildings. Although books are delightful and informative, there is no substitute for the experience of seeing works of art in person. Many galleries and museums offer free admission, and there are magnificent collections in all parts of the UK. There are also many heritage buildings such as cathedrals, churches, town halls and stately homes that contain superb works of art.

Children should experience art not only as viewers but also as creators. They should be encouraged to draw, cut, paste and mould with clay, to imitate styles and artists they have encountered and to develop a style of their own.

# The Language of Art: Style

## Rococo vs. Modernism

In the earlier books in this series, we have looked at the various elements that go towards the creation of a work of art. Do you remember looking at and using the elements of colour, line, shape, texture, form, light and space? All artists have to think about these things when they begin the artistic process, but works of art created in different places and at different times look very different from each other. This is because different artists choose to work in different *styles*.

Some artists want their paintings and sculptures to be as lifelike as possible. For hundreds of years, the highest praise anyone could give a painting or sculpture was to say that it looked as if it was about to breathe, or speak, or step down off its pedestal. Then,

## Activity 1:
## Feeling big and small with architecture

The ancient Greeks used to say that 'man is the measure of all things', which is why you don't feel overwhelmed, even by their greatest buildings like the Parthenon. However, the twentieth-century Swiss architect Le Corbusier

Compare ancient Greek architecture and modern architecture in the Year 3 book to see how each makes you feel.

described buildings as 'machines for living in', and many modern buildings like skyscrapers make you feel very small indeed.

Now look at these photos of two buildings in London: Saint Paul's Cathedral was designed by Sir Christopher Wren using elements of ancient Greek architecture and the Shard is a new, modern-style building. How do you think you would feel if you were standing in front of these two buildings? If you are in London, visit each building and experience the difference.

Can you work like an architect to draw two buildings, one that is more traditional and like an ancient Greek building and one that is as modern as you like?

*St Paul's Cathedral*

*The Shard*

when cameras and other modern technologies had made it very easy to create lifelike images, artists began to say that art should not be competing with technology: the artist should express the things that you *can't* see – the spiritual or other-worldly values.

There have been different opinions about the purpose of art. Some people have wondered why we have art at all, and how it helps our society. Should art seek to solve problems, to teach people how to behave and make them better people? The artist William Hogarth, who created prints like the series *Industry and Idleness* on page 171 to warn people about the consequences of bad behaviour, certainly thought so. (To be *idle* means to be lazy and unwilling to work.) Other artists have believed that art should have nothing to do with the problems of real life: it should try to show us a perfect world in which these problems do not exist, or have been solved. Think about how we saw Jacob van Ruisdael's *Bentheim Castle* in Year 3 and how he changed the real Bentheim Castle to show us a more perfect world, in his eyes.

The sort of art that an artist creates will be influenced by the kind of society he or she lives in. Whether people feel comfortable and safe, or anxious and afraid of what the future may bring, will influence the sort of art they enjoy and want to see. There are differences between the art that appeals to people when they are well off and the art that appeals when times are hard; between the art that appeals when their country is at war compared with the art that appeals in peacetime. Religious and philosophical views are also important. In many societies, art has been mainly about religion.

All of these things will affect the style that an artist develops. Let's look at two very different styles and think about the ways that they reflect the societies people were living in at the time: *rococo* and *modernism*.

## Rococo

Rococo art began in France and was popular in the second half of the eighteenth century. It is decorative and light-hearted, with delicate pastel colours and no hard edges. It appealed to *aristocrats* – wealthy people who led a privileged, luxurious and idle lifestyle in the years leading up to the French Revolution. Some of them lived in the magnificent palace of Versailles, where they had nothing to do except enjoy themselves by eating fine food, wearing beautiful clothes, making music, watching plays and ballets and falling in love. They wanted art that reflected their way of life. They did not want solemn art that tried to teach them a moral lesson or that made them think of the difficult lives of poor people.

One of the greatest painters of this time was Antoine Watteau [wat-oh], who lived from 1684 to 1721. He invented a new type of painting called *fêtes galantes*, or aristocratic parties, to reflect and display this idle way of life. His most famous painting is *The Embarkation for*

*Cythera*, which is sometimes called *Pilgrimage to the Isle of Cythera*. The ancient Greeks and Romans thought that the island of Cythera was the birthplace of Venus, the goddess of Love.

In the painting you can see courting couples who are about to set sail for the island in a beautiful golden boat. Flying cupids are pushing the couples closer together to encourage them to fall in love. A beautiful lady looks back. Do you think she is looking back at her friends, or is she looking at the statue of Venus on the right, wondering how long love will last?

> We learnt about the ancient Romans and their gods in Year 3.

Watteau painted real people but the settings of his paintings were imaginary places of great beauty and tranquillity. The light is soft, the trees are in full-leaf and there is nothing unpleasant in this scene. It is make-believe, not real life. The idleness and luxury of the French aristocracy, together with their unwillingness to live in the real world with its sufferings and hardships, helped to bring about the French Revolution in 1789.

*Pilgrimage to the Isle of Cythera*

Read about the French Revolution on page 136.

French art was admired in other countries during the eighteenth century, and soon rich people in Britain decided that they wanted to see their homes decorated in the new rococo style. Thomas Chippendale was a designer and skilled cabinet-maker – the name given to someone who makes furniture. His aristocratic customers wanted fashionable designs, so Chippendale published a book called *The Gentleman and Cabinet Maker's Director* to show that he could design furniture in the rococo style.

*Thomas Chippendale designed this ribbon-backed chair.*

One of his very popular chair designs was called 'ribbon-backed' because the intricate carving looked like ribbons. They were very beautiful but difficult to carve, as the backs were made from one piece of *mahogany* – a tropical hardwood that was imported into Britain. Chippendale designed the furniture for some of the great mansions being built by rich aristocrats during the eighteenth century. However, by publishing his designs in a book, he also became popular with people who were not aristocrats but who were becoming wealthy, thanks to the industrial revolution. These middle-class customers might not have been able to live in a palace, but they could afford some of Mr Chippendale's chairs for their dining rooms.

## Modernism and Abstract Art

In the twentieth century artists no longer worried about painting the real world; photography could record real life. Artists worried about how to paint, not what to paint. Since what they painted did not matter so much, many artists painted bowls of fruit and flowers, as they wanted to explore how we see things.

They also wanted to see beyond this world; they wanted to show us the *divine*, or spiritual, world. Instead of painting in a realistic style, like Watteau, they started experimenting with *abstract art*. Abstract art doesn't look exactly like the thing the artist is showing us, but it might remind you of the thing by showing you some basic lines and shapes, rather than every detail. Some artists felt that colour, alone, could represent all sorts of things, without looking like the things themselves. They studied theories about colour, light and *optics*.

We read about Isaac Newton's work on optics in Year 4.

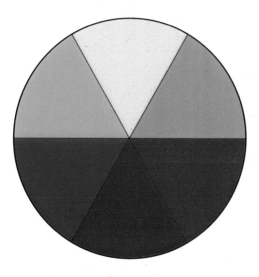

*A colour wheel*

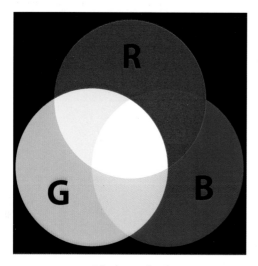

*Light triad*

Colour theory became very important after chemist Michel Chevreul [me-shell shev-rerl] published his research on colour harmonies and contrasts in the nineteenth century. He devised a colour wheel that classified colours and showed that red was the contrasting colour to green across the wheel. We worked with the colour wheel in Year 4 so you know that red, yellow, blue (RYB) are the primary colours that make up the standard artist's colour wheel. The next three colours or *colour triad* are the secondary colours: violet, orange, green (VOG). Artists also used the *light triad*, or red, green, blue (RGB), because, when you lay these colours on top of each other, you see white.

Abstract artists used red, blue, yellow and green, to which they added black and white. These colours have a *symbolic* meaning, so they are used to represent certain ideas. Black and white can stand for man and woman, solid and empty, light and dark. Blue, the colour of the sky, means love and faith. Green is the colour of nature. Red, the colour of blood, stands for suffering and death. Yellow is the glory of heaven. These meanings belong to many cultures. Theo van Doesburg [tay-o van dose-berg] (who lived from 1883 to 1931) used these colours to show particular ideas. He also liked to use geometric shapes.

'Tri' is a prefix meaning three. Learn other prefixes on page 56.

Contra-Composition of Dissonances, XVI *by Theo van Doesburg*

It is said that Theo van Doesburg's paintings are abstract as he does not paint anything you could recognise, like a bowl of fruit or a tree. But they have a meaning, as the colours and shapes are symbols that carry a message. We learnt in Year 4 that emblems are patterns or images that are often repeated, and they can also have special meanings. Abstract shapes are also emblems: squares and rectangles mean 'man' or 'earth'. This meaning is ancient, from a time when people believed the world was flat, with four continents and four rivers. The circle represents the spirit (this is why saints wear a halo). The triangle, pointing up towards heaven, like the spire of a church, stands for hope. Abstract artists painted this way because they thought the lines and colour combinations are beautiful; they create a rhythm or a harmony. Everything is ordered and balanced. As people love bright colours, they wanted to create images that were simple, that everybody could understand and like. You do not have to know about history or mythology to like van Doesburg's red and blue squares, but, if you do know about them and understand these symbols, you will see even more in his abstract art. By using these universal symbols, abstract artists were trying to reach everyone through their art, not just people who knew a lot about art.

This new way of creating art in the twentieth century became known as *modernism*. It was a style that reflected the modern way of life, which was increasingly influenced by new technologies. Modernism was a style not just for paintings but for architecture, furniture and other things that we need and use every day. Modernist designs were *rational* (a chair was for sitting on); *functional* (a chair had to do the job well); and they were *standardised*, meaning that they were simple and repetitive in design, and could therefore be easily reproduced many times

Modernist artists and designers wanted good designs for everybody, not just the rich. This meant designing pieces of art that could be produced by machines. Making things by hand was expensive and time-consuming. Decoration, like the ribbons carved on Chippendale's chairs, was considered unnecessary as they were just showing off how rich someone was. Modernists thought that what was needed was functional art – something plain that would do the job it was supposed to do. Art and Industry would work together so everybody could enjoy well made and good looking things in their homes.

The Wassily chair designed by Marcel Breuer in 1925 is a perfect example of functional modernism; it was also revolutionary and a completely new type of chair as it was made from bent steel tubes rather than wood. Breuer was inspired by the curved handlebars of his bicycle. Compare the Wassily chair with Chippendale's ribbon-backed chair. What differences do you see in their styles? They are completely different! The hand-made Chippendale chair, carved from a costly wood, was very expensive to buy; in the eighteenth century only wealthy people could enjoy good designs. In the twentieth century and today, designs are standardised and more affordable because they can be made by machines.

*Marcel Breuer designed these modernist Wassily chairs.*

## Activity 2: Hidden Meanings

Now you have read about van Doesburg's abstract art, it is your turn to create some art! There are lots of different ways to create abstract art; here are some suggestions to get you started.

Think about what you would like your abstract piece to look like. It is a good idea to look at lots of examples of abstract art first, to give you some ideas. Do you want to use certain shapes that have meaning? Do you want to choose colours that show certain feelings? Some abstract art is busy and bustling with lots going on, other pieces are simpler. What do you want people to feel when they look at your work?

When you have decided what you would like your piece to look like, think about what you will use to create it. Will you use pencils, paint or perhaps cut shapes out from different materials? Will you need a ruler or just draw free hand?

## The Symbolic Meaning of Colours

Red can be used to show death or pain.

White can show day/light/good.

Blue means love and faith.

Yellow can show heaven.

Black can stand for night/dark/evil.

Green is the colour of nature.

## The Meaning of Emblems in Modern Art

Squares or rectangles can be used to show humanity or the earth.

Triangles are like the point of a church spire and show hope.

Circles can show the spirit, which is why saints are often drawn wearing a halo.

# Islamic Art and Architecture

## The Alhambra

During the Middle Ages, Muslim people from northern Africa conquered much of Spain. They developed an architectural style very different from the Gothic style that was used throughout Europe at that time.

*The Alhambra was built on a hilltop overlooking Granada.*

On a hill overlooking the town of Granada [grah-NAH-dah] in Spain, one Muslim leader built a palace that became known as the Alhambra [ahl-HAHM-bra]. Completed in the 1300s, the Alhambra was a home for the royal family. It included an enormous bath, more like an indoor pool than the baths and showers we have today. Europeans called the Alhambra's style Moorish, because they called the Muslim people from North Africa 'Moors'.

From as early as 100 B.C., Spain was part of the Roman Empire. When Muslims took over in Spain in the eighth century A.D., they changed the design of buildings to suit their needs and their sense of beauty. They replaced thick Roman columns with slim, delicate ones. They smoothed the walls of buildings with plaster and drew designs on them before it dried. These designs give the walls a delicate appearance, very different from the solid, bare walls of Roman buildings. You can see this in the Court of the Lions at the Alhambra.

*The Alhambra includes a courtyard called the Court of the Lions because its large, central fountain is ringed by 12 smaller fountains shaped like lions.*

Although the architecture was different in some ways, there were also some similarities. Just as the ancient Romans made mosaics (like the ones we saw of Empress Theodora and Emperor Justinian in Year 4), the Alhambra also had mosaics but of a different style. What other similarities and differences do you see?

*The walls of the Alhambra were carefully decorated with many delicate and detailed designs.*

# The Dome of the Rock

*This is how the Dome of the Rock in Jerusalem looks today.*

The Dome of the Rock was built for Muslims in Jerusalem in 691. Muslims believe that the prophet Muhammad journeyed up to heaven from this spot (see page 108).

One of the first things you notice when you look at the Dome of the Rock is the golden dome on top of the mosque. When Muhammad met someone who didn't believe in God, he would point to the sky and ask who had made the stars and planets. Islamic mosques are built with domed ceilings, to remind the people inside of God's power. Some ceilings are decorated to shine like a starry night sky.

# The Taj Mahal

One of the world's most famous buildings is the Taj Mahal in India. The Taj Mahal was built in the 1600s as a tomb for a Muslim emperor's beloved wife. Many people consider it one of the world's most beautiful buildings.

> We learnt about symmetry in Year 3.

Built at the end of a very long, narrow pool of still water, the Taj Mahal appears to float. When you look at it from a distance, the pool reflects its perfect symmetry, or balance. As you walk closer, the gleaming white building looms bigger and bigger. Slender minarets, or towers, stand at the four corners. Turn over to see a photograph of it!

*The Taj Mahal in India, one of the most famous buildings in the world, was built in the 1600s. Its domes and minarets make it a good example of Islamic architecture.*

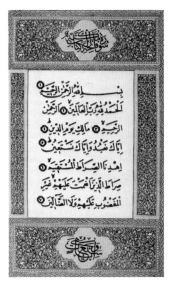

## The Word of Allah, Decorated

The *Qur'an* is the holy book of Islam, just as the Bible is the holy book of Christianity. Muslims believe that the *Qur'an* contains the actual words of God.

Muslims believe only God can create living things. They are not permitted to make images of living things, including people, in their religious books or buildings. So Muslim artists and architects often decorate holy books and mosques with geometric patterns instead. Over the centuries, Muslims have made beautiful copies of the *Qur'an*. Some are so beautiful they are considered works of art, with elegant Arabic lettering and touches of real gold.

*This beautifully decorated prayer from the Qur'an has Arabic writing in the centre and complicated decorations painted along its edges.*

# Art of Africa

## Dancing Antelopes

Long ago, many African people did not write down their histories. They remembered things from the past by singing songs, dancing, acting and telling stories – and by making works of art.

In Mali, a group of people called the Bamana [bah-MAH-nah] believed that, long ago, a special being called Chiwara [chee-WAH-rah] used magical powers to teach the people to farm. To remember their ancestors and to honour the powers of Chiwara, Bamana artists carved tall wooden figures shaped like antelopes, designed to be worn on top of the head. During planting and harvest festivals, young men hid their bodies under costumes made of fibre, wore these tall headdresses and performed a dance like leaping antelopes. The dance told the story of Chiwara.

*These are two different Chiwara headdresses that were worn by dancers during festivals.*

## Activity 3: Make your own Chiwara headdress

Bamana artists didn't try to make their sculptures look exactly like real antelopes. Instead, they suggested the shape of the antelope's body with big, bold curves. Look at these two photos of different antelopes. Using the pictures on the next page and the examples of Chiwara masks that you have seen here, get some ideas for your own

Chiwara mask. Construct the legs, body, head and of course the antlers of your antelope using different pipecleaners. Once you have made the figure of your antelope, make the base separately – this will be the bottom part of your headdress that will sit on the top of your head. Take a few pipecleaners and wrap them around each other to form a circular base and then wrap the legs or feet of your antelope around the circular base to connect them. How do you like your headdress?

## Portraits in Clay and Bronze

The Yoruba [YO-roo-bah] people of West Africa lived in the city of Ife [EE-fay]. From about A.D. 1000 to 1500, artists in Ife carved beautiful sculptures.

Ife sculptures are made of brass (a metal) and terracotta (red clay baked in a hot fire). Ife sculptors made sculptures that looked like real people, with delicate features, dignified expressions and eyes that stare straight ahead.

To make this brass head, the sculptor moulded the head, using a mixture of sand and clay. He covered it with a thin layer of beeswax. Next, using a knife made of bone, he moulded the details of the face into the beeswax, then covered it all with a thin layer of clay. When he put the

*This brass sculpture probably represents the head of an Ife king. You can see it in the British Museum.*

sculpture on a hot fire, what do you think happened? The beeswax melted and drained out, leaving a thin hollow space between two face-shaped shells of clay. The sculptor then poured hot melted brass into the space. After the brass cooled, he broke the clay shells. What remained was this brass sculpture.

## A Portrait Mask of an African Queen

The Edo [Eh-DOE] people lived in Benin [ben-EEN], a kingdom southeast of Ife and west of today's Nigeria. The Edo people considered the king and his ancestors to be like gods, and they created sculptures to show their respect. The mask on this page, carved out of ivory, is a portrait of Idia [id-EE-a], the mother of a king who lived in Benin in the sixteenth century. The king may have worn this mask on his belt for important occasions.

In Benin, every time a hunter killed an elephant, one tusk was given to the king. Ivory carvers lived near the palace and worked for the king. Like the brass and terracotta heads made by the Yoruba, Benin masks represented real people. The artist did not make an exact copy of the person's facial features, though. We can say that he *idealised* the portrait, or made it closer to perfect than any one person can be.

*This ivory mask was created to represent Idia, a queen of the Edo people in Benin. The queen's head is surrounded by bearded men, representing Portuguese traders who brought much wealth to Benin.*

# Prints: Pictures that Go Further

We all enjoy looking at paintings, drawings and other works of art. Do you have a favourite painting, one that you would like to see every day? Buying a work of art such as a painting can be expensive, and impossible if it is in a museum or gallery! So how can you see it whenever you want to? Easy! You can buy a print of it, either from the gallery, from an art shop or from a website, or you can buy or borrow a book that has a reproduction of the painting in it. Perhaps you could look at it on a computer screen at home or at school.

Today, printers use the latest technologies, including digital printing, so that your reproduction will look very like the original,
but of course it is not an original work of art. It is a copy. But a print can be an original work of art too, even when there are lots of copies of it. A print can be a very simple design cut into a block of wood, a piece of lino or even a potato. It can also be a very complicated process using several methods.

We made a 'relief sculpture' like the Parthenon frieze in Year 3.

There are three basic types of prints. A *relief*, like a woodcut, cuts away the areas that need to stay white; *intaglio* [in-TAG-lee-oh], like an engraving or etching, holds ink in grooves; or you can draw on the surface of a plate, which is called *lithography*.

## Woodcuts – Pictures in a Book

Printmaking went hand in hand with the first books and allowed many more people to see pictures, although only in black and white. Johannes [yo-HAN-ez] Gutenberg invented a *printing press* in 1436. This device allowed paper to be 'pressed' against the design again and again, making repeated copies. He started with words, made out of sturdy metal letters. Before the discovery of the printing press, every book had to

*The Gutenberg Bible*

be written out by hand. Being able to make more than one copy of a book at a time made a big difference to the spread of knowledge. How long would it take you to write out every word of this book by hand? A very long time! That's why we printed it.

In 1455, the Gutenberg Bible was printed. It was so beautifully printed that it is now the most valuable book in the world, but when it first appeared it was much cheaper than having a copy of the Bible that someone had written out by hand. Gutenberg's print revolution created best-selling authors, including Martin Luther and Erasmus; by the end of the sixteenth century, many families were able to own a Bible in their own language. The Reformation, which we read about in Year 3, might not have spread so quickly throughout Europe without the printing press. Books were the Internet of the sixteenth century!

We first saw examples of illuminations of the Lindisfarne Gospel in Year 2.

Even though it was printed, the Gutenberg Bible was still decorated by hand; wealthy owners could pay for *illuminations*. That is not a light show, but a style of painting and gilding parts of the pages to make them look beautiful. The *Nuremberg Chronicle*, printed in 1493, was one of the earliest religious books to be illustrated with prints instead of having each page painted by hand. The text and the pictures were printed repeatedly, using the same press. The *Nuremberg Chronicle* used woodcuts for its prints.

*Pages from the*
Nuremberg Chronicle

A woodcut requires carving an image into the surface of a wooden block. It is known as a *relief* print, as the parts that print in black are level with the surface, while the parts cut away with a chisel show white. It is more work than drawing one picture but can then be repeated many times. In the image, you can see the artist Jacques Hnizdovsky cutting the woodblock *Copper Beech* whist following his sketch. He has already carved the light brown areas, and the darker brown areas are waiting to be carved.

You can make your own print in the activity. One thing you will notice straight away is that, as we saw in the tracing activity in Year 4, the image comes out in *reverse*, or back to front. Printed words did the same, so the person who put the letters in frames for printing had to be able to read backwards! The artist Pablo Picasso also created striking prints using this technique by gouging linoleum, more usually used as floor-covering; they are known as *lino cuts*.

*Hnizdovsky carving the woodblock for* Copper Beech

## Activity 4: Potato printing

First, gather some medium-sized potatoes, some paints, thick paper and a vegetable knife (make sure an adult does this part). Next, follow these instructions to make your own potato prints.

1. Cut the potatoes in half.

2. Draw your shape onto the flat part of the potato.

3. Ask an adult to help you cut around the shape with a vegetable knife, leaving the design raised on the surface of the potato.

*These potatoes were carved to make prints for Chinese New Year.*

4. Press your potato into some paint.

5. Wipe off any excess before stamping the potato onto paper. (Be careful, if you push too hard the potato will slide across the page.)

6. You can wash the potato stamp and use a different colour. Can you make a pattern? You can use your potato to print again and again!

You might like to try a small biscuit cutter for a more complicated shape. Push the biscuit cutter into the potato and then ask an adult to help you cut around it. If you mix some paint in a tray using a roller you can make multi-coloured prints. Enjoy your printing!

## Engravings – Into the Groove

Albrecht Dürer [ALB-rekt DYURR-uh], who lived from 1471 to 1528, was a famous printmaker who made some of the best woodcut designs ever produced. His *Rhinoceros* woodcut is based on a written description and a sketch of an

> We saw Dürer's painting *Young Hare* in Year 2.

Indian rhinoceros that had arrived in Lisbon in 1515. This was the first living rhino to be seen in Europe since Roman times. Dürer hadn't actually seen the rhinoceros himself, so his print is not entirely accurate. Nevertheless, it allowed lots of people to get an idea of what a rhinoceros looked like because most people had never seen one, even in pictures.

Dürer had trained to be a goldsmith, so he was used to handling tools that could shape metal. This made it easy for him to engrave a picture on a sheet of copper metal. He used a hard, steel tool called a *burin* to cut the design into the surface of a copper plate.

This is *intaglio* technique. The image is the opposite of a woodcut. The plain areas are white and the cut away parts are black. The ink is rubbed into the gouges cut into the surface but the flat bit is wiped clean.

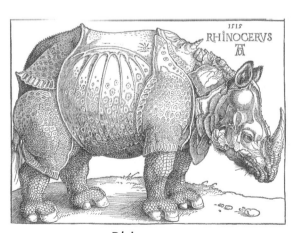

*Rhinoceros*

The copper plate is then pressed onto a sheet of paper, in a printing press; the paper, forced into the engraved lines or gouges, picks up the ink. This process can be repeated many times before the copper plate shows signs of wear.

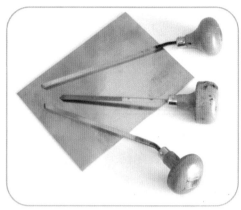

*These burins are tools used for engraving.*

◀ *The American print-maker Jack Baumgartner can be seen lifting the paper on which he has made a print of his image of St Christopher. What do you notice when you compare the print with the engraving?*

## Activity 5: Brass rubbings

In the Middle Ages, when wealthy and powerful people died, it was the custom to have a brass image made of them, which would be fixed into the floor of the church where they were buried. These brass images show us what they looked like and what sort of clothes they wore. People found that it was possible to put a piece of paper over the brass and rub it with a wax stick to make a copy of the image. Because it can wear away the image if a brass is rubbed many

times, there are now brass rubbing centres where you can rub copies of the brass images. This means that the original – which is a valuable historical record – is not harmed. You can purchase a brass rubbing kit at some early learning centres or online, or else from a brass rubbing centre. The website of the Monumental Brass Society has a list of these, as well as instructions on how to make one of these fascinating images.

*In the first scene of the* Industry and Idleness *series, we see the idle and the industrious apprentices at their looms. The idle apprentice has fallen asleep, and the cat is playing with his thread! Their employer takes note.*

William Hogarth, who lived from 1697 to 1764, was trained as an engraver. Hogarth used his skills to make prints that could tell a story which taught a moral, rather like Aesop's fables. He wanted to help people, especially poor people, to avoid doing things that would cause problems in their lives. For example, he created twelve prints in a series called *Industry and Idleness* which traces the lives of two apprentices. One, who works hard, achieves great success and becomes Lord Mayor of London, while the other's idleness leads to a life of crime, for which he is punished.

We read some of Aesop's fables in Years 1 and 2.

Could you tell a story by drawing a sequence of pictures? Hogarth wanted everybody to see his stories, including poor people who would never be able to buy a painting or an expensive work of art. Prints were the ideal way to do this, and Hogarth charged only one shilling (5p) for each of the prints of *Industry and Idleness* so that many people would be able to enjoy the pictures.

In Year 1 we saw Hogarth's portrait of the Graham children. In Year 2 we saw his self-portrait.

He hoped they would listen to his lesson and work hard, too!

*In Plate 12, at the end of the series, we see that the industrious apprentice has been chosen to be Lord Mayor of London.*

Engraving is a very difficult technique to learn. It requires a skilled eye and steady hand plus, as with the other types of print-making we have learnt about, everything has to be cut backwards – in reverse – so that it prints the right way round. To see how difficult this is, try writing backwards and then hold what you have written up to a mirror to see if you can read it the right way around.

Because Dürer had trained as a goldsmith and Hogarth as an engraver, they could cut their own plates. Most artists had to hand the job over to someone else, which meant that they lost control of making the copies. However, another process, called etching, came along which put the artists back in control.

# Etchings – Cutting out the Middle Man

Like an engraving, *etching* is an intaglio method but it does not require cutting directly into the metal. Instead, the copper plate is covered with a waxy *ground*. The artist draws through the ground with a pointed etching needle. The exposed metal is then cut or 'bitten' by dipping the plate in a bath of acid. Don't try this at home!

The waxy ground protects most of the plate, except where the artist has scraped the wax away. Here, the acid can get through and eat away the copper surface, making grooves that will hold ink. The wax has now done its job and can be cleaned off the plate. It is easier drawing with a needle through wax than scratching copper with a burin. Artists could now use this new technique, printing works of art in limited editions, typically from fifty to two hundred prints. Normally etchings are numbered, so a collector will know how many were printed.

Rembrandt van Rijn, Francisco Goya and James McNeill Whistler were master-etchers, transforming the print into a work of art in its own right. Rembrandt created striking lighting effects, or *chiaroscuro*, in his etchings, as seen in *The Three Crosses* which he made in 1653. Look at the way Jesus, on the middle cross, is illuminated in a shaft of light. To create this effect, white is untouched copper plate, protected by the waxy ground. Pale grey is thin scratches, with space between. Dark grey and black are deep scratches, close together. The scene is very dramatic.

**The Three Crosses** *by Rembrandt*

We learnt about chiaroscuro in Year 3.

Compare the Hogarth engravings with the Rembrandt. What differences do you see? Rembrandt's etching looks like a drawing. The lines are free, whereas in Hogarth's engraving they are very regular and rather stiff. But both prints are still 'black and white'.

## Colour

Printing in colour is a tricky process; for a woodcut you have to cut a block for each colour. The Japanese mastered this process. Japanese prints were almost unknown in the West until the mid-nineteenth century, when they were eagerly collected and influenced the Impressionist painters, especially Claude Monet. They also influenced Henri de Toulouse-Lautrec [ON-ree de TOO-loos low-TRECK] who made use of the same sort of bold outlines and vivid colours in his posters. Lautrec's posters were made possible by the invention of the lithograph. Do you remember the woodblock print *The Great Wave off Kanagawa* by the Japanese artist Hokusai which we saw in Year 3?

*The Great Wave off Kanagawa*

## Lithography

*Lithography,* 'writing on stone', is a skill that artists can learn. The advantage is that it can use a flat block, originally a flat piece of limestone. If they drew a picture on limestone with a wax crayon, wiped it with oily ink and pressed it with paper, a copy of the picture came off on the paper. The trouble was that it was often horribly smudged. So before adding the ink, they covered the picture and the whole stone with a special gum and moistened the stone. Now, when ink was wiped over the picture, it only stayed where the crayon had drawn. Everywhere else was wet and the ink was too oily to stick.

Toulouse-Lautrec perfected the lithograph, as you can see in the poster *La Troupe de Mlle Églantine*. Notice the bold yellow background and the *silhouette* of the dancer's legs. A silhouette is an outline filled in with one colour. The floor tips up at a startling angle, showing the influence of Hokusai's print of *The Great Wave off Kanagawa*. Using just a few bold lines, Toulouse-Lautrec has created a startling image that brings to life a dance performance at the Palace Theatre in London.

*La Troupe de Mlle Églantine*

Posters are the perfect way to advertise events or products; they may have been the first form of street art! Posters try to sell us many things, from cars to shampoo. When you are out and about, see how many poster adverts you can spot.

# Suggested Resources

## Artistic Techniques and Activities

*My Art Book: Amazing Art Projects Inspired by Masterpieces* (Dorling Kindersley) 2011

*Draw 3-D: A Step-by-Step Guide to Perspective (Learn to Draw)* by Doug DuBosque (Peel) 1998

*Discovering Great Artists: Hands-On Art for Children in the Styles of the Great Masters* by MaryAnn Kohl and Kim Solga (Bright Ring) 2008

*Complete Book of Art Ideas (Usborne Art Ideas)* by Fiona Watt (Usborne) 2009

*Mini Art Projects (Usborne Activity Books)* by Fiona Watt (Usborne) 2009

*13 Art Techniques Children Should Know* by Angela Wenzel (Prestel) 2013

## Looking At and Talking About Art

*Introduction to Art (Usborne Internet-linked Reference)* by Rosie Dickins and Mari Griffith (Usborne) 2009

*The Museum Book: A Guide to Strange and Wonderful Collections* by Jan Mark (Walker) 2010

*13 Artists Children Should Know* by Angela Wenzel (Prestel) 2009

*13 Paintings Children Should Know* by Angela Wenzel (Prestel) 2009

*A Children's Book of Art* by Sonia Whillock-Moore, Pamela Shiels and Deborah Lock (Dorling Kindersley) *2009*

*Islamic Culture* by Charlotte Guillain (Heinemann) 2012

# Where to Find the Works
# of Art in this Chapter

Christopher Wren, St Paul's Cathedral, London, UK

The Shard, London, UK

Antoine Watteau, *Pilgrimage to the Isle of Cythera*, 1717 (Louvre Museum) Paris, France

Thomas Chippendale, *Ribbon-backed Chair*, made 1850-1880 from Chippendale's design of 1754 (Victoria & Albert Museum) London, UK

Theo van Doesburg, *Contra-Composition of Dissonances*, XVI (Haags Gemeentemuseum) The Hague, Netherlands

Marcel Breuer, *Wassily Chairs or Model B3 Chairs*, 1925-1926 (Bauhaus) Dessau, Germany

The Alhambra, Granada, Spain

Dome of the Rock, Jerusalem

Taj Mahal, India

*Chiwara Headdresses*, 20th century (Brooklyn Museum) New York, USA

*Brass Head with a Beaded Crown and Plume* from Ife, Nigeria, 12th-14th century (British Museum) London, UK

*Ivory Mask from Benin*, 16th century (British Museum) London, UK

*The Gutenberg Bible*, 1455 (British Library) London, UK (accessible online)

*Nuremberg Chronicle*, 1493 (University Library) Cambridge, UK (accessible online)

Jacques Hnizdovsky, *Copper Beech*, 1985 (Artist's Collection)

Albrecht Dürer, *Rhinoceros*, 1847 (British Museum) London, UK

Jack Baumgartner, *St Christopher*, 2008 (Artist's Collection)

Brass Rubbings (Monumental Brass Society) Whitchurch, UK

William Hogarth, *Industry and Idleness Plate 1: The Fellow 'Prentices at their Looms; Plate 12: The Industrious 'Prentice Lord Mayor of London*, 1747 (Tate Britain) London, UK

Rembrandt van Rijn, *Three Crosses*, 1653 (British Museum) London, UK

Katsushika Hokusai, *The Great Wave off Kanagawa*, 1829-33 (British Museum, Print Room) London, UK

Henri de Toulouse-Lautrec, *Troupe de Mlle Églantine*, 1896 (Victoria & Albert Museum) London, UK

# Music

## Introduction

In music, as in art, pupils benefit from learning by doing. Singing, playing instruments and dancing all sharpen a child's sense of how music works. We encourage you to share good music with children by singing some of the songs presented here, attending concerts, listening to radio programmes and to recordings.

## The Elements of Music

### Make a Note of It!

Long ago, people shared music by singing to each other and playing musical instruments. Later, when they wanted to remember more complicated music or share music with people far away, musicians developed musical notation – a way to write down music so that different people, no matter what language they spoke, could read that music and sing or play it.

In Year 4 we learnt that, when composers write music down, they use special marks called notes, and they arrange the notes on a set of parallel lines called a stave. The notes on the stave below give the music for the beginning of 'Twinkle, Twinkle, Little Star'.

When you are learning a piece of music, you can follow the notes across the stave from left to right, just as you follow words across the page when you read.

The position of notes on the stave tells you how high or low the notes are. The higher the note sits on the stave, the higher your voice goes when you sing that note. Can you hear how your voice goes up to a higher pitch as you move from the first 'twinkle' to the second one, and then up again as you sing 'little'? Then the pitch of your voice comes steadily downward until you sing 'are' at the same pitch as the first note.

The shape of the note tells you how long to hold each note. Did you notice that when you sing 'Twinkle, Twinkle, Little Star', you hold the notes for 'star' and 'are' longer than the other notes? That's because these notes are minims, while the other notes in the song are crotchets. A minim is held twice as long as a crotchet.

## Shorter and Longer Notes

The music for 'Twinkle, Twinkle, Little Star' contains only minims and crotchets, but musicians also use other notes, some shorter and some longer. Do you remember the quaver, which is like a crotchet with a little flag on top?

 ◀ A quaver is held for half as long as a crotchet. When two or more quavers are written side by side, they are sometimes connected with a beam, like this ▶

A semibreve is held twice as long as a minim. That means it's held for as long as four crotchets, or eight quavers. It looks like this:

If a composer wants to make a note last longer than a minim but not as long as a semibreve, he or she just adds a little black dot to the right of the note. That dot tells performers to hold the note half as long again.

Another special symbol can be used to show that a note should be held for a long time. Composers use a tie, or a curved line that ties the notes together, to tell the musician to continue to hold the first note through the time of the second. If a note is too long to fit in a bar, write a tie and carry on in the next bar.

Look at the example above. Can you find the tied notes? The dotted notes? How many of each do you see?

# Bars and Time Signatures

Look again at the music for 'Twinkle, Twinkle, Little Star'. Do you see the vertical (up-and-down) lines that separate the notes into groups? These lines are called bar lines. They divide the music into bars. How many bars of 'Twinkle, Twinkle, Little Star' are shown?

Composers use a single bar line to mark the end of a bar. They use a double bar line to mark the end of a piece of music.

See the two numbers sitting on top of one another at the beginning of the music – the ones that look like a fraction? Those numbers make up the time signature. The top number tells you how many beats there are in each bar, and the bottom number tells you what kind of note represents one beat. For 'Twinkle, Twinkle, Little Star,' the time signature is $\frac{4}{4}$. The 4 on the top means that there are four beats per bar, and the 4 on the bottom means each beat lasts as long as a crotchet.

You can see that the first bar of 'Twinkle, Twinkle, Little Star' is made up of four crotchets, each of which is held for one beat: 'twin-kle, twin-kle.' But the second bar is a little different. It only contains three notes. But one of these notes – the one that goes with the word 'star' – is held for twice as long (for two beats). So there are still four beats in this bar, even though there are only three notes.

When the time signature is $\frac{4}{4}$, we say that the song is written in four-four time. Many popular songs are written in $\frac{4}{4}$ time. But you will also see songs in $\frac{2}{4}$ time and $\frac{3}{4}$ time. How many crotchets fill a bar in $\frac{2}{4}$ time? Two.

Now, how many quavers will fit in a bar in $\frac{3}{4}$ time? There would be three crotchet notes or, since a crotchet lasts two times the length of a quaver, there would be six quavers in a bar in $\frac{3}{4}$ time. As you can see, maths skills are important for understanding music.

D E F G A B C D E F G

## The Treble Clef

Musical pitches are named after the first seven letters of the alphabet: A B C D E F G. Each line and each space on the stave corresponds with one of these letters.

Do you see how the letters repeat themselves as you go from low to high? At the bottom of the stave, just below the bottom line, is D. Then you move up to E, F and G. But there's no H. Instead the letters start again, with A.

How can you remember which letters go in which positions on the stave? Here's one way. Notice that the letters that are located on the lines from bottom to top are E, G, B, D and F. You can remember these letters by memorising this sentence: 'Every good boy deserves favour'.

Another way to remember which letters go where on the stave is to look at the treble clef. The treble clef is the fancy, curly symbol located at the beginning of the music. The treble clef is also known as the G clef because the innermost circle of the clef circles around the line that stands for G. If you remember this, you can figure out all the other pitches above and below G.

The lowest note shown on the music on page 181 is D. What would happen if the composer wanted to write a note one note lower than D? He or she would just draw a short line segment below the stave and place the note on the line segment. This particular note actually has a special name. It is called middle C, because the key that sounds this note is located close to the middle of a piano keyboard.

Middle C

The music for 'Twinkle, Twinkle, Little Star' begins and ends at middle C. See if you can identify the other notes in the first few bars of the song by letter.

## The Composer's Language

Composers place notes on a stave to show how they want their music to be performed, but sometimes they give even more specifics.

When the composer wants the music to be played smoothly, without breaks between the notes, he or she writes *legato* in the music. In Italian, *legato* means tied together. In a piece sung *legato*, there's no gap between notes.

When the composer wants the music to be played in the opposite way – with short, bouncy sounds – he or she writes the Italian word *staccato*. *Staccato* means detached or 'separated'.

Other notations, written in Italian words or their abbreviations, tell musicians how loud or soft to play a piece of music.

*mp* = mezzo piano (moderately soft)   *mf* = mezzo forte (moderately loud)

*p* = piano (soft)          *f* = forte (loud)

*pp* = pianissimo (very soft)     *ff* = fortissimo (very loud)

## Play it again!

If you wanted something to be played twice, you would not want to write it all out again. Fortunately, there are signs that mean 'play it again'. They are called repeat signs. When you reach the end-repeat sign, go back to the begin-repeat sign and play or sing it again. The second time you reach the sign, carry on. If you kept going back and repeating you would never finish!

**Begin repeat sign**                    **End repeat sign**

Another instruction you may see written on music is *Da capo al fine. Da capo* means 'from the beginning'. *Al fine* [ahl FEE-nay] means to the end. This instruction is often used when the composer wants the beginning of a piece repeated at the end. When you reach the word 'fine' it's time to stop.

Some people choose to use numbers instead of letters to name the keys of a keyboard. Look at how they number the keys below, then quiz yourself on which letter goes with each number.

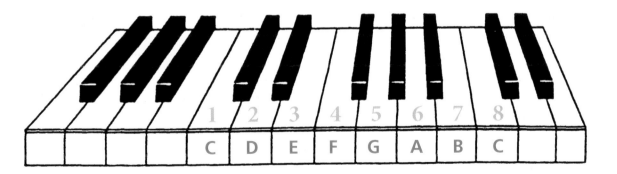

## Sharps and Flats

The notes in a piece of music match the notes on a piano keyboard. The white keys on the piano all have letter names. Can you match the piano keys in the picture on page 183 with the keys written on the stave?

The black keys on a piano are important, too. They don't get their own names, though. They are named according to the keys on either side of them. Find D on the piano keyboard. The black key just to the right of D is called D sharp, which can be written D# for short. D# is a little bit higher in pitch than D.

Now go back to D on the piano keyboard. The black key just to the left of D is called D flat, or D♭ for short. D♭ is a little bit lower in pitch than D. A black key can have two names. It can be called the sharp of a note to the left or the flat of a note to the right. What is the other name for D♭? No matter which name you call that note, it always means the same key.

# Listening and Understanding

## The Orchestra

Half an hour before a performance, the concert hall is quiet. The stage lights shine on empty chairs, arranged in the shape of a fan, all pointing toward a platform at the edge of the stage. Can you spot this platform where the conductor will stand?

Ushers lead the first audience arrivals to their seats, and the hall begins to stir with quiet conversation. Soon, the musicians enter from backstage, carrying their instruments and walking to

*This concert hall is ready to be filled with musicians and the audience before a performance.*

their places. They settle in and, just as athletes stretch and move their bodies before a big sports event, the musicians begin to warm up. The concert hall soon fills with high-pitched toots, deep rumbles and plucked strings. To the audience it sounds a little chaotic, but soon the musicians will be ready for the concert.

From out of all the noise, an oboe sounds the note A. Soon all the other musicians are playing the same note. Violinists draw their bows lightly across all four strings of their instruments; the A is one of them. If any string sounds off-pitch, a violinist turns the tuning pegs to adjust it.

The musicians have spent many hours practising for the concert, and now they are ready to perform. The conductor crosses the stage, steps up on the platform, bows to the audience, turns to the orchestra, lifts his or her baton and signals for the music to begin.

Fanning out in front of the conductor, the orchestra includes four major families of instruments. The strings are played with a bow or plucked with a finger; the woodwind and the brass instruments are blown; the percussion instruments are struck with sticks or mallets.

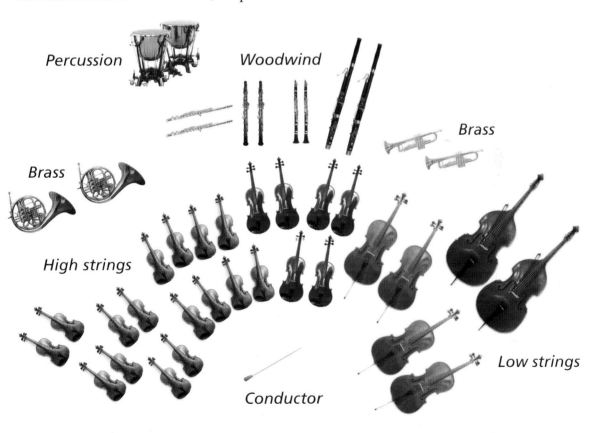

*The orchestra is divided into groups for different kinds of instruments.*

The conductor knows the music and every instrument's part. Even when all the instruments are playing, the conductor can hear if a note is played too high or low, too loud or soft, or out of rhythm. The conductor's job is to help all the instruments blend into a beautiful and well-balanced whole and to make sure the music is played the way the composer meant it to be played.

The conductor reads from a score in which each type of instrument has a stave and the notes they play together are above one another on the page. The conductor is like a coach who tries to get all the members of the team to work together to ensure a winning performance.

*Sir Simon Rattle conducts the Berlin Philharmonic Orchestra. Here he is conducting a symphony by Mozart.*

## A Magical Musical Tour

At first, it can be difficult to work out how an orchestra works. That's why

Visit www.coreknowledge.org.uk/music.php to listen to this piece and try our online activity.

the English composer Benjamin Britten wrote *The Young Person's Guide to the Orchestra*. In this piece of music, you'll hear the same melody, or theme, played a number of times, by different instruments of the orchestra. This makes it easier to identify each of the instrument families, as they take turns. When a piece of music plays the same theme in different ways, it is called a *theme and variations*. Sometimes the theme, like this one, is an old one written by another composer. Henry Purcell first wrote this theme as music for a play, and then Britten wrote the theme and variations in his piece of music.

*The Young Person's Guide to the Orchestra* begins as the whole orchestra plays the main theme. The four major families – woodwinds, strings, brass and percussion instruments – play the theme and variations, then the whole orchestra plays together. If you can, listen to Britten's piece and begin to identify instruments by their sounds.

The **woodwinds** begin with the high notes of the piccolo and the sweet, clear sound of two flutes, accompanied by violins and a harp. The thoughtful-sounding oboe comes in next, followed by the smooth and athletic clarinets, which make sounds that seem to loop all around. The bassoons come in next and make the deepest, fullest sounds.

*Can you make out the conductor Bramwell Tovey and the Vancouver Symphony Orchestra's sections for high strings and low strings?*

The family of **strings** then comes in, led by the violins. Their sound is so important to the orchestra that there are more of them than any other instrument. Violas, a bit larger in size, have a deeper, often sombre-sounding tone. Both the violin and the viola are held against the musician's chin while he or she draws a bow across the strings.

Cellos, much larger than the violas, are held upright on the floor, between the knees of the players. Cellos have a rich, warm sound. The double bass, the largest member of the string family, rumbles when it plays its lowest notes. The harp belongs in this instrument family, too. A harpist plucks its 47 strings while sitting beside it.

Among the **brass instruments**, the horns lead the way. The trumpets come in with higher, bright sounds. The trombone, played by sliding one metal tube in and out of another, adds a deep voice. The bass tuba has an even deeper, heavier sound.

The **percussion instruments** take their turn as the kettle drums, or *timpani* [TIM-pan-ee], make deep, vibrating sounds you can feel as well as hear. There are many rhythmic noisemakers in the percussion family, including the bass drum, cymbals, tambourine and triangle. Wooden blocks clapped together make a sound like the crack of a whip, commanding the whole orchestra to play together again.

*The tuba makes a deep, low sound.*

Benjamin Britten ends his tour of the orchestra with the instruments playing one after another as if singing a round. This gives us another chance to hear the distinctive qualities of each family of instruments. Now we can appreciate the role each has in the full orchestra's sound. The brass instruments ring out at the end of the piece, adding a sort of celebratory icing to the rich cake made by the sound of the rest of the orchestra. Each time you listen to this piece, you will be able to identify more clearly the instruments of the orchestra by the sounds that they make.

## The Instrument We All Can Play

Even without music lessons, you already play the oldest, most universal and most expressive musical instrument of all – the human voice. Babies seem to discover this instrument all on their own. Before they walk, they experiment with making all kinds of sounds. You can practise all the basic elements of music – rhythm, melody, harmony – simply by singing by yourself or with friends.

Everyone has a high note, a low note and notes in between that he or she can sing comfortably. The highest note and the lowest note that you can sing define your *range*.

Think about 'Happy Birthday to You'. That starts low with the first 'Happy'. By the third 'Birthday', 'Birth-' is a high note. Can you think of any songs that need a wider range than 'Happy Birthday'? Do you know 'O Danny Boy' or 'You'll Never Walk Alone'? It's a challenge to sing every note.

## Voices, High and Low

Have you noticed that among the people you know, some sing high and some sing low? The voices of women and men are divided into three main categories of singers.

*When you hear a chorus sing, can you make out the different categories of women's and men's voices?*

| Women's voices | Men's voices |
|---|---|
| High: soprano | High: tenor |
| Middle: mezzo [MET-so] soprano | Middle: baritone |
| Low: alto | Low: bass |

Composers write music with these vocal ranges in mind, and their choices can have dramatic effects.

## Music of the Middle Ages

Stained glass windows like this one show that music was an important part of religion in the Middle Ages.

In Year 2 we first learnt about monasteries during the Middle Ages.

During the Middle Ages, groups of men lived in religious communities, devoting all their time and work to their religion. They were called *monks*, and their homes were called *monasteries*. Monasteries were quiet, protected places where monks could concentrate on their faith. The monks wore plain robes, gave up their personal possessions and promised never to marry. They went to bed late but still got up before sunrise. They did a lot of hard work, much of it to help the poor.

During the Middle Ages, few people knew how to read and write. Monks could read music as well as words, and they spent many hours carefully copying music and Latin texts by hand. (They lived in a time before computers and printing presses, when every book had to be copied by hand.)

Every day, the monks came together to pray and sing. The songs they sang are called Gregorian chants, in honour of Pope Gregory the Great, who was the head of the Catholic Church from 590 to 604 A.D. Gregorian chants are still sung today by monks and in cathedrals.

The words in the chants were mostly taken from the Bible and usually they were sung in Latin, with no instruments playing along. Sometimes two choirs sat across from each other, taking turns at singing. This was called an *antiphon*, which became our word *anthem*.

When you first hear Gregorian chants, they sound very different to the music we are used to, which uses contrasts in rhythm and harmony. Gregorian chants have only one line, the melody line, with no harmony at all. Because it is so simple and uncomplicated, it is also called *plainsong*. Nevertheless, strong voices, singing in a candlelit church, echo and blend into one bigger voice that can sound beautiful, powerful and even a bit mysterious. Try to find a recording of Gregorian chants to hear for yourself or visit a cathedral when the music programme says 'Men's voices only'.

*Monks like St Bede wrote, read, taught and sang.*

Nuns sing plainsong too. They sing the same tunes as the monks but at a higher pitch. You can hear men or women singing plainsong, but not both together.

# George Frideric Handel (1685-1759)

George Frideric Handel [HAN-del] was born in Germany in 1685. He was interested in music as a young boy, but his father wanted him to be a lawyer, not a musician, and would not let him have an instrument. Handel smuggled a small keyboard instrument called a *clavichord* [CLA-vi-cord] into his house. He wanted to play music so much, he played his clavichord in secret. Later, when he was older, he studied music full time, no longer having to keep it a secret.

Handel is best known for his compositions based on stories from the Bible. One of these pieces, called *Messiah* [mes-SYE-ya], is performed by an orchestra and a chorus, with soloists

in all the vocal ranges singing special parts. Each part of *Messiah* tells a different episode in the life of Jesus. For words, Handel used verses from the English Bible and a prayer book. The most famous part of *Messiah* is the thrilling 'Hallelujah Chorus' in which voices proclaim the everlasting glory of God.

There is a story that when Handel's *Messiah* was performed for the first time in London, George II was so moved by the 'Hallelujah Chorus' that he stood up to hear it. Whether the story is true or not, audiences have been standing up to hear that chorus ever since, such is the inspiring effect of Handel's music.

*George Frideric Handel playing the clavichord*

# Franz Joseph Haydn (1732-1809)

When he was very young, Franz Joseph Haydn [HIGH-dun] delighted his family with his singing. He soon became a church choirboy and, by the time he was eight, he was singing in the choir of the cathedral in Vienna, Austria. He also learnt to play the violin, the organ and other instruments.

Find the other Esterházy Palace on our map of Eastern Europe in Year 4.

As he grew older Haydn wrote music, played the piano to accompany singing lessons and taught music to others. Word of his talent spread, and eventually Paul Anton, Prince Esterházy, brought him to live in his new palace in Hungary.

There Haydn's job was to teach, write music and direct concerts for the prince and his many guests. He worked for the family for nearly 30 years and produced music that made him famous throughout Europe.

*Haydn worked for Prince Paul Anton and lived in Eszterháza Palace in Hungary where he produced many of his most famous works.*

At Eszterháza Palace, Haydn often conducted symphonies after dinner. He composed more than one hundred symphonies altogether, and many other works besides. His symphonies are considered so important in the history of music, he is sometimes called the Father of the Symphony.

A *symphony* is a musical composition performed by an orchestra. The word comes from the Greek *sym*, meaning together, and *phonos*, meaning sound. Usually Haydn's symphonies were divided into four movements, or sections, each distinctly different from the others.

As Haydn conducted the palace orchestra, he noticed that the quieter passages in his music actually lulled some guests to sleep. He decided to play a musical joke on the prince and his guests. In one symphony, the second movement begins with a gentle melody for plucked strings only – the kind that might put a drowsy person to sleep.

Can you see in the score what happens at the end? Suddenly the sound of a great chord unexpectedly bursts in from the whole orchestra, with woodwind, trumpets, drums and bowed strings shattering the calm mood. It's where all the crotchets are lined up on the right and marked *ff*. After that, all the musicians go quiet again, as if nothing unusual had happened. Ever since, people have called Haydn's Symphony No. 94 in G the 'Surprise Symphony'. Have a listen!

# Wolfgang Amadeus Mozart (1756-1791)

*Mozart as a young man*

Wolfgang Amadeus Mozart [MOTE-sart] was also born in Austria. His father was a professional musician who could tell from very early on that his son had remarkable musical skills. By the age of four, Mozart played the piano and the violin very well. By the time he was eight, he was composing symphonies!

Through much of his childhood, Mozart toured Europe with his father and older sister, playing music. Everywhere he went, the young boy amazed audiences. When the emperor of Austria heard Mozart play, he called him a 'little wizard'.

Mozart wrote musical compositions of all kinds – for the piano and for small groups of instruments, for orchestras and for singers. He wrote several famous *operas*, which are plays in which the actors sing rather than speak some or all of their lines.

One of Mozart's most famous operas is *The Magic Flute*. *The Magic Flute* is a strange and beautiful love story, full of serpents, sorcerers and spells. It tells the story of the young prince Tamino [tah-MEE-no], who sets out to rescue the beautiful princess Pamina [pah-MEE-na]. Tamino has to pass many tests, some in the company of a funny birdcatcher named Papageno [pa-pa-GAY-no]. In the end, Tamino passes all his tests and is united with Pamina.

*Tamino listens as Papageno sings the words of a new challenge in Mozart's* Magic Flute.

Mozart followed the rules for composing different types of music, but he always added a twist, so that each piece included new, bold musical ideas. For example, Mozart wrote 12 variations of an old French song called *Ah, Vous Dirai-je Maman* for the piano. The song has the same tune as 'Twinkle, Twinkle, Little Star'. Mozart begins with the simple melody, then he changes it around. He changes the *tempo*, or speed of the music. He changes the *dynamics*, or the intensity with which the music is played, so some versions are loud and some are quiet. Some sound proper and formal; some sound exuberant and full of fun; one even sounds a little spooky.

Mozart said that his music came to him in a kind of 'lively dream'. He heard all the parts at once and kept them in his head until he could write them all down. Haydn once said that Mozart was 'the greatest composer known to me', and many people agree with him to this day.

## Scott Joplin (1867-1917)

Some pieces of music become so well known that they define a whole style. If you can, listen to *Maple Leaf Rag* by Scott Joplin. After hearing it, most people remember hearing something very fast but pianists insist that it should not be rushed. The important point is that the rhythm is *syncopated*, meaning that you hear notes with accents between beats.

These are the first two bars. The bottom line, for the pianist's left hand, is steady quavers but the top line, played by the right-hand, has the accents. The first group starts late, after a rest. The second group has a longer note between two short ones. The third group ties its last note to the next crotchet. It is easier to follow if you hear it first. Other composers are known for special rhythms. We think of Chopin in connection with lively mazurkas and also slower waltzes; polkas always suggest the Strauss family.

*The Maple Leaf Rag* sold enough copies to give Scott Joplin an income all his life, but he needed it. His family was poor. His father had previously been a slave in the southern United States. His mother played the banjo and encouraged him to have piano lessons but the piano belonged to a family where she worked as a cleaner. Joplin himself worked as a travelling musician after giving up a more stable but low-paid job as a railway labourer.

In 1893 Joplin was at the World Fair in Chicago, playing the cornet in a band. Joplin also sang in a vocal quartet and wrote pieces for them. As you see, he had a lot of musical talents.

*Scott Joplin*

One of his early piano pieces was the *Great Crush Collision March*. Does the idea of making two trains crash into each other just for fun sound daft to you? At least they were empty at the time, but 30,000 people came to watch. The locomotives exploded and two people watching were killed by flying debris. Joplin's march was written to remember the event, but not in a solemn way. There are sounds that suggest the moment when the trains collided. He might have been there but it is hard to imagine writing such a jolly piece if he had witnessed the disaster. A more famous piece today is called *The Entertainer*, which almost always raises a smile.

Joplin took his music very seriously. He wrote a book to explain how to write in the Ragtime style and wrote an opera, *Treemonisha*, combining ragtime with other musical styles. He wrote the story himself about a heroine who learnt to read and rescued her community by getting them to prefer education to magic. Joplin longed to see his opera performed on stage but never saw the whole thing. His first opera, symphony and piano concerto have very sadly been lost, but a performance of *Treemonisha* has been made into a film. Scott Joplin died in 1917, but his music is very much alive.

# Some Songs for Year 5
## Auld Lang Syne

'Auld Lang Syne' is an old Scottish song, often sung on New Year's Eve. 'Auld lang syne' means old long since, or the old times. In the song two old friends are talking. One asks, 'Should old friends and old times be forgotten?' Then he answers his own question, saying they should have a drink – 'a cup of kindness' – for old times' sake!

Should auld acquaintance be forgot
And never brought to mind?
Should auld acquaintance be forgot
And days of Auld Lang Syne?

For Auld Lang Syne, my dear,
For Auld Lang Syne,
We'll take a cup o' kindness yet,
For Auld Lang Syne!

# Loch Lomond

*Like 'Annie Laurie' and 'On Ilkley Moor Baht 'At' in Year 4, this song uses dialect. Rules in dialect are sometimes different from standard English, but you can usually guess the meaning from the sound. Brae is a hillside, but can you work out the meaning of gloamin'?*

By yon bonnie banks and by yon bonnie braes,

Where the sun shines bright on Loch Lomond,

Where me and my true love were ever wont tae gae,

On the bonnie, bonnie banks of Loch Lomond.


Oh ye'll tak' the high road and I'll tak' the low road,

And I'll be in Scotland afore ye;

But me and my true love will never meet again

On the bonnie, bonnie banks of Loch Lomond.


I mind where we parted in yon shady glen

On the steep, steep side of Ben Lomond.

Where in soft purple hue the Highland hills we view,

And the moon comin' out in the gloamin'.

# Skye Boat Song

## by Sir Harold Boulton

*'Skye Boat Song' is a Scottish folk song about Bonnie Prince Charlie's escape by boat to the Isle of Skye. A claymore is a large, two-edged sword.*

[chorus]

*Speed bonnie boat like a bird on the wing,*
*Onward! The sailors cry;*
*Carry the lad that's born to be King*
*Over the sea to Skye.*

Loud the winds howl, loud the waves roar,
Thunderclaps rend the air,
Baffled, our foes stand by the shore,
Follow they will not dare.

[repeat chorus]

Though the waves leap, soft shall ye sleep,
Ocean's a royal bed.
Rocked in the deep, Flora will keep
Watch o'er your weary head.

[repeat chorus]

Many's the lad fought on that day,
Well the claymore could wield,
When the night came, silently lay
Dead in Culloden's field.

[repeat chorus]

Burned are our homes, exile and death,
Scatter the loyal men.
Yet ere the sword cool in the sheath,
Charlie will come again.

[repeat chorus]

You can read about Bonnie Prince Charlie and Flora MacDonald on page 125.

197

# With a Little Help from My Friends

## by John Lennon and Paul McCartney

*The Beatles were a popular music group from the 1960s who made this song famous. It was written by two members of the group. Here, the brackets show which words are questions sung by the singer's friend.*

What would you think if I sang out of tune,

Would you stand up and walk out on me?

Lend me your ears and I'll sing you a song,

And I'll try not to sing out of key.

Oh, I get by with a little help from my friends.

Mm, I get high with a little help from my friends.

Mm, gonna try with a little help from my friends.

What do I do when my love is away?

(Does it worry you to be alone?)

How do I feel by the end of the day?

(Are you sad because you're on your own?)

Oh, I get by with a little help from my friends.

Mm, I get high with a little help from my friends.

Mm, gonna try with a little help from my friends.

(Do you need anybody?)

I need somebody to love.

(Could it be anybody?)

I want somebody to love.

(Would you believe in a love at first sight?)

Yes I'm certain that it happens all the time.

(What do you see when you turn out the light?)

I can't tell you but I know it's mine.

Oh, I get by with a little help from my friends.

Mm, I get high with a little help from my friends.

Mm, gonna try with a little help from my friends.

(Do you need anybody?)

I need somebody to love.

(Could it be anybody?)

I want somebody to love.

Oh I get by with a little help from my friends.

Mm going to try with a little help from my friends.

Oh I get high with a little help from my friends.

Yes I get by with a little help from my friends.

With a little help from my friends.

## Waltzing Matilda

*'Waltzing Matilda' is sometimes described as the unofficial national anthem of Australia, but it isn't about a woman named Matilda who liked to waltz. A 'matilda' is a knapsack that Australian bushmen carried in the late 1800s. To go 'waltzing matilda' meant to walk around, looking for work, with all your belongings in your knapsack. In this song, a 'swagman', or bushman, sits by a lake (billabong) waiting for his billy, or kettle, to boil. When he sees a jumbuck, or a sheep, he stuffs it into his knapsack but is caught in the act!*

Once a jolly swagman camped by a billabong,

Under the shade of a coolibah tree,

And he sang as he watched and waited till his billy boiled,

'You'll come a-waltzing matilda with me.'

'Waltzing matilda, waltzing matilda,
'You'll come a-waltzing matilda with me.'
And he sang as he watched and waited till his billy boiled,
'You'll come a-waltzing matilda with me.'

Down came a jumbuck to drink at that billabong.
Up jumped the swagman and grabbed him with glee.
And he sang as he stuffed that jumbuck in his tucker bag,
'You'll come a-waltzing matilda with me.

You can read
about Australia
on page 95.

'Waltzing matilda, waltzing matilda,
'You'll come a-waltzing matilda with me.'
And he sang as he stuffed that jumbuck in his tucker bag,
'You'll come a-waltzing matilda with me.'

Up rode the squatter, mounted on his thoroughbred;
Down came the troopers, one, two, three.
'Where's that jolly jumbuck you've got in your tucker bag?
'You'll come a-waltzing Matilda with me.'

'Waltzing matilda, waltzing matilda,
'You'll come a-waltzing matilda with me.
'Where's that jolly jumbuck
you've got in your tucker bag?
'You'll come a-waltzing Matilda with me.'

Up jumped the swagman and sprang
into that billabong.
'You'll never take me alive,' said he.
And his ghost may be heard as you
pass by that billabong:
'You'll come a-
waltzing Matilda
with me.'

# Heart of Oak

*'Heart of Oak' is the official march of the Royal Navy. It was written for a pantomime that opened at the Theatre Royal, Drury Lane in 1759 – the 'Year of Miracles' that we read about on page 130.*

Come, cheer up my lads! 'tis to glory we steer,
To add something more to this wonderful year;
To honour we call you, as free men not slaves
For who are so free as the sons of the waves?

[chorus]

*Heart of oak are our ships, jolly tars are our men;*
*We always are ready; steady, boys, steady;*
*We'll fight and we'll conquer again and again.*

We ne'er see our foes but we wish them to stay,
They never see us but they wish us away;
If they run, why, we follow, and run 'em ashore,
For if they won't fight us we cannot do more.

[chorus]

They swear they'll invade us, these terrible foes,
They frighten our women, our children and beaux;
But should their flat-bottoms in darkness get o'er,
Still Britons they'll find to receive them on shore.

[chorus]

We still make 'em feel and we still make 'em flee,
And drub them ashore as we drub them at sea.
Then cheer up my lads, with one heart let us sing,
Our soldiers, our sailors, our statesmen, and King.

# The British Grenadiers

*This marching song became popular with regiments of grenadiers (soldiers who use grenades or artillery) in the eighteenth century and is still played every year at the Trooping of the Colour on the Queen's birthday.* Palisades *and* glacis *are parts of a fort. A* fusee *is a short firearm.*

Some talk of Alexander and some of Hercules,
Of Hector and Lysander and such great names as these;
But of all the world's brave heroes there's none that can compare,
With a tow row row row row row,
To the British Grenadiers.

None of those ancient heroes e'er saw a cannonball,
Or knew the force of powder, to slay their foes withal;
But our brave boys do know it and banish all their fears,
Sing tow row row row row row,
To the British Grenadiers.

When e'er we are commanded to storm the palisades,
Our leaders march with fusees and we with hand grenades;
We throw them from the glacis about the enemies' ears,
Sing tow row row row row row,
To the British Grenadiers.

Then let us fill a bumper, and drink
a health to those
Who carry caps and pouches and wear
the louped clothes;
May they and their commanders
live happy all their years,
With a tow row row row row row,
For the British Grenadiers.

## The Bare Necessities

**by Terry Gilkyson from Walt Disney's *The Jungle Book***

Look for the bare necessities, the simple, bare necessities.
Forget about your worries and your strife.
I mean the bare necessities, oh, Mother Nature's recipes
That bring the bare necessities of life.

Wherever I wander, wherever I roam,
I couldn't be fonder of my big home.
The bees are buzzing in the tree
To make some honey, just for me.
When you look under the rocks and plants,
Take a glance at the fancy ants
And maybe try a few! (Thanks, Balloo.)
The bare necessities of life will come to you.
Will come to you.

[Tuba solo]

When you pick a paw-paw or a prickly pear

And you pick a raw paw, well, next time, beware.

Don't pick the prickly pear by the paw;

When you pick a pear, try to use the claw,

But you don't need to use the claw

When you pick a pear of the big paw-paw.

(Have I given you a clue?)

The bear necessities of life will come to you.

They'll come to you, (They'll come to me?) They'll come to you. (They'll come to me!)

They'll come to you. (They'll come to you! Oh, yeah!)

## I Wanna Be Like You

**by Richard Sherman and Robert Sherman
from Walt Disney's *The Jungle Book***

Now I'm the king of the swingers

Oh, the jungle VIP

I've reached the top and had to stop

And that's what's botherin' me

I wanna be a man, mancub

And stroll right into town

And be just like the other men

I'm tired of monkeyin' around!

Oh, oobee doo

I wanna be like you

I wanna walk like you

Talk like you, too

You'll see it's true

An ape like me

Can learn to be human, too

Now don't try to kid me, mancub

I made a deal with you

What I desire is man's red fire

To make my dream come true

Now give me the secret, mancub

Come on, clue me what to do

Give me the power of man's red flower

So I can be like you

[Ad lib]

You!

I wanna be like you!

I wanna walk like you

Talk like you, too

You see it's true

Someone like me

Can learn to be

Like someone like me

Can learn to be

Like someone like you

Can learn to be

Like someone like me!

# Suggested Resources

## Radio

*Discovering Music*, BBC Radio3 series (90 – 92 FM or digital radio and online at www.bbc.co.uk/programmes/b012r8c2)

## Audio Recordings

*Young Person's Guide to the Orchestra* by Britten, performed by Richard Baker and the New Philharmonia Orchestra, conducted by Raymond Leppard, from *Peter and the Wolf and other pieces* (Classics for Pleasure) 2006

*Messiah*, by Handel, performed by the Academy of Ancient Music and the Choir of New College Oxford, conducted by Edward Higginbottom (Naxos) 2006

*Symphony no. 94 ('The Surprise')*, by Haydn, performed by the Academy of Ancient Music, conducted by Christopher Hogwood (Decca) 2007

*The Magic Flute (highlights)*, by Mozart, performed by the RIAS Chamber Choir, the Berlin Philharmonic Orchestra and soloists, conducted by Karl Böhm (Deutsche Grammophon Opera for Kids) 2009

*Treemonisha* by Joplin, performed by Houston Grand Opera, conducted by Gunther Schuller (Deutsche Grammophon) 2005

*Maple Leaf Rag* by Joplin, performed by Scott Joplin (piano), from *Original Piano Rolls 1899-1916* (Jazz Anthology) 2008

## Books About Music

*The Orchard Book of Opera Stories* by Adèle Geras (Orchard) 1997

*Meet the Instruments of the Orchestra* by Genevieve Helsby (Naxos Books) 2007

*The Story of Classical Music* by Darren Henley (Naxos Books) 2010

*The Orchestra* by Liz Miles (Raintree) 2009

## Songbooks

*Hook, Line and Singer: A Sing-a-long Book* by Cerys Matthews (Particular Books) 2013

*Strawberry Fair* edited by Emily Haward (A & C Black) 2001

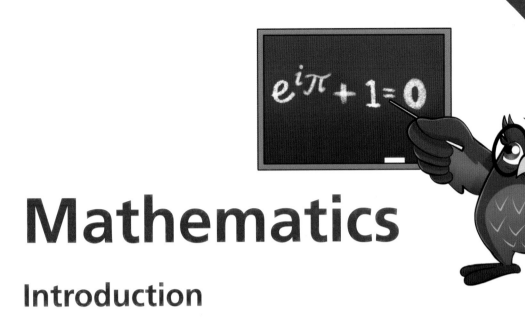

$$e^{i\pi} + 1 = 0$$

# Mathematics

## Introduction

This chapter offers a brief overview of essential maths topics for Year 5, including number sense, fractions and decimals, computation, measurement and geometry. Success in learning maths comes through practice: not mindless, repetitive practice but thoughtful practice, with a variety of problems. While it is important to work toward the development of higher-order problem-solving skills, such skills depend on a sound grasp of basic facts and an automatic mastery of fundamental operations. Since practice is the secret to mastery, practice is a prerequisite for more advanced problem-solving.

Some well-meaning people fear that practice in mathematics – memorising arithmetic facts or doing timed worksheets, for example – constitutes joyless, soul-killing drudgery for children. Nothing could be further from the truth. It is not practice but anxiety that kills the joy in mathematics. And one way of overcoming anxiety is by practising until the procedures become so easy and automatic that anxiety evaporates.

One effective way to practise is to have children talk out loud while doing problems, explaining computational steps along the way. In this way the child's mental process becomes visible to you, and you can correct misunderstandings as they happen. This brief outline presented here does not constitute a complete maths programme, since it does not include as many practice problems as a child ought to do while learning this material. To learn maths thoroughly, children need to be shown these concepts and then encouraged to practise, practise, practise. We therefore urge that parents and teachers select a maths programme that allows plenty of opportunities to practise.

The best maths programmes incorporate the principle of incremental review: once a concept or skill is introduced, it is practised again and again through exercises of gradually increasing difficulty (including word problems). One result of this approach is that a child's arithmetic skills become automatic. Only when children achieve automatic command of basic facts – when they can tell you instantly what 6 times 6 equals, for example – are they ready to tackle more challenging problems. Maths programmes that offer both incremental review and varied opportunities for problem-solving achieve the best results.

# Numbers and Number Sense

## Place Value

In Year 4, we learnt how to work with numbers up to hundred thousands. What comes after 999,999? One million, which is written 1,000,000.

You can write the numbers from 1,000 to 9,999 with or without a comma: 9,672 or 9672. However, whenever you write numbers ten thousand or greater, it is often better to write them with commas to mark off each group of three to help you see the place values. Therefore, you would write 10,403 rather than 10403.

When you read a number, always begin with the largest place value. How would you read this number?

### 4,315,825

The four is one digit to the left of the millions comma. It is in the millions place. 4,315,825 is read: 'four million, three hundred and fifteen thousand, eight hundred and twenty-five'. Now can you read this next number?

### 462,977,003

The 4 is three digits to the left of the millions comma. It is in the hundred millions place. 462,977,003 is read: 'four hundred and sixty-two million, nine hundred and seventy-seven thousand and three'. Notice how the commas make the number easier to read, by dividing the digits up into groups of three.

When you read numbers with this many digits, you have to pay attention to the place value of each digit. Draw boxes like the ones below and fill them in with 462,977,003.

| millions | | | thousands | | | ones | | |
|---|---|---|---|---|---|---|---|---|
| hundreds | tens | ones | hundreds | tens | ones | hundreds | tens | ones |
| | | | | | | | | |

Beginning at the right, the values of the places are: ones, tens, hundreds; then there are thousands, ten thousands, hundred thousands; followed by millions, ten millions, hundred millions. Each place has a value 10 times greater than the place to its right. This system of writing numbers is called the *decimal system*.

'Decimal' means having to do with 10. In the decimal system, the place values are based on groups of 10. In the decimal system, whenever we have 10 of a certain place value, we write it as 1 in the next highest place value. For example, there are *10* tens in *1* hundred. There are *10* hundreds in *1* thousand.

## The Value of Digits

Can you write 936,455,171 in expanded form?

In the number 9**3**6,**4**55,171, the bold 3 is in the ten millions place. Its value is 30,000,000. The bold 4 is in the hundred thousands place. How would you write its value? 400,000.

Another useful way to look at place value is to see how many of each place value a number has. For example, take 43,289. You can write the number in terms of how many ten thousands, thousands, hundreds, tens and ones it has. It has 4 ten thousands, 43 thousands, 432 hundreds, 4,328 tens or 43,289 ones. Learning to use place value in this way is very useful in both subtraction and division.

## Comparing Numbers

When you compare numbers, always begin by comparing the digits with the largest place values. For example, to compare 286,563 and 97,800, you begin at the left, with the largest places.

Think: 286,563 _____ 97,800

200,000 > 90,000

So, 286,563 > 97,800

Remember that the sign > stands for 'is greater than'. The sign < stands for 'is less than'. A statement like '286,563 > 97,800' is called an *inequality* because it shows how the numbers are not equal.

Another way to practise comparing numbers is to write a double inequality: find a number that fits between the two numbers in order to compare them. 286,563 is greater than 200,000. 200,000 is greater than 97,800. You write:

$$286,563 > 200,000 > 97,800$$

So, $286,563 > 97,800$.

## Standard Form and Expanded Form

You know that the standard way to write a number is to express it as a single number with digits. For example:

8,532,706 is in standard form.

You can also write the number in expanded form, separating the digits in each place. There are two ways to write the same number in its expanded form. You can write:

$$8,532,706 = 8,000,000 + 500,000 + 30,000$$
$$+ 2,000 + 700 + 6.$$

Or, you can multiply each digit by its place value, like this:

$$8,532,706 = (8 \times 1,000,000) + (5 \times 100,000)$$
$$+ (3 \times 10,000) + (2 \times 1,000) + (7 \times 100) + (6 \times 1).$$

Now, how would you write 5,367,824 and 6,928,284 in each of the two ways of writing expanded form?

## Using a Number Line

You can also compare numbers using a number line. Suppose your friends have been selling lemonade. They sold 7 glasses on Monday, 5 on Tuesday, 1 on Wednesday, 16 on Thursday and 11 on Friday.

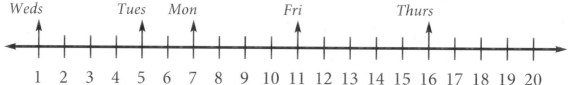

By placing these numbers on a number line, you can see which day was the best for sales. The farther to the right a number is on the number line, the larger it is. The farther left, the smaller the number.

## Negative Numbers

*Positive numbers* are numbers greater than 0. There is another set of numbers that are less than 0. They are called negative numbers. Negative numbers are written with a minus sign.

*Negative numbers* are a bit harder to understand than positive numbers, but they can be very useful. For instance, suppose you are keeping track of how much money your friend Jerome owes you. Let's say that at first Jerome owes you £5. Then Jerome pays when you have a doner kebab that costs £2. Subtract 2 from 5 by moving your finger two notches to the left on the number line below.

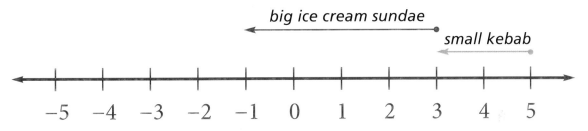

*big ice cream sundae*

*small kebab*

$$-5 \quad -4 \quad -3 \quad -2 \quad -1 \quad 0 \quad 1 \quad 2 \quad 3 \quad 4 \quad 5$$

After that, Jerome only owes you £3. Suppose he buys you a big ice cream sundae, with sprinkles and sauce, for £4. If you move four more ticks to the left, you move past zero to −1. What does it mean to say Jerome owes you −£1? It means you owe him a pound! How much would you owe him if he lent you £3 more?

See if you can put these numbers in order from the least to the greatest:

$$1 \quad -3 \quad 2 \quad 0 \quad -5$$

By using the number line, you can see that the order would be −5, −3, 0, 1, 2. Don't be fooled into thinking that −5 must be greater than −3 because 5 is larger than 3. The number line shows you that −5 is farther to the left of zero than −2, which means it is less.

## Comparing positive and negative numbers

$$-5 < -2$$

Any negative number is always less than any positive number.

$$-3 < 1 \qquad -1{,}000 < 5 \qquad -6 < 6$$

Any positive number is always greater than any negative number.

$$2 > -5 \qquad 2 > -450 \qquad 3 > -3$$

If both numbers are negative, the number farther from zero is less. You can think of it as larger and negative, meaning less.

$$-3 < -1 \qquad -6 > -7 \qquad -6 = -6$$

It's your turn. Supply the signs >, < or = between these numbers.

$$-5 \underline{\quad} 5 \qquad 21 \underline{\quad} -21 \qquad -12 \underline{\quad} -12 \qquad -7 \underline{\quad} -5$$

$$-8 \underline{\quad} -6 \qquad 9 \underline{\quad} -20 \qquad -4 \underline{\quad} -3 \qquad -1 \underline{\quad} -1$$

Draw yourself a number line if it helps.

## Rounding

You know from Years 3 and 4 that you can use 'round' numbers sometimes when you do not need to know an exact value for a number. Let's practise rounding.

What is 137 rounded to the nearest ten and the nearest hundred?

What is 151 rounded to the nearest ten and hundred?

What is 187 rounded to the nearest ten and hundred?

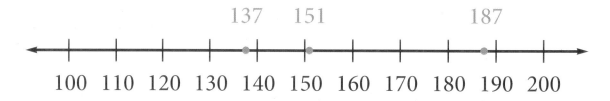

Now let's round 3,417 to the nearest thousand. When you look in the thousands place, you see 3. Your choice is to round the number up to 4,000 or round it down to 3,000.

Because the digit in the place just to the right is a 4, you should round **down** to 3,000. Notice that when you round a number to a certain place value, all the digits to the right of that place become zeros. Now, what is 8,568 rounded to the nearest thousand?

## Perfect Squares

When you take a number and multiply it by itself, you square the number. If you square a whole number, the resulting product is called a perfect square. In Year 4 we saw a few examples of perfect squares. Now look at these:

$1 \times 1 = 1$          $7 \times 7 = 49$

$2 \times 2 = 4$          $8 \times 8 = 64$

$3 \times 3 = 9$          $9 \times 9 = 81$

$4 \times 4 = 16$         $10 \times 10 = 100$

$5 \times 5 = 25$         $11 \times 11 = 121$

$6 \times 6 = 36$         $12 \times 12 = 144$

You can see why 9, 16, 25 and the other products above are called perfect squares if you draw pictures that stand for the numbers.

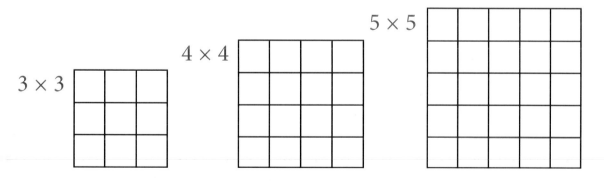

You can read the equation '5 × 5 = 25' as '5 times 5 equals 25'. Or you can say: '5 squared equals 25'. There is also a special symbol to mean 'squared'. It is $^2$.

$$5 \times 5 = 5^2 = 25$$

Why $^2$? It is above the line so it does not look like an ordinary digit. $5 \times 5$ is not 52. It is a 2 because five is a factor twice in the product.

For $10 \times 10 = 10$ squared $= 10^2 = 100$, 2 is also the number of zeroes in **100**. That only works with 10 squared.

## Square Roots

When we take the square root of 25, we ask what number multiplied by itself equals 25.

Since $5 \times 5 = 25$, the square root of 25 is 5.

Let's try that again. What number multiplied by itself equals 81? $9 \times 9 = 81$. So the square root of 81 is 9.

We use a special symbol to mean 'square root of': $\sqrt{\phantom{x}}$. We read $\sqrt{64}$ as 'the square root of 64'. What does $\sqrt{64}$ equal? How about $\sqrt{100}$? $\sqrt{144}$? You can look at the perfect squares on the previous page for a clue.

## Roman Numerals

In Year 4 we first learnt about Roman numerals. Let's review the Roman numerals from 1 to 10. Look at them carefully, especially the numerals for 4 and 9.

I    II    III    IV    V    VI    VII    VIII    IX    X

We learnt in Year 4 that there are some more Roman numerals, and you can use these symbols to write numbers into the thousands. The symbols are:

L is 50     C is 100     D is 500     M is 1,000

Now do you remember the two rules of using Roman numerals?

### Rule 1

When a Roman numeral that is the same size or smaller comes after another Roman numeral, you add their values together.

XV is $10 + 5 = 15$     XXX is $10 + 10 + 10 = 30$

### Rule 2

When a Roman numeral that is smaller comes just before one that is larger, you subtract the smaller one from the larger one.

$$IV \text{ is } 5 - 1 = 4$$
$$IX \text{ is } 10 - 1 = 9$$
$$XL \text{ is } 50 - 10 = 40$$

*What time is it?*

*It's 2:56.*

Often, you need to use both these rules to write numbers in Roman numerals. The example below shows you how grouping numbers within a long Roman numeral helps you read it:

$$CDXLVIII$$
$$= CD + XL + VIII$$
$$= (500 - 100) + (50 - 10) + (5 + 3)$$
$$= 400 + 40 + 8$$
$$= 448$$

Sometimes people still use Roman numerals for years. For example, you might find a book published in the year MCMLXXXVII.

$$M + CM + LXXX + VII$$
$$= 1000 + (1000 - 100) + (50 + 30) + (5 + 2)$$
$$= 1000 + 900 + 80 + 7$$
$$= 1987$$

What year is it now? Can you write the year in Roman numerals? What famous historical event happened in MDCLXVI? How about MCCXV or MCDXCII?

# Multiplication

## Multiplication Review

Remember that multiplication is a quick way of adding the same number over and over again. You can solve $4 + 4 + 4 + 4 + 4$ in two ways. You can write the numbers in a column and add them, or you can multiply $4 \times 5$. $4 \times 5 = 20$. In this equation, 4 and 5 are the *factors*, and 20 is the *product*.

Do you know the basic multiplication facts, from $1 \times 1$ to $10 \times 10$? Can you fill in the blanks in the following equations?

$$4 \times 8 = \underline{\quad} \qquad \underline{\quad} \times 7 = 35 \qquad 6 \times \underline{\quad} = 24$$

$$7 \times 6 = \underline{\quad} \qquad \underline{\quad} \times 9 = 63 \qquad 8 \times \underline{\quad} = 40$$

If it takes you more than a second or two to solve any of these, you should practise your multiplication facts.

## A Property of Multiplication

Remember also that multiplication has a special property. This property allows you to find a product by first multiplying with one part of a number and then multiplying with the other part, then adding the two partial products together, to find the whole product. Here is an example with $9 \times 4$. If you didn't remember that $9 \times 4 = 36$, you could work it out this way:

$$
\begin{aligned}
9 \times 4 &= (6 + 3) \times 4 \\
&= (6 \times 4) + (3 \times 4) \\
&= 24 + 12 \\
&= 36
\end{aligned}
$$

Because of this property of multiplication, there is an easy way to multiply numbers of more than one digit in your head. You can multiply the value in each digit separately, and then add to find the whole product. Here's an example:

$$
\begin{aligned}
3 \times 17 &= 3 \times (10 + 7) \\
&= (3 \times 10) + (3 \times 7) \\
&= 30 + 21 \\
&= 51
\end{aligned}
$$

Now look at this problem: $3{,}624 \times 5$. You can multiply 5 by the ones, then by the tens, then by the hundreds, then by the thousands. Then you add those numbers together.

$$3{,}624 \times 5 = (4 \text{ ones} \times 5) + (2 \text{ tens} \times 5) + (6 \text{ hundreds} \times 5) + (3 \text{ thousands} \times 5)$$
$$= (4 \times 5) + (20 \times 5) + (600 \times 5) + (3{,}000 \times 5)$$
$$= 20 + 100 + 3{,}000 + 15{,}000$$
$$= 18{,}120$$

You know from Year 4 that there is a quicker way to work through these same stages of multiplication. First, write the two numbers to be multiplied one on top of another. Then multiply the ones, tens, hundreds and thousands columns, 'carrying' numbers to the next column, as needed.

$$
\begin{array}{r}
{\scriptstyle 3\ \ 1\ 2} \\
3{,}6\,2\,4 \\
\times \qquad 5 \\
\hline
1\,8{,}1\,2\,0
\end{array}
$$

First multiply $4 \times 5$.

$4 \times 5 = 20$, or 2 tens, 0 ones. Write zero in the ones place and carry the two tens by writing a 2 over the tens column.

Now move to the tens place. $5 \times 2$ tens $= 10$ tens, plus 2 tens carried over from the ones column $= 12$ tens. Write 2 in the tens column and carry the 1 hundred to the hundreds column.

Continue to multiply and add in this way until you have multiplied each digit by the 5 and added in the numbers carried over from the last place.

# Multiples

24 is a multiple of 6, because $6 \times 4 = 24$. A multiple of a number is the product of that number and any whole number. 36 is also a multiple of 6 because $6 \times 6 = 36$.

Here are some multiples of 2: $2, 4, 6, 8, 10, 12, 14\ldots$

Here are some multiples of 6: $6, 12, 18, 24, 30\ldots$

Here are some multiples of 7: $7, 14, 21, 28, 35\ldots$

18 is a multiple of 6, because $6 \times 3 = 18$. But 18 is also a multiple of 9, because $9 \times 2 = 18$.

We say that 18 is a common multiple of 6 and 9. Another common multiple of 6 and 9 is 36, because 6 × 6 = 36 and 9 × 4 = 36. Can you find three common multiples for 4 and 6?

Notice that all the multiples of 2 are even. You can define even numbers this way – even numbers are numbers that are multiples of 2.

Here are some multiples of 10: 10, 20, 30, 40, 50...

Notice that all multiples of 10 end in zero. All whole numbers that end in zero are multiples of 10.

## Multiplying by Tens

Whenever you multiply a number by ten, you make it ten times as large. In the decimal system, you make a whole number ten times as large just by adding an extra zero to it. So it is easy to multiply by ten – just add an extra zero to the number you're multiplying by. The numbers move a place to the left to make room for the zero.

$$
\begin{array}{r} 4 \\ \times\ 10 \\ \hline 40 \end{array}
\qquad
\begin{array}{r} 54 \\ \times\ 10 \\ \hline 540 \end{array}
\qquad
\begin{array}{r} 184 \\ \times\ 10 \\ \hline 1{,}840 \end{array}
$$

You can use this knowledge to multiply by any multiple of ten. Suppose you wanted to multiply 23 × 60. You already know how to multiply 23 × 6, and you know how to multiply by ten. By combining these two skills you can get your answer:

$$23 \times 60 = 23 \times (6 \times 10)$$
$$= (23 \times 6) \times 10$$

So, the product of 23 × 60 is equal to the product of 23 times 6, times 10:

$$
\begin{array}{r} 1\phantom{0} \\ \times\ 23 \\ 6 \\ \hline 138 \end{array}
$$

Then multiply 138 × 10, which is as easy as adding a zero: 138 × 10 = 1,380.

So 23 × 60 = 1,380.

Now try multiplying 14 × 70.

# Multiplying by Two-Digit Numbers

Once you know how to multiply by tens, you can multiply by any two-digit number: you just break the problem down into two parts. First you multiply by ones, and then you multiply by tens and write this product below the first product. After this, you add. Here's how you would find the product of $23 \times 58$.

Think: $23 \times 58$ is $(20 \times 58) + (3 \times 58)$

$$
\begin{array}{r}
58 \\
\times \quad 23 \\
\hline
174 \\
\end{array}
\qquad \textit{Multiply 58 by 3 ones}
$$

Multiply 58 by 2 tens. Be sure to write a zero in the ones place to show you are working with the tens now.

$$
\begin{array}{r}
58 \\
\times \quad 23 \\
\hline
174 \\
1{,}160 \\
\end{array}
\qquad \textit{Then add} \qquad
\begin{array}{r}
58 \\
\times \quad 23 \\
\hline
174 \\
+ \ 1{,}160 \\
\hline
1{,}334 \\
\end{array}
$$

You can multiply larger numbers by two-digit numbers in the same way. Here's an example.

$$
\begin{aligned}
372 \times 48 &= 372 \times (40 + 8) \\
&= (372 \times 40) + (372 \times 8)
\end{aligned}
$$

$$
\begin{array}{r}
372 \\
\times \quad 48 \\
\hline
2{,}976 \\
+ \ 14{,}880 \\
\hline
17{,}856 \\
\end{array}
\begin{array}{l}
\\
\\
= 372 \times 8 \\
= 372 \times 40 \\
= 372 \times 48 \\
\end{array}
$$

# Multiplying by Hundreds

When you multiply a whole number by 100, you add *two* zeros to it. Multiplying by 100 is like multiplying by 10 twice. The numbers move two places to the left.

$$100 \times 6 = (10 \times 10) \times 6$$
$$= 10 \times (10 \times 6)$$
$$= 10 \times 60$$
$$= 600$$

$$\begin{array}{r} 6 \\ \times\ 100 \\ \hline 600 \end{array} \qquad \begin{array}{r} 87 \\ \times\ 100 \\ \hline 8{,}700 \end{array} \qquad \begin{array}{r} 942 \\ \times\ 100 \\ \hline 94{,}200 \end{array}$$

To multiply by any multiple of 100, write zeros in the ones place and the tens place of the product, because you are multiplying by 100. Then multiply using the digit in the hundreds place.

Write zeros in the ones place and the tens place, then multiply.

$$\begin{array}{r} 487 \\ \times\ 300 \\ \hline 00 \end{array} \qquad\qquad \begin{array}{r} 487 \\ \times\ 300 \\ \hline 146{,}100 \end{array}$$

# Multiplying by Three-Digit Numbers

Once you know how to multiply by hundreds, you can multiply by three-digit numbers. First multiply by the ones, then by the tens, then by the hundreds. Then add. Here is an example.

*Multiply by 4 ones*

$$\begin{array}{r} 565 \\ \times\ 394 \\ \hline 2{,}260 \end{array} = 4 \times 565$$

*Write a 0 in the ones place and then multiply by 9 tens*

$$
\begin{array}{r}
565 \\
\times \quad 394 \\
\hline
2{,}260 \\
50{,}850 = 90 \times 565
\end{array}
$$

*Write a 0 in the ones place, a 0 in the tens place and then multiply by 3 hundreds*

$$
\begin{array}{r}
565 \\
\times \quad 394 \\
\hline
2{,}260 \\
50{,}850 \\
169{,}500 = 300 \times 565 \\
\hline
222{,}610 = 394 \times 565
\end{array}
$$

## Multiplying by Thousands

You know that when multiplying a whole number by 10, you add one zero. When multiplying by 100, you add two zeros. How many zeros do you suppose you will add when multiplying a whole number by 1,000? Did you say three zeros? If so, you spotted the pattern. Multiplying by 1,000 is like multiplying by 10 three times. The numbers move three places to the left and you fill in zeroes wherever there is a blank.

$$
\begin{array}{r}
7 \\
\times 1{,}000 \\
\hline
7{,}000
\end{array}
\qquad
\begin{array}{r}
23 \\
\times 1{,}000 \\
\hline
23{,}000
\end{array}
\qquad
\begin{array}{r}
981 \\
\times 1{,}000 \\
\hline
981{,}000
\end{array}
$$

To multiply by any thousand, write zeros in the ones, tens and hundreds places of the product. Then multiply by the digit in the thousands place:

*Write zeros in the ones, tens and hundreds places*

$$
\begin{array}{r}
64 \\
\times 2{,}000 \\
\hline
000
\end{array}
$$

*Multiply*

$$
\begin{array}{r}
64 \\
\times 2{,}000 \\
\hline
128{,}000
\end{array}
$$

# Multiplication with Zeros

Sometimes you need to multiply numbers that end in several zeros. There is a handy shortcut for multiplying numbers that end in zeros. Let's say you wanted to multiply 300 × 500. You can do this as you would normally. Write two zeros in the product. Multiply 500 by 3.

$$
\begin{array}{r}
500 \\
\times \ \ 300 \\
\hline
00
\end{array}
\qquad\qquad
\begin{array}{r}
500 \\
\times \ \ \ \ \ 300 \\
\hline
150{,}000
\end{array}
$$

Or you can take a shortcut. You can rule off all the zeros at the ends of the numbers, and write *all four* of the zeros in the product straight away. Then multiply 5 by 3

$$5\,|\,00 \times 3\,|\,00 = \underline{\phantom{15}}\,|\,0{,}000$$
$$= 15\,|\,0{,}000$$

If you write the sum vertically, notice how the two zeros from the 500 and two more zeros from the 300 push the 15 over to the left. You have multiplied hundreds by hundreds and got tens of thousands.

$$
\begin{array}{r}
5\,|\,00 \\
\times \quad 3\,|\,00 \\
\hline
|\,0{,}0 \ \ 00
\end{array}
\qquad\qquad
\begin{array}{r}
5\,|\,00 \\
\times \qquad 3\,|\,00 \\
\hline
15\,|\,0{,}0 \ \ 00
\end{array}
$$

Use this strategy to multiply 2,000 × 600 and 600 × 800.

# Checking Multiplication

There are two different ways of checking multiplication: by estimating or by changing the order of the factors you are multiplying. Estimation lets you know if your answer is about right. Changing the order of the factors gives you an exact check. To check a multiplication problem by estimation, round each factor to the nearest ten, hundred or thousand. (You do not need to round one-digit factors.) Then multiply and check to be sure the estimate is close to the answer you came up with.

Check this problem

$$
\begin{array}{r}
254 \\
\times \quad 49 \\
\hline
2,286 \\
+\ 10,160 \\
\hline
12,446
\end{array}
$$

*Round both factors to the nearest ten and multiply*

$$
\begin{array}{r}
254 \\
\times \quad 49
\end{array}
\longrightarrow
\begin{array}{r}
250 \\
\times \quad 50 \\
\hline
12,500
\end{array}
$$

See if the original product is close to the estimate. If it's not, go back and multiply again.

## 12,446 is close to 12,500 ✔

Based on this check, you can't say that your multiplication is absolutely correct, but you know you are close.

You can also check multiplication by changing the order of the factors and multiplying again.

To check this problem, reverse the order of the factors and multiply

$$
\begin{array}{r}
68 \\
\times \quad 37 \\
\hline
476 \\
+\ 2,040 \\
\hline
2,516
\end{array}
\qquad
\begin{array}{r}
37 \\
\times \quad 68 \\
\hline
296 \\
+\ 2,220 \\
\hline
2,516
\end{array}
$$

If your answer is correct, the product will be the same both times.

## Multiplying Three Factors

You've just seen how you can check a multiplication problem by changing the order of the two factors to be multiplied. You can also do this when multiplying three factors. When you multiply three numbers, you can multiply them in any order, but one particular order may be easiest.

Look at $879 \times 5 \times 6$, for example. In this problem, you can save time if you multiply $5 \times 6$ in your head to get 30, and then multiply $30 \times 879$.

## Multiplication Word Problems

Joe went to the toyshop 13 times last month. He bought 5 marbles each time he went. How many marbles did Joe buy last month?

Fifteen friends were going to the theme park. They each went on thirteen rides. How many rides did they go on in total?

The class is going to the theatre and each ticket costs £6. How much do 26 tickets cost?

# Division

## Division Review

Division and multiplication are *inverse operations*. That means that one inverts, or reverses, the other. Take the equation $10 \times 10 = 100$. You could invert this by dividing: $100 \div 10 = 10$. The first equation says if you combine ten groups, each containing ten items, you'll have a hundred items all told. The second says, if you break that collection of a hundred items into ten equal groups, each group will have ten items.

In Years 2, 3 and 4 we learnt the division tables for the divisors 1 to 10. Before you learn more complicated division, make sure you know the facts of simple division. For example, since you know that $8 \times 4 = 32$, you should also know that $32 \div 4 = 8$, and $32 \div 8 = 4$.

Finally, remember two important rules about division: You cannot divide by 0, and any number divided by 1 equals that number.

Now, do you remember what dividends, divisors and quotients are? In the equation $32 \div 8 = 4$, 32 is the *dividend*, 8 is the *divisor* and 4 is the *quotient*. The dividend is the number you are dividing, the divisor is the number you are dividing by and the quotient is the answer.

$e^{i\pi} + 1 = 0$

The Year 2 book explains why these rules are true.

# Factors

A *factor* is a number that divides another number evenly, without leaving a remainder.

What are the factors of 4?

$$4 \div 1 = 4$$
$$4 \div 2 = 2$$
$$4 \div 3 = \text{DOES NOT DIVIDE EVENLY}$$
$$4 \div 4 = 1$$

So the factors of 4 are 1, 2 and 4 because they all divide 4 evenly. 3 does not divide 4 evenly and so is not a factor of 4.

The factors of 20 are 1, 2, 4, 5, 10, 20. The factors of 24 are 1, 2, 3, 4, 6, 8, 12, 24. How many factors do 20 and 24 have in common? There are three: 1, 2 and 4. Factors shared by two or more numbers are called *common* factors.

What are the common factors of 28 and 42? Of 30 and 45?

## Prime Numbers and Composite Numbers

Every whole number larger than 1 has at least two factors. The number can be divided evenly by itself and it can be divided evenly by 1. If a number has only two factors, it is called a *prime number*. 11 is a good example of a prime number. You can divide 11 evenly by 1 ($11 \div 1 = 11$) and you can divide it by 11 ($11 \div 11 = 1$). But you cannot divide 11 evenly by 3 or 4 or 6, or any other whole number. So 11 is a prime number.

2 is considered the first prime number (1 is a special case). Can you pick out the other prime numbers between 2 and 20? Hint: there are seven of them, not counting 2.

What do we call a number that's not a prime number? We call it a *composite* number. A composite number is a number that is divisible by at least one other number besides itself and 1.

6 is a good example. 6 is evenly divisible by 1, 2, 3 and 6.

So it is a composite number. Is 21 composite? How about 37?

## Three Ways of Writing Division Problems

You can write a division problem in three ways. 28 divided by 7 can be written:

$$28 \div 7 \qquad\qquad 7\overline{)28} \qquad\qquad \frac{28}{7}$$

All three ways mean the same thing: 28 divided by 7. Now can you write 33 divided by 5 in these three different ways?

## Dividing Vertically

$$\begin{array}{r} 6 \text{ R3} \\ 5 \overline{)\ 33} \\ -\ 30 \\ \hline 3 \end{array}$$

First we look to see if the divisor is smaller than the first digit of the dividend. It's not (5 > 3), so we have to look at the next digit of the dividend and divide 5 into 33.

$5 \times 6 = 30$

$33 - 30$ leaves a remainder of 3

So 33 divided by 5 is 6 with a remainder of 3. We abbreviate this quotient '6 R3'.

Because multiplication and division are inverse operations, you can use your multiplication skills to check your division. To check a division problem, you multiply the quotient by the divisor, and you add the remainder (if there is one). Your answer should equal the dividend.

$$(\text{quotient} \times \text{divisor}) + \text{remainder} = \text{dividend}$$
$$(6 \times 5) + 3 =$$
$$30 + 3 = 33\ \checkmark$$

You can begin to use this same form – a multiplication and an addition – as a way of writing division answers.

$$33 = (6 \times 5) + 3 \qquad 3 < 5$$

You write the inequality $3 < 5$ to show that the remainder is less than the divisor. Remember that if the remainder is not less than the divisor, the quotient is too small and you need to go back and redo your division.

## Understanding Remainders in Word Problems

When you do division word problems, you may need to think about your remainders in different ways. Suppose that 31 students are going on a trip in some school minibuses. Each minibus can hold 7 students. How many minibuses are needed?

When you divide 31 by 7, you get 4 ($7 \times 4$ = 28) with a remainder of 3. Does the answer 4 with a remainder of 3 mean you only need 4 minibuses? No. If you only had 4 minibuses, 3 people would not be able to go on the trip. In this problem the remainder tells us an extra minibus will be needed. Altogether, 5 minibuses will be needed for the trip.

Now try the following problem: Mrs Pauli is making surprise baskets for a fair. She has 6 baskets and 52 treats to place in them. If she wants all the baskets to have the same number of surprises, how many treats should go in each basket? How many will be left over for her grandchildren?

## Zeros in Quotients

Sometimes when you divide, you need to write a zero as one of the digits of the quotient.

Consider $922 \div 3$

First divide the hundreds. ▶

$$
\begin{array}{r}
3\phantom{22} \\
3\overline{)922} \\
-9\phantom{22} \\
\hline
0\phantom{22}
\end{array}
$$

Think: $0 < 3$

$$
\begin{array}{r}
30\phantom{2} \\
3\overline{)922} \\
-9\phantom{2}\downarrow \\
\hline
02
\end{array}
$$

Bring down the tens and try to divide them. Since you cannot divide 2 by 3, write a zero in the tens place of the quotient and bring down the ones as well. ▶

Divide 22 by 3 ▶

$$
\begin{array}{r}
307 \text{ R1} \\
3\overline{)922} \\
-9\downarrow\downarrow \\
\hline
022 \\
-21 \\
\hline
1
\end{array}
$$

Think: $1 < 3$

Check by multiplying the quotient by the divisor and adding the remainder. ▼

$$
\begin{array}{r}
307 \\
\times\ 3 \\
\hline
921 \\
+\ 1 \\
\hline
922
\end{array}
$$

Practise writing your answer as a multiplication and an addition, followed by an inequality.

$$922 = (3 \times 307) + 1 \qquad 1 < 3$$

## The Number of Digits in a Quotient

Before you begin solving a division problem, work out first how many digits there will be in the quotient. For example, in the problem $496 \div 3$, you know straight away that there will be **three** digits in the quotient, because you can divide 4 hundreds by 3. Another way to think of this is that $496 > 3 \times 100$. You know the quotient will be at least 100, which is the smallest possible three-digit number.

In the problem $519 \div 6$, you know straight away that the quotient will have **two** digits. You cannot divide the 5 in the hundreds place by 6 but you can divide 51 tens by 6. Another way to think of this is that $519 < 6 \times 100$. You know the quotient will be less than 100.

## Dividing Larger Numbers

You can use the same method to divide larger numbers by one-digit numbers. Here is an example of dividing a number in the thousands.

$$8 \overline{)\, 8254}$$

You can divide 8 thousands by 8. Begin by dividing the thousands. The quotient will have four digits.

$$
\begin{array}{r}
1031 \text{ R6} \\
8\overline{)8254} \\
-\,8\phantom{254} \\
\hline
025\phantom{0} \\
-\,24\phantom{0} \\
\hline
14 \\
-\,8 \\
\hline
6
\end{array}
$$

In this problem, notice that you cannot divide the 2 in the hundreds place by 8. So you write a zero in the hundreds place, bring down the 5 and divide 8 into 25 tens.

# Mental Division

Sometimes you can do a division problem in your head, without writing out all the steps. Here's an example.

$$3 \overline{)\,936}$$

Think: 9 hundreds ÷ 3 = 3 hundreds

3 tens ÷ 3 = 1 ten

6 ones ÷ 3 = 2 ones

So, $3 \overline{)\,936}^{\,312}$

Try solving $2\overline{)684}$, $7\overline{)749}$ and $9\overline{)3636}$ in your head.

# Dividing by Tens

When dividing by tens, remember that division is the opposite of multiplication. Here's an example:

$$30 \overline{)\,90}$$

Think: how many × 30 = 90?

Try different numbers.

2 × 30 = 60

3 × 30 = 90

$$\begin{array}{r} 3 \\ 30\overline{)90} \\ -\,90 \\ \hline 0 \end{array}$$

Now try 80 ÷ 4.

# Dividing by Two-Digit Numbers

When the divisor is a two-digit number, but not an even ten, round it to the nearest ten to estimate what the quotient will be. Here is an example.

$$28\overline{)\,640}$$

To divide the 64 tens by 28, first round 28 to 30.

Think: **how many × 30 is about 64?**

$$2 \times 30 = 60$$

$$\begin{array}{r} 2\phantom{00} \\ 28\overline{)640} \\ -\ 56\phantom{0} \\ \hline 8\phantom{0} \end{array}$$

Think: **8 < 28**

When you bring down the 0, you will need to divide the 80 ones by 28.

Think: **how many × 30 is about 80?**

$$2 \times 30 = 60$$

$$3 \times 30 = 90$$

**3 × 30 is too large.**

$$\begin{array}{r} 22 \text{ R24} \\ 28\overline{)640} \\ -\ 56\phantom{0}\downarrow \\ \hline 80 \\ -\ 56 \\ \hline 24 \end{array}$$

Check: **24 < 28**

Check your answer by multiplying the quotient by the divisor and adding the remainder.

$$
\begin{array}{r}
22 \\
\times\ 28 \\
\hline
176 \\
+\ 440 \\
\hline
616 \\
+\ \ 24 \\
\hline
640
\end{array}
$$

As before, practise writing your answer as a multiplication and an addition, followed by an inequality.

$$640 = (28 \times 22) + 24 \qquad 24 < 28$$

## Adjusting the Quotient

Sometimes when you round the divisor to the nearest ten, the quotient you try will be too large or too small. Then you need to adjust the quotient. Here's an example:

$$36\,\overline{)\,146}$$

You can't divide 14 tens by 36. Divide 146 ones by 36. Round 36 to 40. $40 \times 3 = 120$.

Try 3 as a quotient.

$$
\begin{array}{r}
3\ \ \\
36\overline{)146} \\
-\ 108 \\
\hline
38
\end{array}
\qquad\qquad 38 > 36
$$

The remainder is greater than the divisor. So the quotient you tried was too small. Make the quotient one number larger. Try 4.

$$
\begin{array}{r}
4\ \text{R2} \\
36\overline{)146} \\
-\ 144 \\
\hline
2
\end{array}
\qquad\qquad 2 < 36
$$

Here's a similar problem for you to try:

$$13 \overline{\smash{\big)}\ 851}$$

It can happen that your estimate of the quotient is too big. You can tell because when you multiply the quotient by the divisor, you get a product bigger than your original dividend. When that happens, try with a smaller quotient.

$$13 \overline{\smash{\big)}\ 851}$$

You need to divide 85 tens by 13

$8 \times 10 = 80$ so start with 8.

$$
\begin{array}{r}
8\phantom{00} \\
13\overline{\smash{\big)}\ 851} \\
-\ 104\phantom{0} \\
\hline
\end{array}
$$

For the next step, you are trying to subtract 104 from 85 but it is too big. The product of quotient and divisor is greater than the dividend. Try a smaller quotient. 7 is still too big but 6 works.

$$
\begin{array}{r}
6\phantom{00} \\
13\overline{\smash{\big)}\ 851} \\
-\ 78\phantom{0}\downarrow \\
\hline
71\phantom{0}
\end{array}
\qquad
\begin{array}{r}
65\ \text{R}6 \\
13\overline{\smash{\big)}\ 851} \\
-\ 78\phantom{0}\downarrow \\
\hline
71\phantom{0} \\
-\ 65\phantom{0} \\
\hline
6\phantom{0}
\end{array}
$$

$$851 = (13 \times 65) + 6$$

$$6 < 13$$

When you estimate the quotient,

if you **round up** the divisor, your quotient could be **too small**.

if you **round down** the divisor, your quotient could be **too big**.

Practise with some more examples:

$$16 \overline{\smash{\big)}\ 256}$$

$$18 \overline{\smash{\big)}\ 325}$$

$$54 \overline{\smash{\big)}\ 325}$$

# Dividing Thousands

You divide numbers in the thousands by two-digit numbers in the same way as for hundreds:

$$32 \overline{)\, 6{,}659}$$

1. Divide 66 hundreds by 32.

2. Subtract 64 from 66. Bring down the 5 tens. You cannot divide 25 tens by 32, so write a zero in the tens place of the quotient.

3. Bring down the 9 ones. Divide 259 ones by 32. Think: how many times 30 is about 259?

4. Check your work by multiplying the quotient by the divisor, and adding the remainder to that product.

```
         208 R3                     Check:        208
    32)6,659                                  ×     32
     – 6,4↓↓                                       416
        259                                    + 6,240
      – 256                                      6,656
          3                                    +      3
                                                 6,659
```

Practise writing your answer like this:

$$6{,}659 = (32 \times 208) + 3 \qquad 3 < 32$$

Long division is a very good way to practise both multiplication and division. Here are a few long division problems you can use for practice:

$$39\overline{)4{,}132} \quad 27\overline{)1{,}007} \quad 45\overline{)2{,}503} \quad 16\overline{)224} \quad 15\overline{)224}$$

## Estimating Quotients

When you estimate a quotient, you can round the dividend or the divisor to a number that makes the division easy, rather than to the greatest place value. Here are two examples:

$$6 \overline{)\, 383}$$

Round the dividend (383) to 360 because you can divide 360 by 6 easily. (You cannot divide 400 by 6 easily.)

$$\begin{array}{r} 60 \\ 6\overline{)360} \end{array}$$

$383 \div 6$ is about 60.

$$\text{Estimate: } 28\overline{)1{,}143}$$

Round the divisor to the greatest place value. 28 rounds to 30. 30 does not go into 1,000 easily. 30 does go into 1,200 easily.

$$\begin{array}{r} 40 \\ 30\overline{)1{,}200} \end{array}$$

$1{,}143 \div 28$ is about 40.

## Division Word Problems

Michelle read 137 pages of her book over 4 days. Roughly how many pages did she read each day? Why do we say roughly? Was there a remainder?

5,785 people wanted tickets for an event at the Edinburgh Festival Fringe, but only 65 tickets were available. How many people competed for each ticket?

# Working with Numbers and Letters in Equations

## Letters That Stand for Numbers

Sometimes in maths we use a letter to stand for a number. Here's an example:

$$A = 6 + (8 \times 5)$$

In an equation like this, A stands for a mystery number and your job as a maths detective is to work out what A equals. In this case, you can solve the mystery by multiplying and then adding:

$$A = 6 + (8 \times 5)$$
$$= 6 + 40$$
$$= 46$$

So A = 46. See if you can work out the mystery number in this equation:

$$B = (8 \times 3) - 4$$

## Equality Properties

Equality properties are rules that can help you solve equations like the ones above. One equality property says that **equals added to equals are equal**. This property can help you work out the mystery number in the following equation.

Do you remember learning this equality property first in Year 3 in our example of making orange juice?

$$Y - 25 = 15$$

This equality property says that, if you add an equal quantity to both sides of any equation, it will still be an equation. Look what happens if we add 25 to both sides of this equation.

$$Y - 25 = 15$$
$$(Y - 25) + 25 = 15 + 25$$
$$Y = 40$$

If you subtract 25 from Y and then add 25, the addition and subtraction cancel each other out, and you are left with just Y on the left side of the equation. On the right side of the equation, you add 25 to 15 and get 40. So you know that Y = 40.

Use the same technique to solve Z − 12 = 17 and P − 29 = 17.

Now let's learn another equality property: **equals multiplied by equals are equal**. This is also very useful for solving equations. Here's an example:

$$Y \div 2 = 37$$

This equality property tells us that we can multiply both sides of an equation by the same number and we will still have an equation. Look what happens when we multiply by 2.

$$Y \div 2 = 37$$
$$(Y \div 2) \times 2 = 37 \times 2$$
$$Y = 74$$

If we divide Y by 2 and then multiply it by 2, the multiplication undoes the division, and we are left with just Y on the left side of the equation. Meanwhile, on the right side of the equation, we multiply 37 by 2 and get 74. So Y = 74.

Try to solve another problem of this sort on your own: Z ÷ 6 = 23

Remembering these equality properties will help you as you begin to study the kind of maths called *algebra*.

# Fractions and Decimals

## Review: Fractions

Can you read these numbers?

$$\frac{1}{2} \quad \frac{1}{3} \quad \frac{1}{4} \quad \frac{1}{5} \quad \frac{1}{6} \quad \frac{1}{7} \quad \frac{1}{8} \quad \frac{1}{9} \quad \frac{1}{10}$$

These numbers are all *fractions*. They are all smaller than one but larger than zero. Each one is made up of two parts, the *numerator* and the *denominator*.

Can you identify the numerator and denominator for each fraction? Sometimes it is easier to write a fraction with a sloping line in the middle. It means the same thing. The numerator is above and to the left; the denominator is below the line and to the right.

$$\frac{3}{4} \longleftarrow \text{numerator} \longrightarrow \frac{3}{5}$$
$$\longleftarrow \text{denominator} \longrightarrow$$

These numbers are all fractions, too.

$$\frac{3}{4} \qquad \frac{3}{5} \qquad \frac{5}{6} \qquad \frac{7}{11} \qquad \frac{11}{12}$$

# Improper Fractions

When the numerator of a fraction is equal to or greater than the denominator, the fraction is called an *improper* fraction. Here are some examples of improper fractions:

$$\frac{5}{5} \qquad \frac{7}{4} \qquad \frac{12}{3} \qquad \frac{18}{5}$$

When the number in the numerator equals the number in the denominator, as in ⅘, the fraction equals the whole number 1. (Remember that the bar in a fraction means the same thing as a division sign, and any number divided by itself equals 1.) The fraction ⅘ means the same thing as 5 ÷ 5, and 5 ÷ 5 = 1.

These fractions all equal 1:

$$\frac{1}{1} \qquad \frac{2}{2} \qquad \frac{3}{3} \qquad \frac{100}{100} \qquad \frac{197}{197}$$

When the numerator of an improper fraction can be divided evenly by the denominator, with no remainder, the improper fraction equals a whole number.

$$\frac{12}{4} \quad \longrightarrow \quad 4\overline{)12} \atop {\phantom{4)}\underline{-12} \atop \phantom{4)}0} \quad \longrightarrow \quad \text{So, } \frac{12}{4} = 3$$

# Mixed Numbers

When the numerator of an improper fraction cannot be divided evenly by the denominator, the fraction cannot be written as a whole number. Instead, it must be written as a mixed number, which we started learning about in Year 4. Mixed numbers have one part that's a whole number and one part that's a fraction.

These are all mixed numbers:

$$2\tfrac{2}{3} \qquad\qquad 5\tfrac{1}{4} \qquad\qquad 1\tfrac{1}{6}$$

The improper fraction ¹⁸⁄₅ can be written as a mixed number.

Remember that ¹⁸⁄₅ means 18 ÷ 5. If you solve this division problem, you will get a whole number and a remainder.

$$
\begin{array}{r}
3 \text{ R3} \\
5{\overline{\smash{\big)}\,18}} \\
-15 \\
\hline
3
\end{array}
$$

¹⁸⁄₅ is the same as the mixed number 3³⁄₅. To write the remainder as a fraction instead of 'R3', use the remainder (3) as the numerator of the fraction and the divisor (5) as the denominator of the fraction. A remainder always shows that there is a fractional part left over after a division. The answer to every division problem you have solved that had a remainder could be written as a whole number plus a fraction.

Improper fractions can always be written as either whole numbers or mixed numbers. Take a look at the improper fractions below. Which ones can be written as whole numbers? Which ones can only be written as mixed numbers?

$$\frac{9}{9} \qquad \frac{8}{3} \qquad \frac{8}{2} \qquad \frac{16}{5}$$

## Equivalent Fractions

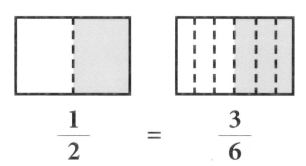

$$\frac{1}{2} = \frac{3}{6}$$

In Year 4, we saw that even if two fractions have different numbers in the numerator and denominator, they can name the same amount. Such fractions are called *equivalent* fractions.

You can make an equivalent fraction by multiplying or dividing both the numerator and the denominator by the same number. Here are two examples:

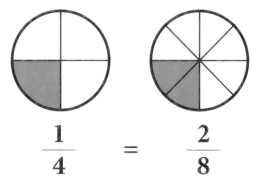

$$\frac{1}{4} = \frac{2}{8}$$

Multiply the numerator and denominator by 2.

$$\frac{1}{4} = \frac{1 \times 2}{4 \times 2} = \frac{2}{8}$$

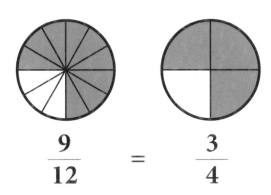

$$\frac{9}{12} = \frac{3}{4}$$

Divide the numerator and denominator by 3.

$$\frac{9}{12} = \frac{9 \div 3}{12 \div 3} = \frac{3}{4}$$

Can you work out what should go in place of the question mark in the problems below?

$$\frac{2}{3} = \frac{?}{12} \qquad \frac{3}{4} = \frac{?}{100} \qquad \frac{8}{16} = \frac{1}{?}$$

## Putting Fractions in their Lowest Terms

A fraction is in its lowest terms when its numerator and denominator have no common factor greater than 1; in other words, when no number larger than 1 can divide into both the numerator and denominator without a remainder. So, to put a fraction in its lowest terms, divide the numerator and denominator by common factors, until there is no common factor left greater than one.

Here is an example. Put ⅜ in its lowest terms. You can divide both 3 and 9 by 3. They have 3 as a common factor.

$$\frac{3}{9} = \frac{3 \div 3}{9 \div 3} = \frac{1}{3}$$

1 and 3 have no common factor greater than 1. Therefore, $\frac{1}{3}$ is in its lowest terms.

Now try putting $\frac{12}{18}$ in its lowest terms. You can divide both 12 and 18 by 2.

$$\frac{12}{18} = \frac{12 \div 2}{18 \div 2} = \frac{6}{9}$$

But you can go further. You can divide both 6 and 9 by 3.

$$\frac{6 \div 3}{9 \div 3} = \frac{2}{3}$$

There are no more common factors greater than 1.

$$\frac{12}{18} = \frac{6}{9} = \frac{2}{3}$$

$\frac{2}{3}$ is the only one of these equivalent fractions that is written in its lowest terms. You could have done this problem in one step by noticing that 12 and 18 have 6 as a common factor. 6 is the greatest common factor of 12 and 18.

$$\frac{12 \div 6}{18 \div 6} = \frac{2}{3}$$

When you divide the numerator and denominator by their greatest common factor, you put a fraction into its lowest terms in one step.

## Comparing Fractions

You can compare two fractions with the same denominator by comparing their numerators. For example, the fractions $\frac{2}{6}$, $\frac{4}{6}$ and $\frac{5}{6}$ have a common denominator.

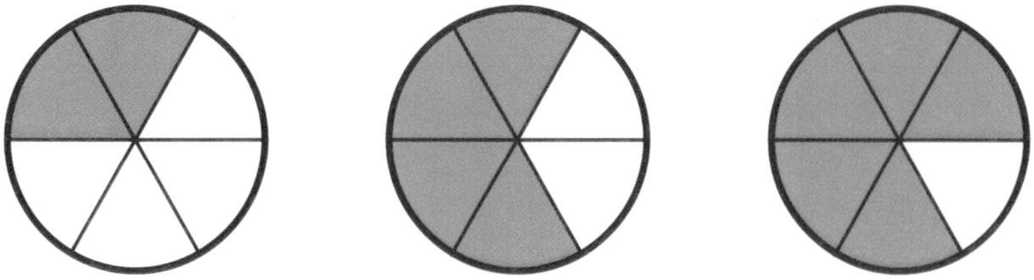

$$\frac{2}{6} < \frac{4}{6} < \frac{5}{6} \text{ because } 2 < 4 < 5$$

To compare fractions with different denominators, you must first give them a common denominator. Once their denominators are the same, you can easily compare them. Which fraction is larger, $\frac{2}{3}$ or $\frac{3}{6}$ ?

First, you need to find the equivalent fraction for $\frac{2}{3}$ with a denominator of 6. You can make an equivalent fraction by multiplying the numerator and the denominator by the same number.

$$\frac{2}{3} = \frac{?}{6}$$

Ask yourself, what do I need to multiply my denominator 3 by to get 6? The answer is 2, because $3 \times 2 = 6$. Now you can find the equivalent fraction by multiplying both the numerator and the denominator by 2.

$$\frac{2}{3} = \frac{2 \times 2}{3 \times 2} = \frac{4}{6}$$

Therefore, $\frac{2}{3}$ is equivalent to $\frac{4}{6}$.

You can now compare $\frac{2}{3}$ and $\frac{3}{6}$ because you have common denominators.

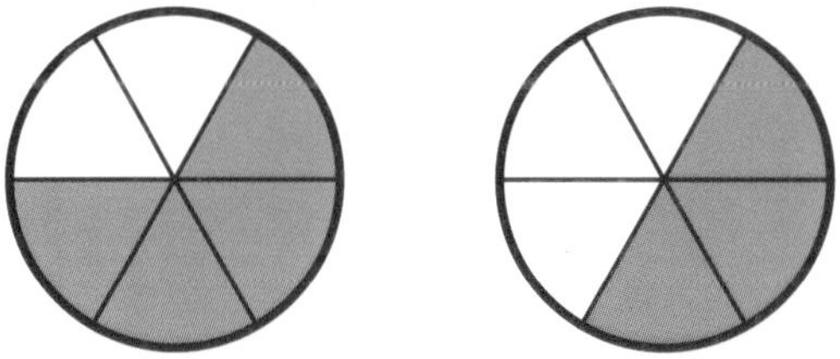

Since 4 is greater than 3, the fraction $\frac{4}{6}$, or $\frac{2}{3}$, is greater than $\frac{3}{6}$. Can you compare $\frac{3}{6}$ and $\frac{5}{12}$? Which fraction is larger?

# Adding Fractions

You can add fractions with the same denominator by adding the numerators. You write each sum in its lowest terms.

$$\frac{2}{5} + \frac{1}{5} = \frac{3}{5} \qquad\qquad \frac{4}{9} + \frac{3}{9} = \frac{7}{9}$$

Be sure to add only the numerators. The denominators stay the same. The picture below shows why. You are adding the equal parts shown in each numerator. You are not changing the size of the equal parts shown in the denominator.

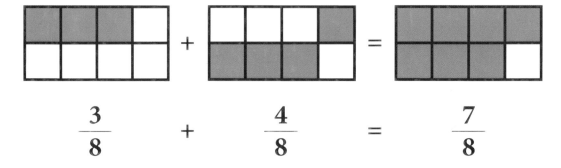

$$\frac{3}{8} \qquad + \qquad \frac{4}{8} \qquad = \qquad \frac{7}{8}$$

Practise adding fractions that have the same denominator. Make sure to write the sum in its lowest terms. If the sum is an improper fraction, write it as a whole number or a mixed number in its lowest terms. Here are three examples.

$$\frac{5}{9} + \frac{7}{9} = \frac{12}{9} = 1\frac{1}{3} \qquad\qquad \frac{5}{12} + \frac{1}{12} = \frac{6}{12} = \frac{1}{2}$$

$$\frac{7}{13} + \frac{6}{13} = \frac{13}{13} = 1$$

# Subtracting Fractions

You can subtract two fractions that have the same denominator by subtracting the numerators. The denominators remain the same. Here is an example:

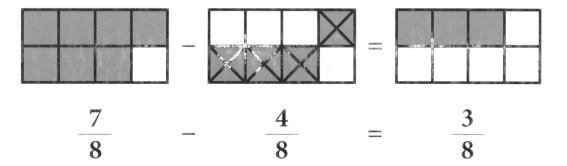

$$\frac{7}{8} - \frac{4}{8} = \frac{3}{8}$$

When you subtract fractions, make sure to write the difference in its lowest terms. Here are two examples.

$$\frac{5}{16} - \frac{3}{16} = \frac{2}{16} = \frac{1}{8} \qquad \frac{5}{12} - \frac{5}{12} = \frac{0}{12} = 0$$

Notice that $\frac{0}{12} = 0$

All fractions with a numerator of 0 equal 0.

## Expressing Simple Outcomes

Sometimes we use fractions to express simple outcomes. For instance, suppose you were at Wembley Stadium and took a survey to see how many fans at a football match were rooting for England and how many for the visitors. After asking a lot of people, you found that for every 4 fans you asked, 3 supported England and only 1  supported the visitors. You could use fractions to explain these outcomes. You might say that ¾ of the crowd was rooting for the home team and only ¼ for the visitors.

Suppose there are 25 students in your class, 15 girls and 10 boys. That means ¹⁵⁄₂₅ of the class are girls. Can you put that fraction in its lowest terms? What fraction, in its lowest terms, would tell what proportion of the class is boys?

# Decimals

We learnt in Year 4 that you can write the fraction ⅒ as the decimal 0.1. They both mean the same thing – one tenth. You also say the decimal is 'nought point one', or just 'point one'. *Nought* is another word for zero. The dot to the left of the 1 is called a *decimal point*. The decimal point shows that the value of the digits to its right is anywhere between 0 and 1, like a fraction. A *decimal* is any number that uses places to the right of the decimal point to show a fraction. The first place to the right of the decimal point is the tenths place.

You can write the mixed number 1⅞₀ as the decimal 1.7. They both mean the same thing: one and seven tenths. You can also say the decimal is 'one point seven'.

| ones | . | tenths |
|------|---|--------|
| 1 | . | 7 |

The second place to the right of the decimal point is the hundredths place. ⅟₁₀₀ can also be written 0.01, 'nought point nought one'. Sometimes you will hear people say 'point O one'. We can understand what they mean but it is a good habit to use 'nought' or 'zero'. 0 is a digit, not a letter, even though it looks like the letter O.

So, ⅟₁₀₀ and 0.01 both mean the same thing: one hundredth.

$$\frac{1}{100} =$$

$$2\frac{47}{100} =$$

| ones | . | tenths | hundredths |
|------|---|--------|------------|
| 0 | . | 0 | 1 |
| 2 | . | 4 | 7 |

2⁴⁷⁄₁₀₀ and 2.47 both mean the same thing but we read the mixed number as 'two and forty-seven hundredths' and the decimal as 'two point four seven'.

Notice that when there are both tenths and hundredths in a decimal, you read the tenths and hundredths together in terms of hundredths. Also remember to put an 'and' between the whole number part and the fractional part of a decimal, just as in mixed numbers.

The third place to the right of the decimal point is the thousandths place. You can write ⅟₁₀₀₀ as 0.001. They both mean the same thing: one thousandth.

| ones | . | tenths | hundredths | thousandths |
|------|---|--------|------------|-------------|
| 0 | . | 0 | 0 | 1 |

Notice that as you move from the left to the right, each place value gets 10 times smaller: first tenths, then hundredths, then thousandths. In the decimal system, each place has a value one-tenth as large as the one to its left.

$$3\frac{857}{1000} = 3.857$$

You understand both as three and eight hundred and fifty-seven thousandths. Notice that, because there are thousandths in the decimal, you read the tenths and hundredths in terms of thousandths.

## Reading and Writing Decimals

Practise writing decimals in words. 0.27 is twenty-seven hundredths; 3.8 is three and eight tenths. Also practise writing decimals that are in words with digits. Five hundred and one and fourteen hundredths is 501.14. Three hundred and fifty-four thousandths is 0.354. But it could also be interpreted as 300.054. Can you write seven hundred and eleven thousandths in two ways? When the meaning isn't clear, you need to add extra words, such as 'seven hundred *units* and eleven thousandths' for 700.011 or '*the fraction* seven hundred and eleven thousandths' for 0.711.

Practise writing decimals in expanded form.

$$176.04 \text{ is } 100 + 70 + 6 + 0.04.$$

What is $600 + 40 + 0.7 + 0.08$?

## Decimals as Fractions

You can write decimals as fractions and fractions as decimals. $\frac{39}{100}$ can be written as 0.39; and 0.02 can be written $\frac{2}{100}$. Rewrite $\frac{25}{100}$ and $\frac{101}{1000}$ as decimals. Now rewrite 0.16 and 0.599 as fractions. Are you ready for something more challenging? Find the decimal equivalents of the fractions that follow. You'll need to convert the fractions to equivalents with a denominator of 100.

$$\frac{1}{2} \qquad \frac{1}{4} \qquad \frac{1}{10}$$

Now try ⅛. That one needs a denominator of 1000

Now let's go the other way. Convert these decimals to fractions, in their lowest terms:

0.25      0.75      0.050      0.875

## Reading Decimals on a Number Line

We can show decimals on a number line.

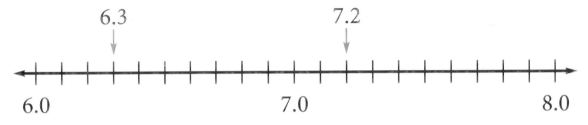

On this number line, each mark shows a tenth. The first arrow is at 6.3, three tenths past 6. The second arrow is at 7.2. You can see from the number line that 7.2 > 6.3.

## Rounding Decimals

You round decimals the same way you round whole numbers. To decide whether to round a decimal up or down, look at the digit to the right of the place to which you are rounding.

Round 6.85 to the nearest tenth. The tenths place is also called the first decimal place. Look at the digit to the right of the 8 in the tenths place. It's a 5, so round up to 6.9.

Round 7.453 to the nearest hundredth. That is the second decimal place. Look at the digit to the right of the 5 in the hundredths place. It's a 3, so round down to 7.45.

Rounding a decimal to the nearest whole number means rounding it to the ones place, so that there is no fractional part left. Round 76.47 to the nearest whole number. Look at the digit to the right of the ones place. Four is less than five. 76.4 is closer to 76 than 77. So round down to 76.

## Comparing Decimals

Remember that when you compare numbers, you start with their greatest place values. Compare 7.77 and 7.82.

| ones | . | tenths | hundredths |
|:---:|:---:|:---:|:---:|
| 7 | . | 7 | 7 |
| 7 | . | 8 | 2 |

$$7 = 7 \qquad 0.7 < 0.8$$

First, compare the ones: 7 = 7. Next, compare the tenths: 0.7 < 0.8. So 7.77 < 7.82

Compare 7.77 and 7.7. Remember that you can write 7.7 as 7.70. Then you can compare 7.77 and 7.70. Compare the ones: 7 = 7. Compare the tenths: 0.7 = 0.7. Compare the hundredths: 0.07 > 0.00, so 7.77 > 7.7

Practise comparing decimals in problems like these. Remember that you can add zeros to the end of decimals without changing their value.

## Comparing Decimals and Fractions

You can also compare decimals and fractions. For example, compare $1\frac{7}{10}$ and 1.15. First rewrite the mixed number $1\frac{7}{10}$ as a decimal: 1.7. Now compare 1.7 and 1.15. Compare the ones: 1 = 1. Compare the tenths: 0.7 > 0.1. So 1.70 > 1.15

Which is greater, ¼ or 0.27? Hint: convert 0.27 to a fraction and then convert ¼ to a fraction with the same denominator.

## Adding and Subtracting Decimals

You add and subtract decimals the same way that you add and subtract whole numbers. You must make sure the decimal points and the place values are lined up correctly. Line up the tenths with the tenths, the hundredths with the hundredths and the thousandths with the thousandths. Here are two examples:

Add 0.167 and 2.346

$$
\begin{array}{r}
0.167 \\
+\ 2.346 \\
\hline
2.513
\end{array}
$$

Make sure you put the decimal point in your answer.

Subtract 1.846 from 5.072.

4 10 6 12

$$
\begin{array}{r}
5.0\!\!\!/7\!\!\!/2 \\
-1.846 \\
\hline
3.226
\end{array}
$$

Make sure you put the decimal point in your answer.

Sometimes it is helpful to put in zeros when you are adding decimals to help you line up the place values correctly. It is not necessary to add zeros, however, as long as you can keep the place values straight.

$$\text{Add } 9.307 + 8 + 0.53 + 6.2$$

One way is to put in decimal points and zeros:

$$\begin{array}{r} 9.307 \\ 8.000 \\ 0.530 \\ + \; 6.200 \\ \hline 24.037 \end{array}$$

Another way is to leave the numbers as they are. Think hard about 8:

$$\begin{array}{r} 9.307 \\ 8 \\ 0.53 \\ + \; 6.2 \\ \hline 24.037 \end{array}$$

When you subtract decimals, often you must put in zeros. Here is an example. When you subtract 2.63 from 5, you *must* write 5 with a decimal point and two zeros, to match 2.63. Then subtract.

$$\begin{array}{r} {\scriptstyle 4\;\;9\;10} \\ 5.00 \\ - \; 2.63 \\ \hline 2.37 \end{array}$$

## Giving Change

We express pounds and pence using decimals. We write three pounds and forty-five pence like this:

$$£3.45$$

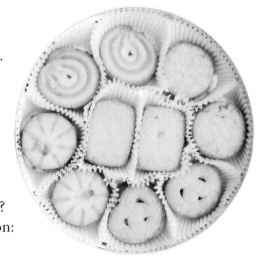

Suppose you are selling biscuits to raise money for your favourite club. Each box of biscuits costs £2.75. A man gives you £5.00 for one box. How much change should you give him? Line up the decimal points and do the subtraction:

$$£5.00$$
$$- £2.75$$
$$\overline{£2.25}$$

You should give the customer two pounds and 25 pence in change. You could give him two pound coins, a twenty pence piece and a five pence piece; or two pound coins and twenty-five pennies.

## Multiplying Decimals

$$\begin{array}{r} 17 \\ \times\ 3 \\ \hline 51 \end{array}$$

You have practised multiplication many times. This calculation is nothing new.

How is it different if the first factor is a decimal?

$$1.7 \times 3 = ?$$

It is the same calculation but the place values change.

| tens | ones | . | tenths |
|------|------|---|--------|
| 0 | 1 | . | 7 |
| 0 | 3 | . | 0 |

First, write the problem in columns:

$$\begin{array}{r} 1.7 \\ \times\ 3 \\ \hline \end{array}$$

The decimal point in the product goes under the decimal point in the factors.

$$\begin{array}{r} 1.7 \\ \times\ 3 \\ \hline \end{array}$$

When you multiply by ones, you multiply 3 ones by 7 tenths. This is 21 tenths, or 2 ones and 1 tenth. Write the 1 tenth directly underneath the first factor (7 tenths) and carry the 2 ones.

$$\begin{array}{r} 2 \\ 1.7 \\ \times\ \ 3 \\ \hline .1 \end{array}$$

Next, work from right to left as usual.

$$\begin{array}{r} 2 \\ 1.7 \\ \times\ \ 3 \\ \hline 5.1 \end{array}$$

Have a look again at these two examples:

$$\begin{array}{r} 17 \\ \times\ \ 3 \\ \hline 51 \end{array} \qquad\qquad \begin{array}{r} 1.7 \\ \times\ 3 \\ \hline 5.1 \end{array}$$

The only difference is place value. 1.7 has the same digits as 17, but shifted one place to the right. The same happens to the product.

Moving a factor's digits to the right is the same as dividing by 10. If you divide a factor by 10, you will also divide the product by 10.

Here's one more example, then it's your turn. $2.5 \times 6 = ?$

$$\begin{array}{r} 2.5 \\ \times\ 6 \\ \hline . \end{array} \qquad\qquad \begin{array}{r} 3 \\ 2.5 \\ \times\ 6 \\ \hline .0 \end{array}$$

Notice that you started putting the product in the tenths column, but 30 tenths is the same as 3 ones and 0 tenths.

$$\begin{array}{r} 3 \\ 2.5 \\ \times\ 6 \\ \hline 15.0 \end{array}$$

How does that compare with $25 \times 6$?

Try these:

$$1.3 \times 3 = ? \qquad 6.1 \times 4 = ? \qquad 9.5 \times 6 = ?$$

The method works for hundredths as well, so you can multiply with two decimal places, for tenths and hundredths.

$$1.24 \times 4 = ?$$

Write it vertically, with the decimal points in line.

$$
\begin{array}{r}
1.24 \\
\times\, 4 \\
\hline
\phantom{0}.\phantom{0}
\end{array}
$$

Multiplying by ones, start writing the product in the same column as the factor, working from right to left.

$$
\begin{array}{r}
1 \\
1.24 \\
\times\, 4 \\
\hline
.\,6
\end{array}
\qquad\qquad
\begin{array}{r}
1 \\
1.24 \\
\times\, 4 \\
\hline
4.96
\end{array}
$$

As a check, try rounding to the nearest one.

$$1 \times 4 < 1.24 \times 4 < 2 \times 4$$

$$4 < 4.96 < 8$$

Can you work these out?

$$2.33 \times 3 \qquad 5.62 \times 5 \qquad 4.99 \times 4$$

## Multiplying with Money

You should just have calculated that

$$4.99 \times 4 = 19.96$$

Does 4.99 look familiar? How about £4.99? It is a price tag on many things in shops. You have learnt that it means 4 pounds and 99 pennies. Is it closer to 4 pounds or to 5 pounds?

If you need to multiply money, treat it as a decimal with two decimal places and include a £ sign.

$$
\begin{array}{r}
3\,3 \\
£4.99 \\
\times \quad 4 \\
\hline
£19.96
\end{array}
$$

Can you think of a quick way to check that? £4.99 is a penny less than five pounds. 1p = £0.01. You have learnt that:

$$4 \times (£5 - 1p)$$
$$= (4 \times £5) - (4 \times 1p)$$
$$= £20 - 4p$$

The product should be 4p less than £20. Is it?

# Dividing by 10 or 100 or 1,000 with Whole Numbers and Decimals

You have looked at multiplying by ten already. Everything is done by changing place value. The digits move one place to the left. Ones become tens. Tens become hundreds. Hundreds become thousands. If you start with a whole number, you add a zero in the ones place.

$$
\begin{array}{r}
234 \\
\times \quad 10 \\
\hline
2,340
\end{array}
$$

If you multiply a decimal by 10, then the tenths move up into the ones place and any hundredths move into the tenths place.

$$
\begin{array}{r}
246.53 \\
\times \quad 10 \\
\hline
2,465.3
\end{array}
$$

Multiplying by 100, everything moves two places. Multiplying by 1,000 moves three places.

$$\begin{array}{r} 12 \\ \times\ 100 \\ \hline 1,200 \end{array} \qquad \begin{array}{r} 135.42 \\ \times\ 1,000 \\ \hline 135,420 \end{array}$$

Try some examples for practice:

| | | |
|---|---|---|
| $1 \times 100$ | $34 \times 10$ | $3.4 \times 100$ |
| $2.1 \times 100$ | $9.53 \times 10$ | $3 \times 1,000$ |
| $19 \times 100$ | $9.53 \times 1,000$ | $6.43 \times 1,000$ |

Division is just the same but in reverse. The decimal point stays where it is, the digits move to the right. For ten they move one place. Use decimals if you need them.

$$10\overline{)2{,}340} = 234 \qquad 10\overline{)2{,}465.3} = 246.53$$

To divide by 100, move the digits two places to the right. For dividing by 1,000, move three places. Think about the decimal places if you need them.

$$100\overline{)1{,}200} = 12 \qquad 1{,}000\overline{)135{,}420} = 135.42$$

Did you notice that, when dividing by 1,000, the digits after the comma are now on the right of the decimal point?

Try some examples:

| | | |
|---|---|---|
| $100 \div 100$ | $340 \div 10$ | $340 \div 100$ |
| $210 \div 100$ | $95.3 \div 10$ | $3,000 \div 1,000$ |
| $1,900 \div 100$ | $9,530 \div 1,000$ | $6,430 \div 1,000$ |

# Per Cent

The term *per cent* means 'per hundred'. For example, 40 per cent means ⁴⁰⁄₁₀₀ or 40 out of 100. The symbol % stands for per cent. You write 11 out of 100 as 11%. A number written per cent is called a *percentage*.

Often a percentage is a part of a whole. The whole is 100%. If 45% of a Year 5 class are boys, then 55% of the class are not boys. They are girls. 100% of the class are either boys or girls.

> Do you remember the Roman numeral for 100? It's C, which stands for *centum* in Latin, which can help you remember that a percentage is a fraction of 100.

| Boys | | Girls | | Whole Class |
|------|---|-------|---|-------------|
| 45% | + | 55% | = | 100% |

$$\frac{45}{100} + \frac{55}{100} = \frac{100}{100}$$

Notice that 100% = ¹⁰⁰⁄₁₀₀ = 1. 100% means 'all the parts'. For example, if 100% of your friends came to a party, they all came.

## Percentages and Fractions

Remember that a percentage is always in hundredths. So to write a percentage as a fraction, write the percentage over a denominator of 100. Then reduce the fraction to lowest terms.

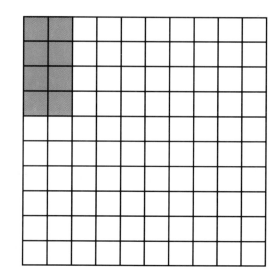

8% or ²⁄₂₅ of the square is shaded.

What would 35% be, written as a fraction in lowest terms?

To write a fraction as a percentage, first write an equivalent fraction that has a denominator of 100. Then you can write the percentage.

$$\frac{1}{4} = \frac{1 \times 25}{4 \times 25} = \frac{25}{100} = 25\%$$

## Percentages and Decimals

To write a percentage as a decimal, remember that a percentage is always in hundredths. 35 per cent is the same as 35 hundredths, and 8 per cent is the same as 8 hundredths.

$$35\% = \frac{35}{100} = 0.35$$

$$8\% = \frac{8}{100} = 0.08$$

To write a decimal as a percentage, think of the decimal in hundredths. Then you can write it as a percentage. 7 tenths (0.7) is the same as 70 hundredths (0.70), which is the same as 70%.

$$0.7 = 0.70 = \frac{70}{100} = 70\%$$

$$0.04 = \frac{4}{100} = 4\%$$

A quick way to write a decimal as a percentage is to multiply the decimal by 100. This method works because percentages are already in hundredths.

$$0.70 \times 100 = 70 \qquad 0.70 = 70\%$$
$$0.04 \times 100 = 4 \qquad 0.04 = 04\% = 4\%$$

A quick way to write a percentage as a decimal is to divide by 100.

$$35\% = \frac{35}{100} = 0.35$$

$$8\% = \frac{8}{100} = 0.08$$

Hint: to divide by 100, keep the decimal point where it is and move the numbers two places to the right.

$$\begin{array}{r} 0.08 \\ 100\overline{)8.00} \end{array}$$

## Writing Fractions, Decimals or Percentages

Fractions, decimals and percentages are often used interchangeably: people sometimes use a fraction, sometimes a decimal or sometimes a percentage to mean the same thing.

For example, we might say 25% of Jim's marbles are red, or ¼ of Jim's marbles are red, or 0.25 of Jim's marble collection is red.

$$25\% = \frac{1}{4} = 0.25$$

Since we are talking about a part of a whole, we could also say that 75% of Jim's marbles are not red, or ¾ of Jim's marbles are not red, or 0.75 of Jim's marble collection is not red.

$$75\% = \frac{3}{4} = 0.75$$

Practise writing statements like these for problems like '40% of the pizza was pepperoni'.

Also learn to complete a table like the one on the next page, writing a number as a fraction, a decimal or a percentage.

| Fraction | Decimal | Percentage |
|----------|---------|------------|
| ⅕ | | |
| | 0.1 | |
| | | 65% |
| | 0.5 | |

You may want to memorise the percent equivalents of some common fractions:

¼ is 25%

½ is 50%

⅒ is 10%

# Measurement

## Measuring Length in Metric Units

In the United Kingdom, we often use metric units to measure things. In Europe, people almost always use this system, too. Some important metric units for measuring length are shown below:

1 centimetre (cm) = 10 millimetres (mm)

1 metre (m) = 1,000 millimetres (mm)

1 metre (m) = 100 centimetres (cm)

1 kilometre (km) = 1,000 metres (m)

A ruler is typically divided into centimetres and millimetres. Can you measure the paper clip here?

The paper clip is about 4 centimetres long, or 40 millimetres long. Since there are 10 millimetres per centimetre, you multiply by ten to convert 4 cm into 40 mm.

Now gather some small objects around your home and measure them to the nearest tenth of a centimetre, or to the nearest millimetre.

Because the metric system is based on the decimal system, it is easy to change from one metric unit to another. It's like working with place value. Here are two examples:

1. How many metres are there in 3 kilometres? Since 1 km = 1,000 m, multiply by 1,000 to change kilometres to metres. 3 × 1,000 = 3,000. So 3 km = 3,000 m.

2. How many metres are there in 400 centimetres? Since 100 cm = 1 m, you divide by 100 to change centimetres to metres. 400 ÷ 100 = 4, so 400 cm = 4 m.

## Measuring Length in Imperial Units

In the UK, we sometimes measure length using imperial units: inches, feet, yards and miles. The following chart shows you the imperial units and their abbreviations. It also shows some *equivalences* among the units. An equivalence shows that two things that appear different are really of equal value.

$$1 \text{ foot (ft)} = 12 \text{ inches (in)}$$
$$1 \text{ yard (yd)} = 3 \text{ feet}$$
$$1 \text{ mile} = 5{,}280 \text{ feet}$$
$$1 \text{ mile} = 1{,}760 \text{ yards}$$

A yard is a bit shorter than a metre. A ruler often measures one foot. To help you measure lengths more quickly, many rulers have lines that mark the inches and fractions of an inch.

The longest lines on the ruler mark the inches and the half (½) inches. The lines marking each quarter (¼) of an inch are a bit shorter, and the lines for the eighths (⅛) are even shorter. The shortest marks on many rulers mark sixteenths of an inch (¹⁄₁₆).

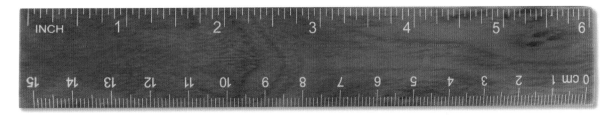

Notice that only the inches are labelled. You have to be able to recognise the halves, quarters and eighths.

When measuring the length of a real object, we often estimate to the nearest unit. Look at the screw in the picture.

To the nearest inch, the screw is 2 inches.

To the nearest half inch, the screw is 1½ inches.

To the nearest quarter inch, the screw is 1¾ inches.

To the nearest eighth of an inch, the screw is 1⅝ inches.

The smaller the unit of measure, the more precise your measurement of the length of the screw will be.

Find some more small items around your home and measure them to the nearest eighth of an inch using the ruler above or a ruler of your own.

It's also helpful to practise converting from one unit to another. For instance, you should be able to work out how many feet there are in half a mile. You know from the table of equivalences that 1 mile equals 5,280 feet. To find ½ of any number, you divide it by 2.

$5{,}280 \div 2 = 2{,}640$, so half a mile equals 2,640 ft. How many feet are in a quarter of a mile?

You should memorise the equivalences listed in this book. That way you can switch from one unit to another without having to look at a table.

## Measuring Weight in Metric Units

The main units for weight in the metric system are the milligram, the gram and the kilogram. Here are some equivalences:

$$1 \text{ gram (g)} = 1{,}000 \text{ milligrams (mg)}$$

$$1 \text{ kilogram (kg)} = 1{,}000 \text{ grams}$$

Notice again how the metric system is based on the decimal system, with each unit 10 times, 100 times or 1,000 times larger than another unit. There are 1,000 grams in a kilogram. You could also say that one gram equals 1/1000th of a kilogram.

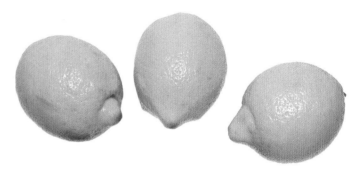

If one lemon weighs 40 grams, how much would three lemons weigh? Multiply 40 g by three, or 40 × 3 = 120 g. How many milligrams is this? 120 g × 1,000 = 120,000 mg.

If one egg weighs 84 grams, how much would a dozen eggs weigh? To find the answer, you multiply 84 by a dozen, or 12.

84 × 12 = 1,008 grams.

How else could you say that? One kilogram and eight grams.

## Measuring Weight in Imperial Units

In the UK, we sometimes measure weight using ounces, pounds, stones, hundredweight and tons.

$$1 \text{ pound (lb)} = 16 \text{ ounces (oz)}$$

$$1 \text{ stone} = 14 \text{ pounds}$$

$$1 \text{ hundredweight (cwt)} = 8 \text{ stone}$$

$$1 \text{ ton (t)} = 20 \text{ hundredweight}$$

$$1 \text{ ton} = 2{,}240 \text{ pounds}$$

What unit of measurement would you use to measure the following? Match these items with the best unit of measurement for them.

Pounds and ounces

Tons

Stones

Hundredweight

*Newborn baby*

*Toddler*

*Three Sacks of Potatoes*

*Cargo in a lorry*

When a baby is born, we usually describe its weight in pounds and ounces, like 8 pounds, 3 ounces. When a child gets older and bigger, we usually express his or her weight in pounds and stone, estimating to the nearest pound. We might use hundredweight for a sack of potatoes or tons if we were measuring the amount of cargo a lorry or an aeroplane can transport.

If you have bathroom scales at home you can practise weighing household items in pounds. First weigh yourself. Then weigh yourself holding an object. The difference between what you weigh holding the object and what you weigh by yourself is the weight of the object.

Practise converting from pounds to ounces and ounces to pounds. How many ounces does the newborn baby weigh if she weighs 8 lb, 3 oz? To solve this problem, find out how many ounces are in 8 pounds, and then add 3 ounces. From the table of equivalences you know that 1 pound = 16 ounces.

So 8 pounds would be 8 × 16 ounces.
8 lb 3 oz = (16 × 8) oz + 3 oz
= 128 oz + 3 oz
= 131 oz

How many pounds are there in a hundredweight of potatoes? It is 8 stones, with 14 pounds in each stone, so 14 × 8. Is that about a hundred?

## Measuring Capacity in Metric Units

Here are the metric units for capacity, or volume:

1 centilitre (cl) = 10 millilitres (ml)
1 litre = 1,000 millilitres (ml)
1 litre = 100 centilitres (cl)

If you had a one-litre jug of water and you poured half of it into a vase, how many millilitres would be left?

If your teapot holds 750 ml of tea and you serve yourself and your mum 250 ml of tea each, how much tea will you have left in centilitres?

# Measuring Capacity in Imperial Units

When we prepare food, we often use measuring jugs that have scales showing how much of an ingredient we are pouring. When you buy milk or juice, you often buy a pint or two. These measurements tell how much liquid is inside.

Here are the equivalences for the imperial measurements of capacity.

<h2 style="text-align:center">1 pint (pt) =<br>20 fluid ounces (fl oz)</h2>

<h2 style="text-align:center">1 gallon (gal) = 8 pints</h2>

This measuring jug shows litres and millilitres on the left and fluid ounces and pints on the right. How many fluid ounces of milk are in the measuring jug? About how much is this in pints?

# Adding and Subtracting with Different Units

When you add or subtract lengths that are in different imperial units, you need to regroup in different ways.

Imagine you have two wooden sticks. One is 3 ft 7 in (3' 7") and one is 2 ft 8 in (2' 8"). How far would they reach if you glued them together end-to-end?

*Add the inches first,*

*regroup 15 in as 1 ft 3 in,*

*then write the 3 below and carry the 1*

```
  1
  3 ft  7 in
+ 2 ft  8 in
_____
        15
  6 ft  3 in
```

Imagine you need to plug a television into a socket that is 21 feet 4 inches away but the cable you have is only 15 feet 9 inches in length. How long an extension lead do you need to connect the television to the socket?

*You can't take 9 in from 4 in.*

*Regroup 21 ft 4 in as 20 ft 16 in.*

```
 20      16
 2̶1̶ ft  4̶ in
-15 ft   9 in
_____
  5 ft   7 in
```

You can also regroup in the same way to add or subtract feet and yards, or yards and miles.

When you add metric measurements, you write the measurements in the same unit first. To add 2.68 litres and 27 millilitres, you can write both measurements in either litres or millilitres.

$$27 \text{ ml} = 0.027 \text{ l}$$
$$2.68 \text{ l} = 2{,}680 \text{ ml}$$

$$
\begin{array}{r}
2.68 \text{ l} \\
+\ 0.027 \text{ l} \\
\hline
2.707 \text{ l}
\end{array}
\qquad\qquad
\begin{array}{r}
2{,}680 \text{ ml} \\
+\ \ 27 \text{ ml} \\
\hline
2{,}707 \text{ ml}
\end{array}
$$

Always convert metric measurements into the same units before you add them.

## Changing Units of Time

There are 24 hours in a day, 60 minutes in an hour, and 60 seconds in a minute. So how many minutes are there in 5 hours and 11 minutes? To find out the answer to this question, first multiply 5 by 60 to find out how many minutes are in 5 hours. Then add 11 minutes. $(5 \times 60) + 11 = 300 + 11$. There are 311 minutes in 5 hours and 11 minutes.

If Jacob swam one lap of the pool in 147 seconds, what was his time in minutes and seconds?

## Adding and Subtracting Time

When you add and subtract time, you may need to regroup, but in a different way. Instead of regrouping so that 10 ones make 1 ten, when you add hours and minutes, regroup 60 minutes as one hour whenever there are 60 minutes or more. Here is an example of adding two times:

If a train journey from London to Aberdeen lasts 7 hours and 45 minutes and the train leaves at 1:43 PM, when will it arrive in Aberdeen?

*hours*   *minutes*

```
  1
  1 : 43
+ 7 : 45
─────────
    : 88
  9 : 28
```

88 minutes =
1 hour 28 minutes.

Add the 1 hour to
the other hours

You add or subtract minutes and seconds in the same way. When you subtract minutes and seconds, you may need to regroup 1 minute as 60 seconds.

Emily ran a race in 37 minutes and 22 seconds. Stella ran it in 28 minutes and 47 seconds. How much less was Stella's time?

# Twenty-Four Hour Clock

You know that there are twenty-four hours in each day. When we tell the time, we can think of the twelve hours before noon (AM) and the twelve after noon (PM). We can also use the 24-hour clock that we learnt about in Year 4.

In 24-hour time, we say hours and minutes rather than minutes past or to each hour:

12-Hour Time                              24-Hour Time

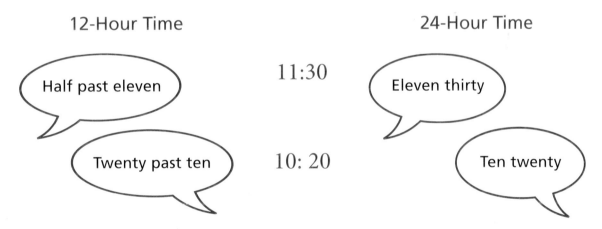

Half past eleven        11:30        Eleven thirty

Twenty past ten        10: 20        Ten twenty

If it is afternoon, we add twelve to the hours, so it is the number of complete hours since midnight.

13:00, not 1 PM. You say 'Thirteen hundred'.

18:55, not five to seven in the evening. You say 'Eighteen fifty-five'.

If it is before ten in the morning, we start with a zero, calling it 'O' like the letter O.

08:35 for twenty-five to nine in the morning. You say 'O eight thirty-five'.

00:15 for quarter past midnight. You say 'O O fifteen'.

12:15 for quarter past midday. You say 'Twelve fifteen'.

Most digital clocks show you the last whole minute, not the nearest minute, even if it is only a second until the next minute starts. If you are meeting someone at 15:00 and the clock says 14:59, you may have a whole minute or you may have only a second.

Write each of these times as they would appear on the face of a digital, twenty-four hour clock:

*Half past nine in the morning.*

*Ten minutes to midday.*

*Twelve minutes past four in the afternoon.*

*2 PM*

*Quarter past seven in the evening.*

# Geometry

## Planes, Points and Segments

A *plane* is a flat surface that keeps going on forever in all directions. It has no thickness. Here's a diagram of a plane.

Plane geometry is the study of points, lines, segments and figures that can be drawn on a plane or flat surface. Let's learn about some of these.

*This plane, labelled T, stretches in all four directions.*

Take a pencil and make the tiniest dot you can. In geometry, a tiny dot like that is called a *point*.

Now draw a second point and connect the two points with a ruler. This is called a *line segment*, or a segment. In ordinary English, we just call it a line but in maths a line has a special meaning: it goes on forever.

Points are named with letters, and so are segments. The two points in the illustration on the next page are G and H. The segment could be called either $\overline{GH}$ or $\overline{HG}$. The bar over the name tells us this is a segment.

G                                  H

## Lines and Rays

What's the difference between a line and a line segment? You know that a segment has a beginning and an end point and that, in maths, a line goes on forever in both directions. Since it's not possible to draw a line that goes on forever, we draw an arrow on both ends of a line, to show that it keeps on going in both directions. A line can be named after any two points along the line. This is line BE, or $\overleftrightarrow{BE}$.

B                                  E

A *ray* is part of a line. (You will not hear the term very often but it is useful for defining an angle.) A ray has one end point, and continues forever in only one direction away from its end point. To name a ray, begin with its end point and add another point along the ray. This is ray EF, or $\overrightarrow{EF}$.

E                              F

An angle is formed by two rays that have the same end point. The end point is called the *vertex* of the angle. Vertex is a mathematical word for a corner. Here is angle WXY.

Point X is the vertex of angle WXY. When you name an angle, you put the vertex in the middle. You can begin by naming either of the other two points, so this angle can also be called angle YXW. The word 'angle' is sometimes abbreviated like this: ∠YXW.

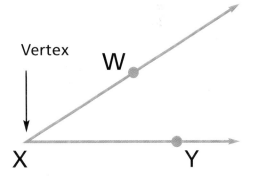

## Types of Angles

There are all sorts of angles, like right angles, acute angles and obtuse angles. Here's what they look like:

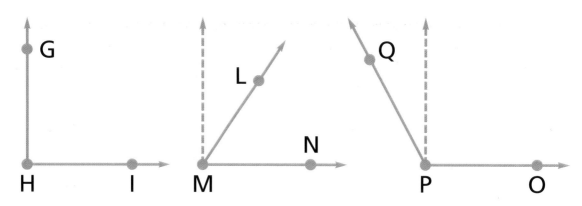

∠GHI is a right angle. A right angle *forms a square corner.*

∠LMN is an acute angle. *An acute angle is less or sharper than a right angle.*

∠QPO is an obtuse angle. *An obtuse angle is greater or wider than a right angle.*

Look around you for angles. What kind of angle does the corner of a windowpane form? How about the corner of a slice of cake?

## Intersecting, Perpendicular and Parallel Lines

When two lines meet, we say they intersect. Here are two intersecting lines.

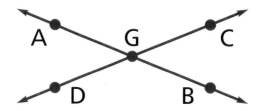

$\overleftrightarrow{DC}$ and $\overleftrightarrow{AB}$ intersect at point G.

When two lines intersect to form right angles, we say they are *perpendicular.*

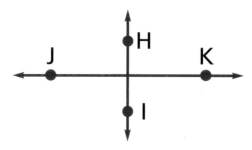

Lines $\overleftrightarrow{HI}$ and $\overleftrightarrow{JK}$ are perpendicular. Where they meet, they form 4 right angles. Lines AB and DC above are not perpendicular.

Parallel lines are lines that never intersect. They go on forever, always staying the same distance apart. Line $\overleftrightarrow{BE}$ and line $\overleftrightarrow{GH}$ are parallel lines.

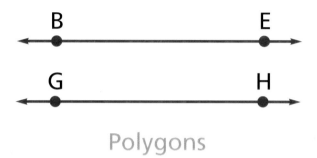

## Polygons

When sides join up to make a closed flat figure around a space, you have a polygon. Can you draw a closed figure with just one straight side? How about two? Even if you return to your starting point, all you have is a straight line segment. For a polygon, you need at least three. The name comes from a Greek word for 'many angles'.

Polygons have the same number of sides, vertices and angles. Every side makes an angle with the next side around. Every angle is positioned at a vertex.

A triangle has three angles. How many sides?

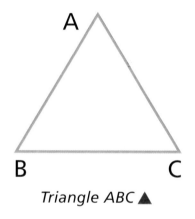

*Triangle ABC* ▲

A quadrilateral has four sides. How many angles?

*Quadrilateral DEFG* ▶

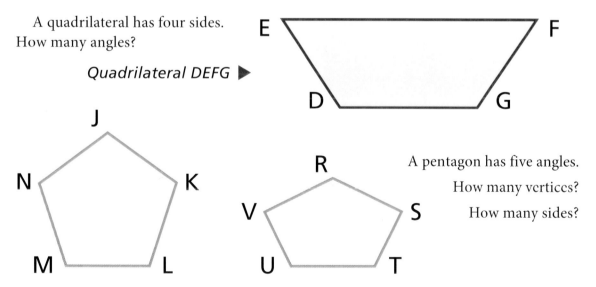

A pentagon has five angles.
How many vertices?
How many sides?

▲ *Regular pentagon JKLMN and* ▲ *irregular pentagon RSTUV*

269

We say that a polygon is *regular* when all of its angles are equal and all of its sides are the same length. An *irregular* polygon has some angles that are different or some sides that are different lengths.

To give polygons names, we put letters at the vertices. Look at triangle FGH and hexagon LMNOPQ. Can you work out what a hexagon is? It is a polygon with six sides, six vertices and six angles.

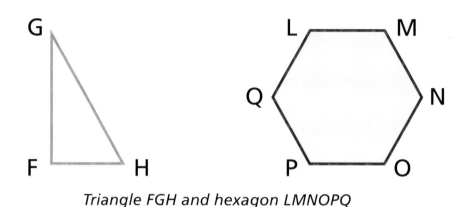

*Triangle FGH and hexagon LMNOPQ*

## Triangles

Some special kinds of triangles:

### Right-angled

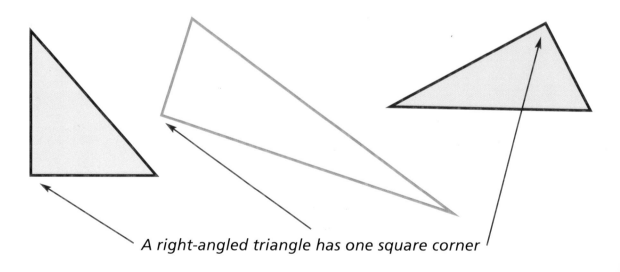

*A right-angled triangle has one square corner*

## Isosceles

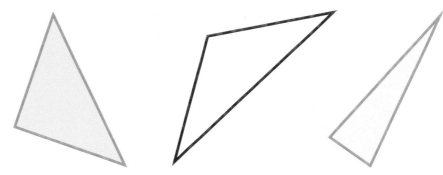

*Isosceles triangles have two sides the same and one different*

## Equilateral

The prefix 'equi-' means equal, and it can help you work out the meanings of different words. Equilateral triangles have sides that are equal lengths. What do you think equidistant means?

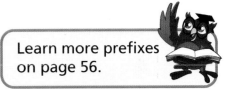

Learn more prefixes on page 56.

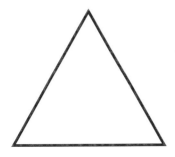 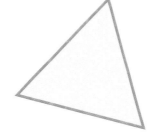 

*Equilateral triangles have all three sides the same.*

## Opposites

What do you understand by the word 'opposite'? In geometry it means on the other side of the centre. In a triangle, a side is opposite the angle made from the other two sides.

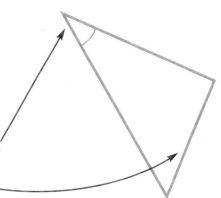

*Opposite side and angle*

In a quadrilateral, two sides are opposite if they do not share an angle and there is another side between them. Opposite angles do not have a side in common.

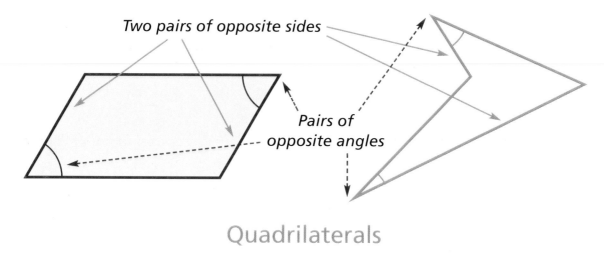

*Two pairs of opposite sides*

*Pairs of opposite angles*

## Quadrilaterals

The prefix 'quadri-' means four and 'lateral' means side. Quadrilaterals are polygons with four sides.

The figures below are quadrilaterals.

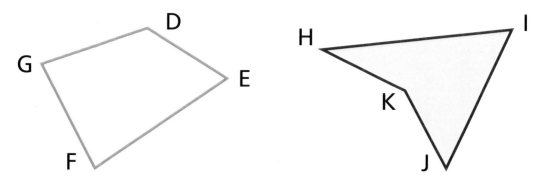

Here are some special types of quadrilaterals:

## Trapezium

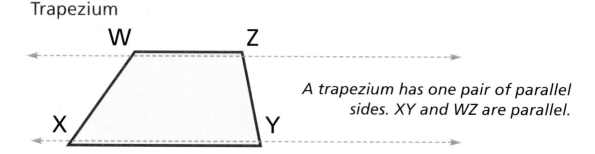

*A trapezium has one pair of parallel sides. XY and WZ are parallel.*

# Parallelogram

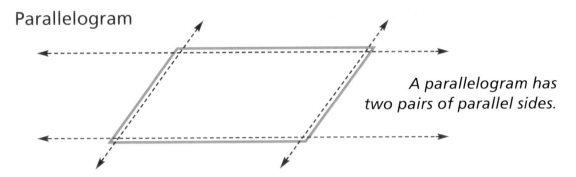

*A parallelogram has two pairs of parallel sides.*

As both pairs of sides of a parallelogram are parallel, then the opposite sides will have the same length and the opposite angles will be equal too.

# Rectangle

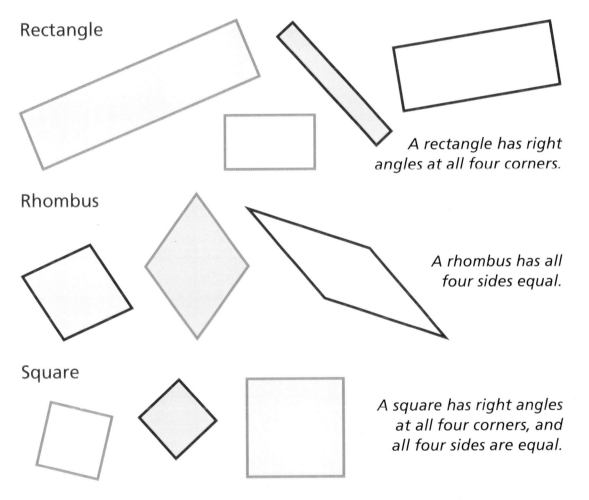

*A rectangle has right angles at all four corners.*

# Rhombus

*A rhombus has all four sides equal.*

# Square

*A square has right angles at all four corners, and all four sides are equal.*

If a quadrilateral is both a rectangle and a rhombus, then it must be a square. Do you see why?

# Other Polygons

A polygon with five sides is called a pentagon. A polygon with six sides is called a hexagon. A polygon with eight sides is called an octagon.

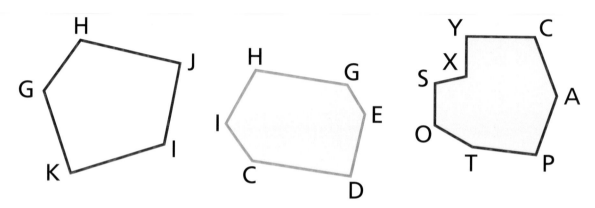

You learnt that a regular polygon has sides of equal length and angles of equal measure. Are the polygons above regular or irregular? What about the three polygons shown below? Which well-known, red traffic sign is shaped like a regular octagon?

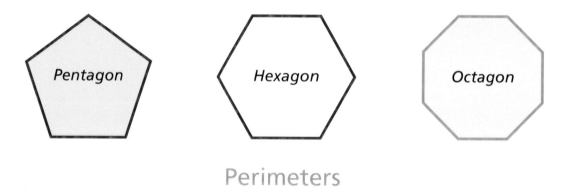

# Perimeters

If a polygon is regular and you know the length of one side, you can calculate the length of its perimeter. Since the perimeter is the length of all the sides added together and the sides are all the same, the perimeter is:

## length of one side × number of sides

A square is a regular quadrilateral. The perimeter of a square with a side 11 m long is:

$$4 \times 11 \text{ m} = 44 \text{ m}$$

Use a ruler to measure a side of each regular polygon on page 274 and calculate their perimeters.

# Circles

A circle is a closed figure, but not a polygon. Polygons have straight line segments for sides. A circle curves in such a way that every point along the circle is exactly the same distance from the centre of the circle.

*On this circle with centre D you can see three segments of equal length, $\overline{DR}$, $\overline{DS}$ and $\overline{DT}$*

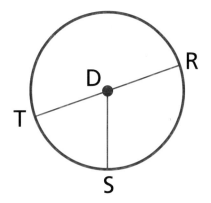

The most important parts of a circle are the centre and the edge. A line segment from the centre to the edge is called a *radius* of the circle. Radius is a Latin word, and the plural is *radii* [RAY-dee-eye]. Segments $\overline{DT}$, $\overline{DR}$ and $\overline{DS}$ are radii of the circle above. Since all the radii of a circle have the same length, we also call the length of any radius of a circle its radius.

A line segment from the edge of a circle, through the centre to the opposite edge is called a *diameter* of the circle. Segment RT is a diameter of the circle above. All the diameters of a circle have the same length. The diameter of a circle is always twice as long as its radius. Do you see why?

With a pair of compasses, practise drawing circles with a certain radius or a certain diameter. To do this, make a dot for the centre of the circle you want to draw, and open the compasses to the length of the radius of the circle. Put the sharp point of the compasses on the centre dot. Keeping that point still, swing the pencil arm of the compasses around on the paper so it draws a circle.

# Congruent Figures

*Congruent* figures have both the same shape and the same size. We say two figures are *similar* when they have the same shape, but not necessarily the same size. When two figures have the same shape and the same size, they are both similar and congruent. All congruent figures are similar, but not all similar figures are congruent.

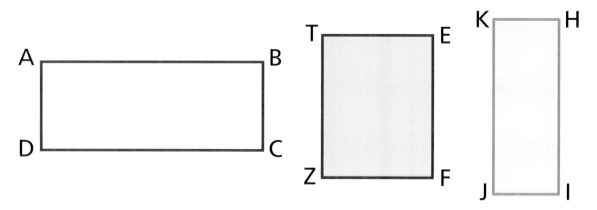

For example, rectangles ABCD and HIJK are similar. Though they have different sizes, they have the same shape.

Rectangles ABCD and EFZT are not similar. They do not have the same shape.

All squares are similar, and all circles are similar.

# Nets of Solids

Can you remember what these solid shapes are called?

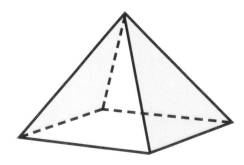 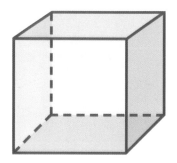

They are a square-based pyramid and a cube. Now imagine what flat shapes you could fold up to make these solids. If the faces are squares and triangles, you will need the same number of squares and the same number of triangles. A cube has six square faces.

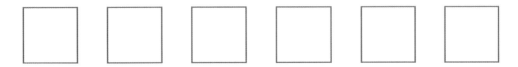

A pyramid has one shape for the base – ours is a square – and a triangle for each edge of the base.

Now we need to put them together to make what we call a *net*. In geometry, a net is the way you arrange flat shapes with their edges touching so that they can be folded up to become the faces of a solid figure. There is more to making a good net than just having the correct number of faces. We must only put faces together when they share an edge and we must ensure that each vertex has the correct number of edges meeting there.

▼ *Would this arrangement work for a square-based pyramid?*

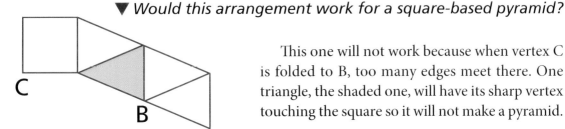

This one will not work because when vertex C is folded to B, too many edges meet there. One triangle, the shaded one, will have its sharp vertex touching the square so it will not make a pyramid.

*Could you fold this shape up to make a pyramid?*
▼

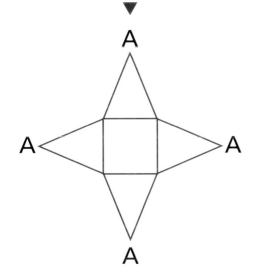

Can you see how to fold the triangles up so that they meet at the top or *apex* (A)?

There are other possible nets. This one works if you make A the apex again and put together all the vertices with the same letters:

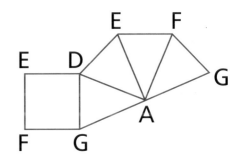

## Making Cubes

When you make a cube, you need to be able to fold each square so every vertex touches three faces and three edges. You need top, bottom, left, right, front and back faces. Which two of these nets will work and which ones will not? Can you say why?

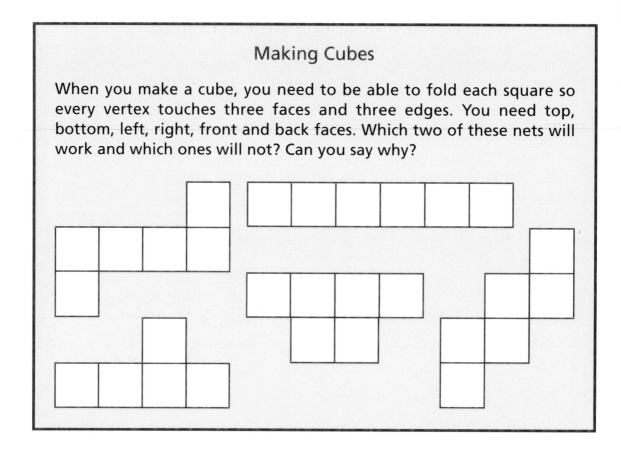

# The Area of a Rectangle

In Year 4 we started learning about area, which is the space inside a closed figure. The *dimensions* of a rectangle are its length and width. The length of a rectangle is the length of either of its two longer sides. The width of a rectangle is the length of either of its two shorter sides.

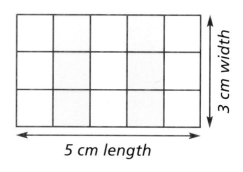

3 cm width

5 cm length

There are 5 × 3 square centimetres in this rectangle. Its area is 15 cm². You can find the area of a rectangle by multiplying its length by its width.

Here is the formula for the area of a rectangle. A *formula* is an equation written with letters that tells you a relationship that is always true. In this formula, $A$ stands for the area of a rectangle, $l$ for its length and $w$ for its width.

$$A = l \times w \text{ or Area} = \text{length} \times \text{width}$$

You can always find the area of a rectangle by substituting real numbers for l and w, and then multiplying the rectangle's length by its width. This is one of many useful formulas in mathematics.

## Square Units

You always measure area in square units.

**Some metric units of area:**

**km²** (square kilometre)

**Hectare** (ha)

**m²** (square metre)

**cm²** (square centimetre)

**mm²** (square millimetre)

**Some imperial units of area:**

**sq. mile** (square mile)

**Acre** (ac)

**sq. yd** (square yard)

**sq. ft** or **ft²** (square foot)

**sq. in** or **in²** (square inch)

What is the area of this rectangle? To find the area of a rectangle, you multiply its length by its width. $22 \times 220 = 4{,}840$. The area of this rectangle is 4,840 square yards. It has a special name too. Remember many imperial units are useful labels. Two old ones are the *chain* and the *furlong*. A chain is the length of a cricket pitch, but once was used as a standard tool for measuring land. A furlong is used today for the distances horses race, but was once used as a farmers' measure of land. Our special rectangle is a chain wide and a furlong long. Its area is an *acre*.

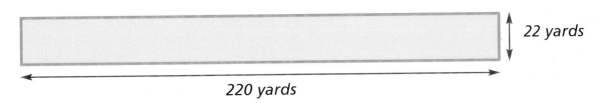

22 yards

220 yards

How many square inches are there in a square foot? Remember that there are 12 inches in 1 foot. $12 \times 12 = 144$

There are 144 in² (square inches) in 1 ft² (square foot). Notice that there are not 12 square inches in a square foot, even though there are 12 inches in a foot! Changing units of area is different from changing units of length. Work out how many mm² there are in 1 cm², how many ft² there are in 1 yd² and how many cm² there are in 1 m². All these answers are perfect squares (see page 213) and can be surprisingly large numbers.

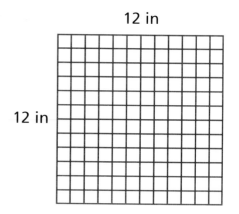

12 in

12 in

Now, in another example, you know the length of a rectangle (12 cm) and its total area (84 cm²). Find its width. You know that 12 cm × ___ cm = 84 cm². So you must divide the area by the length to find the width:

$$\begin{array}{r} 7 \\ 12\overline{)84} \\ -84 \\ \hline 0 \end{array}$$

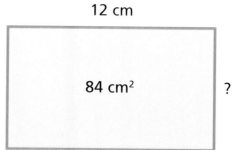

12 cm

84 cm²

?

The width is 7 cm.

When you know the measurement of one dimension of a rectangle and its total area, you can divide to find the measurement of the other dimension.

## Volume

Let's look at some more three-dimensional figures.

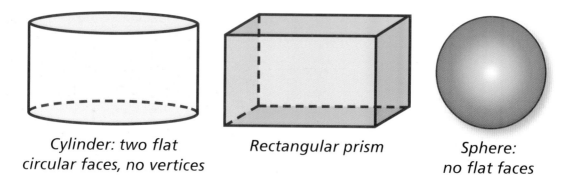

*Cylinder: two flat circular faces, no vertices*

*Rectangular prism*

*Sphere: no flat faces*

A rectangular prism looks like a box. Notice that all of the faces of this prism are rectangles. There are six faces in all: top and bottom, left and right, front and back.

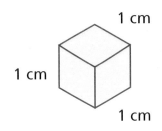

The volume of a three-dimensional figure is how much space it occupies. You measure space in cubic units. One example of a cubic unit is a cubic centimetre. The abbreviation for cubic centimetre is cm$^3$.

Notice that a cubic centimetre is a cube. All cubic units are cubes.

By counting cubic units, you can find the volume of a figure – how much space it occupies. Sometimes you have to count cubic units that you know are there but you cannot see. You can count cubic units that are hidden by thinking about the pattern of those that you can see. On one layer of this rectangular prism, there are 8 cubes. There are two layers. $8 \times 2 = 16$.

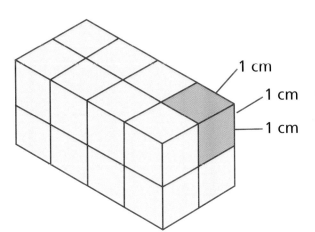

Or, you can say that the volume of this rectangular prism is its length multiplied by its width multiplied by its depth. 4 cm $\times$ 2 cm $\times$ 2 cm = 16 cm$^3$.

Either way, there are 16 cubic centimetres in the rectangular prism.

See if you can work out the volume of the next figure. Notice that there are two sections: the top section is a cube 2 cm on each side. The bottom section is a rectangular prism 4 cm $\times$ 4 cm $\times$ 2 cm. To work out the total volume, you'll have to work out each section separately and then add them together. What did you find for its volume?

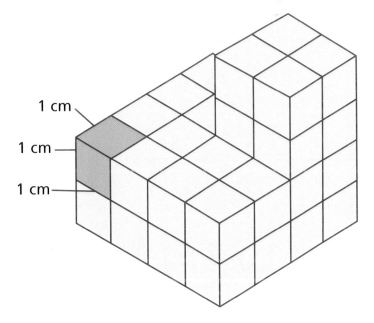

# Graphs

Information, or data, is often given to us in numbers. Sometimes those numbers are used to make pictures, called graphs, that can help us understand the numbers.

Learn about York and Yorkshire on page 91.

A bar graph is a good way to show different amounts. Charlie kept track of how much rain fell each day for a week in York. Here is his table of data that we will use to make a bar graph.

Along the bottom of the graph we write the days of the week. Along the side of the graph we choose a convenient way to show the millimetres of rain: in intervals of 2 millimetres. We title the graph, label the information along the bottom and the sides and draw a bar to show each day's rainfall.

| Day of week | Thu | Fri | Sat | Sun | Mon | Tue | Wed |
|---|---|---|---|---|---|---|---|
| Rain in mm | 24 | 7 | 6 | 0 | 11 | 2 | 9 |

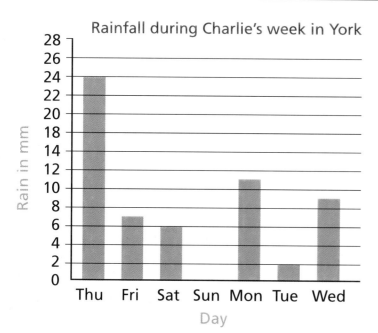

You can see right away from this graph that there was far more rain on Thursday than on any other day. How much more rain was there on Thursday than on Friday? $24 - 7 = 17$ mm. So there were 17 mm more rain on Thursday than on Friday. On which day was there no rain?

A line graph can show how amounts or numbers change.

A line graph can show how amounts or numbers change.

Mrs Sinclair is going to France to do some Christmas shopping. In France, they buy and sell things in euros (€) instead of pounds. She has £100 to spend but the things she wants to buy cost 120 euros. Can she afford them? The number of euros you can buy for each pound does not stay the same. She checked the newspapers to see how many euros she could buy for £100 and made a graph of her findings. Here is her table of data:

| Date | 3 Nov | 6 Nov | 11 Nov | 14 Nov | 19 Nov |
|---|---|---|---|---|---|
| How many euros will £100 buy? | €124 | €124 | €123 | €116 | €119 |

To make a line graph, we put the dates along the bottom of the graph. Along the side, we choose money amounts in intervals that will make the graph a reasonable size and show the data clearly. Here, we can mark every €20 along the side, starting at 0. We give the graph a title and labels along the bottom and side.

## Plotting Points on a Grid

The location of a point on a grid is named by a pair of numbers, called *co-ordinates*. For example, on the grid on the next page the location of point A is named by the co-ordinates (2, 1). The first number of the co-ordinates tells you how many units to the right a point is from zero. The second number tells you how many units up a point is from zero.

Point A is at (2, 1): you get to point A from zero by going 2 units to the right, then 1 unit up. Point B is at (5, 3): 5 units to the right of zero and 3 units up.

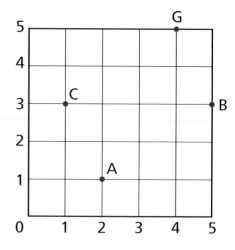

Draw a grid like our one and mark the positions of A, B, G and C. Draw edges to join up the points. What sort of shape have you drawn?

On some squared paper, draw lines to make axes. It needs to be twelve little squares in each direction. 'Axes' is the plural of axis, which is a line that tells you how far you are from a starting point. This starting point is called an *origin*. Another sort of axis is an axis of symmetry, which you have seen before in Years 3 and 4.

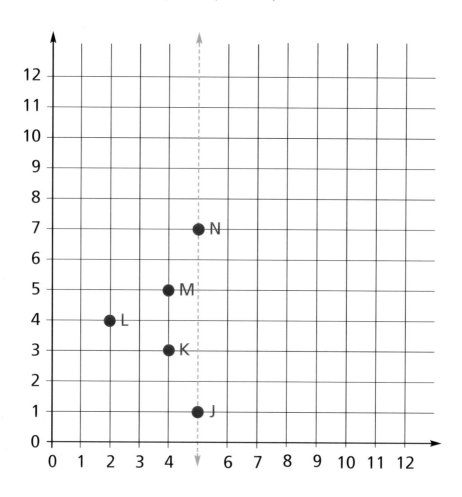

Look at points JKLMN. They are at the locations (5,1), (4,3), (2,4), (4,5) and (5,7). They come from a shape that has vertical symmetry along the dotted line. Knowing that, it is possible to draw the other points PQR that make up the shape. How?

How far is each point from the axis of symmetry? The shortest distance is at right angles. That is called perpendicular distance.

Because of the symmetry, there will be a point on the right of the axis of symmetry the same perpendicular distance away from it as each point on the left. Because this axis of symmetry is vertical, the distance along a horizontal line will be perpendicular to it.

Two points, N and J, are on the axis of symmetry. They do not change. M is one unit to the left, so draw a point P one unit to the right. Its position is (6,5).

Do you see how the line through M and P is perpendicular to the axis of symmetry? The line crosses the axis at (5,5). The points we know on this line are (4,5), (5,5), (6,5). If all the second numbers are the same, 5 in this case, then the line is horizontal.

Can you repeat the process by looking at point K to find the location of R? Now L is 3 to the left of the axis of symmetry, so where should you position Q?

Draw the outline of the shape in the order JKLMNPQR. Can you see any more axes of symmetry?

Well done if you found line LQ. Even better if you found KP and MR as well.

## Translation

As well as changing words from one language to another, *translation* means moving a shape on a grid without twisting or flipping it over. Let's try it.

We have eight co-ordinates. We are going to translate the shape 5 to the right and 1 down. To do this, we add 5 to the first number in the co-ordinates and subtract 1 from the second.

Work out the locations of the last three points and mark them on your graph with little crosses. Now join up the outline. Is it the same shape as your JKLMNPQR? It should be, translated 5 to the right and down 1.

| J | (5,1) | → | (10,0) |
|---|-------|---|--------|
| K | (4,3) | → | (9,2) |
| L | (2,4) | → | (7,3) |
| M | (4,5) | → | (9,4) |
| N | (5,7) | → | (10,6) |
| P | (6,5) | → | ? |
| Q | (8,4) | → | ? |
| R | (6,3) | → | ? |

# Suggested Resources

## Books

*See Inside Maths* by Alex Frith and Minna Lacey (Usborne) 2008

*Mental Arithmetic*, Books 1 and 2, by T R Goddard, J W Adams and R P Beaumont (Schofield & Sims) 1999, 2000

*Junior Maths Book 2* by David Hillard (Galore Park) 2008

*What's Maths All About?* by Minna Lacey (Usborne) 2012

*Practice in the Basic Skills*, Books 3 and 4, by Derek Newton and David Smith (Collins) 2003

*Be the Best at Maths* by Rebecca Rissman (Raintree) 2013

*Magnetic Tangrams: Explore the World of Tangram Pictures* by Jon Tremaine (Barron's) 2009

*Maths Dictionary* by Carol Vorderman (Dorling Kindersley) 2009

*Maths Made Easy Times Tables Ages 7-11 Key Stage 2* by Carol Vorderman (Dorling Kindersley) 2011

## Online Resources

A Maths Dictionary for Kids by Jenny Eather: www.amathsdictionaryforkids.com/dictionary.html

## Mobile Apps

Arithmetic Wiz (The Rocket Studio) app for iPad or iPhone [free]

Crazy Tangram Puzzle of Animals (XiaoFang Li) app for iPad [free]

Division Wiz (The Rocket Studio) app for iPad or iPhone [free]

Multiplication + (The App Gate Inc.) app for iPad or iPhone [free]

Tangram XL Free (Javier Alonso Gutierrez) app for iPad [free]

# Science

## Introduction

This chapter explores the circulatory and respiratory systems, electricity, atoms, chemistry, geology and meteorology. It also profiles several eminent scientists.

Parents and teachers can supplement this chapter by taking children to science museums and doing simple science experiments. Many books of fun, safe experiments are now available. Children should also be encouraged to view the world scientifically: to ask questions about nature and seek answers through observation; to collect, count and measure; to start a rock collection or monitor weather conditions; or learn about wind by flying a kite.

There are many excellent places where you can go to explore science. You cannot go wrong starting with London's world-famous Science and Natural History Museums in Kensington, which also offer a wealth of online material that may prompt you to make a visit in person. The National Museum of Scotland in Edinburgh and the Discovery Museum in Newcastle each offer a wide range of interactive resources for exploring science. The At-Bristol Science Centre offers a fantastic, hands-on experience and, at the Eden Project in Cornwall, you can see jungles and waterfalls in the world's largest undercover rainforest.

Hands-on experience is so important that some educators now reject the very idea of teaching young children about science from books. But book learning should not be neglected altogether. It helps bring system and coherence to a young person's developing knowledge of nature and provides essential building blocks for later study. Book learning also provides knowledge not likely to be gained by simple observations; for instance, books can teach us about things that are not visible to the naked eye, like white blood cells, subatomic particles and continental drift. Different kinds of experiences – experiments, field trips *and* book learning – are necessary to ensure that gaps in knowledge will not hinder later understanding.

# The Human Body

## Circulation and Respiration

Put your hand on your chest and feel your heart beat. Now take a deep breath and feel the air expanding your chest. Every time your heart beats, blood pumps through a network of blood vessels, from the heart to all the parts of your body. Every time you breathe in, air fills your lungs. Oxygen in that air travels from your lungs into your bloodstream, ready to refresh the cells in your body.

The heart and the blood vessels are parts of your body's circulatory system. The lungs and windpipe are parts of your respiratory system. These two systems work together to keep you alive. To understand them, though, let's study them separately.

## The Heart

The heart is a powerful muscle. It works every second of every day, from the moment you are born until the day you die. Most of the time, you don't even know it is working. But if you sprint up some stairs, you can feel it working harder, thump-thump-thumping as it pumps blood through your body.

Your heart is about the size of your fist. It is divided into four chambers. The top two chambers are called the *atria* (each one is called an *atrium*); the bottom two, the *ventricles*. Valves in between the ventricles and atria open and close to allow the blood to flow through the heart.

Blood needing oxygen comes into the heart through the right atrium. It squeezes through a valve and into the right ventricle. From there, it flows out to the lungs for a new supply of oxygen.

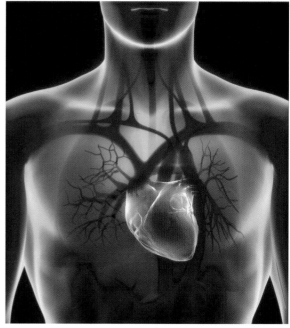

*Can you put your hand over your own heart and feel it beat? (Run around the room and try it again if you can't feel it at first.)*

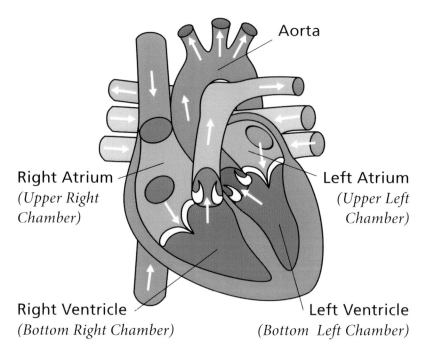

**Aorta**

**Right Atrium**
*(Upper Right Chamber)*

**Left Atrium**
*(Upper Left Chamber)*

**Right Ventricle**
*(Bottom Right Chamber)*

**Left Ventricle**
*(Bottom Left Chamber)*

From the lungs, it flows back into the left atrium of the heart, squeezes through a valve into the left ventricle and then is pumped out of the heart through the *aorta*, the biggest blood vessel of all. Can you trace the flow of blood through the heart on our diagram? The aorta divides and branches out to take the blood to all the different parts of the body.

## The Blood Vessels

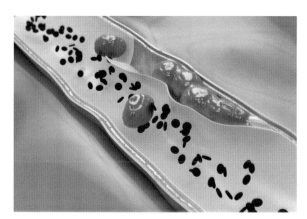

*Your blood flows through blood vessels.*

The heart pumps blood through your body in hollow, stretchy tubes called blood vessels. The blood vessels that carry the oxygen-rich blood away from your heart are called *arteries*. The blood vessels that carry blood back to your heart for more oxygen are called *veins*.

Smaller blood vessels, called *capillaries*, branch off from arteries and veins. The tiny capillaries bring blood in contact with the cells in the body. Capillary walls are so thin that nutrients, oxygen and waste products pass back and forth through them easily. Capillaries connect arteries and veins. They are the endpoint of arteries, through which oxygen and nutrients are delivered, and the starting point of veins, which pick up and carry waste materials away.

You can see some capillaries by looking in the mirror and gently pulling down on your lower eyelid. See those tiny red squiggles on your eyeball? Those are capillaries.

*This diagram shows the circulatory system. Arteries are shown in red and veins are shown in purple.*

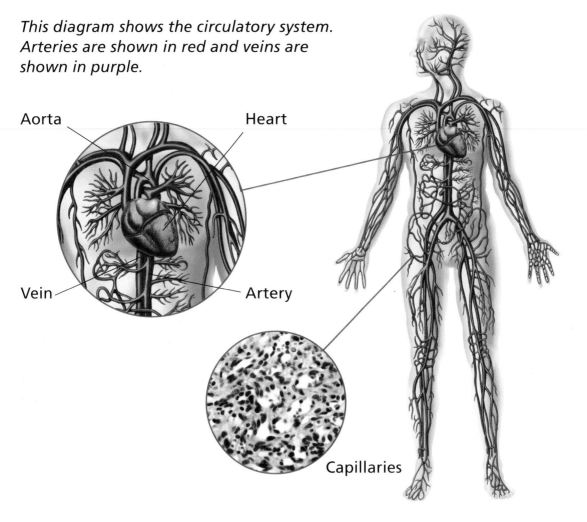

Aorta

Heart

Vein

Artery

Capillaries

## Blood Pressure and Heart Rate

Each time the heart pumps, the stretchy blood vessels swell and shrink as the blood flows through them. The pushing force, caused by the pumping heart, that moves blood through the body is called blood pressure. Blood pressure is one of the things that nurses and GPs check to make sure that your circulatory system is working properly.

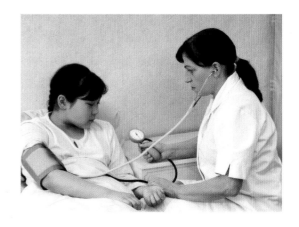

*A doctor is taking the girl's blood pressure.*

Your *pulse*, or heart rate, indicates how often your heart squeezes to pump blood through your body. To measure your heart rate, press your fingertips on the pulse point in your wrist. Use a watch or timer and count the number of pulses you feel in 30 seconds. The average human heart rate is about 90 pulses a minute, so you will probably count about 45 in half a minute.

But what happens to your heart rate when you exercise? Hop on one leg ten times, then circle your arms over your head ten times. Now measure your heart rate again. When you exercise, your cells use lots of oxygen and soon need more. That's why exercise makes you breathe harder and makes your heart pump faster.

## What Is Blood and Why Do We Need It?

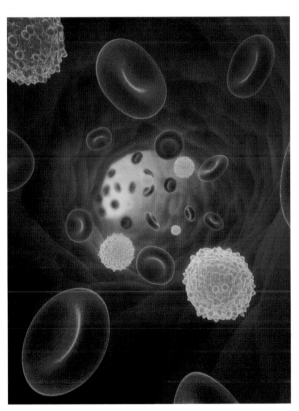

Blood never stops moving through your body. It delivers nutrients from food and oxygen to the cells in organs, muscles, bones and nerves. It picks up waste materials from the cells in your body and carries that waste to organs that can process it. Cells give off a gas called carbon dioxide, which the blood carries to the lungs. When you breathe out, you release carbon dioxide.

If you look at blood under a microscope, you can see tiny objects of several different shapes, all floating in a thin, clear liquid. The liquid part of blood is called the plasma. The most common shapes you would see floating in the plasma are the *red blood cells*. There are over 25 trillion – that's 25,000,000,000,000! – red blood cells in

*This photo of red and white blood cells shows them as they would appear under a microscope, magnified to many times their real size. Can you see the red blood cells, which look like doughnuts with the centres not quite punched out? The white cells with the bumpy surfaces (lymphocytes) are designed to fight infection.*

one person's body. Red blood cells contain a substance called *haemoglobin*. It's the haemoglobin that does the work of carrying oxygen and carbon dioxide.

Looking through the microscope, you would also see *white blood cells*. White blood cells are like a team of soldiers that travels in the blood, ready to fight disease at a moment's notice. When an infection develops, white blood cells attack.

If you have ever had a cut, then you've seen *platelets* in action. Platelets are tiny solids in the blood. Their job is to help stop bleeding. Platelets make blood *coagulate*, or get thicker, so a scab develops, protecting the wound while it heals.

## Cleaning the Blood

Because your red blood cells work hard, they only last for about four months before they die and are replaced by new ones. Red blood cells die at a rate of eight million a second! That means a lot of dead red blood cells are floating in your blood right now.

Removing those dead blood cells is one of the jobs of the *liver*, your body's largest organ. The liver breaks down dead cells and reuses what it can as nutrients. The *spleen*, another cleansing organ, helps to filter your blood and remove harmful wastes.

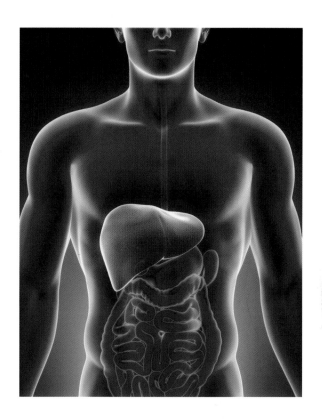

*The liver helps keep your blood healthy.*

## Understanding and Preserving Your Heart

For a long time, people did not know that the heart pumps blood in a circuit through the body. One of the people who helped us to understand this was an English doctor named William Harvey who lived from 1578 to 1657.

Harvey suggested that the heart was at the centre of a blood-circulating system. For a while no one believed him. A few years later, though, the newly invented microscope was used to investigate his claim. Through the microscope, doctors watched blood flowing in the tail of a live fish and realised Harvey had been right.

Today we know much more about the circulatory system and how to keep it healthy. For example, we understand that exercising makes your heart muscle grow stronger, and can help you live longer.

Eating sensibly is another key to a healthy heart. If you eat more fat than your body can use, it may build up on the inside of blood vessels like crud in an old sink pipe or limescale inside a kettle. Then less blood flows through and less oxygen gets to the fingers and toes, brain and heart. When the heart does not receive enough oxygen, heart muscle cells die. The result is called a *heart attack*.

*Jogging is a good way to keep your heart healthy.*

## What's Your Blood Group?

In 1900 Karl Landsteiner, a doctor from Austria, discovered that not everyone has the same type of blood. For years doctors had been trying to perform transfusions – that is, helping badly injured people by giving them blood from another person. It seemed like a good idea, but the patients often died.

Landsteiner noticed that when he mixed blood from two different people in a lab, the blood cells would often clump together and clot. After many experiments, he concluded that there were four different types of blood, called *blood groups*. He named them Type A, Type B, Type AB and Type O. One type of blood just wouldn't flow well in the veins of a person with a different type of blood. From that point on, doctors understood that people donating and receiving blood had to match in blood type.

## The Lungs

You breathe in and out more than 20,000 times a day. Each time, you replenish the oxygen in your body's systems and release carbon dioxide that your body cannot use. Your lungs and your respiratory system work together with your heart and circulatory system to keep you healthy and keep your cells alive.

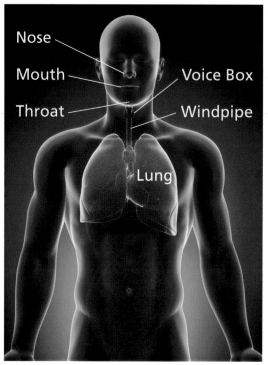

*Your lungs are put to work each time you breathe in and out.*

Inside your chest, on either side of your heart, are two inflatable sacs called 'lungs'. They are like warm, wet sponges inside. They expand and contract as your breathing fills them with air, then pushes the air out again. Take a deep breath and imagine the air filling those two warm, wet sacs inside your chest.

As you take a breath, air flows through your nose or your mouth and travels down the windpipe, or *trachea* [TRA-kee-ah]. It moves past the voice box and into tubes inside your lungs called *bronchi* [BRON-key]. Bronchi branch into smaller and smaller tubes. At the very ends of the tiniest bronchi are air sacs called *alveoli* [al-VEE-oh-lye]. These alveoli contain tiny capillaries where the respiratory and the circulatory systems meet. Haemoglobin in red blood cells absorbs the oxygen from the breath you took and carries it to all the cells in your body.

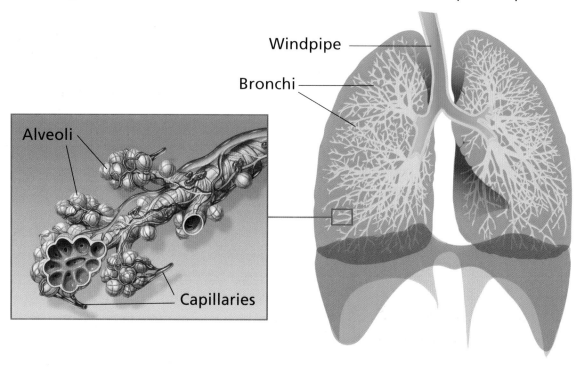

The process happens in reverse, too. As blood circulates through your body, it picks up carbon dioxide, which is of no use to your body. When the red blood cells carrying the carbon dioxide reach the capillaries in the alveoli, they unload the waste products into the lungs. Then you breathe out and get rid of the unneeded gas.

Breathing in and out happens because of the *diaphragm* [DIE-uh-fram], which is a stretchy sheet of muscle underneath your lungs. When the diaphragm arches down, it opens up space in your lungs and air rushes in to fill them. When the diaphragm arches up, it pushes the lungs together and forces air out of them, through the windpipe.

## What about Smoking?

Smoking cigarettes is one of the worst things you can do to your lungs and heart. Every pack of cigarettes carries a health warning, like this:

### Smoking kills

or

### Smoking seriously harms you and others around you

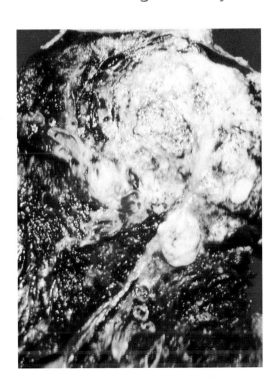

When a person inhales cigarette smoke, 4,000 different chemicals invade the lungs. Some of these chemicals are poisons that cause lung cancer. Others make the platelets sticky so that your blood clots when you don't want it to, and you may have a heart attack. Cigarette smoke also contains sticky, black tar. When tar clogs the nooks and crannies of a smoker's lungs, the alveoli can become so stiff that they cannot expand and pass oxygen to the blood. With less of their lungs working, smokers cannot exercise without running out of breath. The heart pumps harder and harder, but less oxygen reaches their cells.

*An unhealthy, smoker's lung is covered in black tar and white poisons.*

# Chemistry

## Cutting a Cube

Have you ever wondered what would happen if you tried to cut something into smaller and smaller pieces? Could you go on doing this forever? Or is there some 'smallest' piece, beyond which you cannot go?

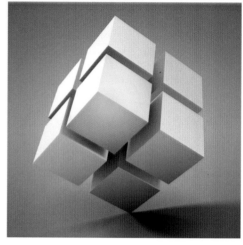

Take a look at the big cube on the right. Let's imagine it is made from only one elemental material, like aliminium, gold or graphite. Now, imagine using a knife to cut the cube in half along all three directions, so that the big cube becomes eight smaller cubes. Next, you cut each of the small cubes into eight smaller cubes. How many cubes do you have now? If you said 64, you are correct!

How many rounds of cutting can we do? Eventually, we will have to use a different cutting technique, because our knife will be too thick. But, no matter what we do, and no matter what element the cube is made of, we can only perform about 30 rounds of cutting. After that, we will have reached the very smallest piece of the material that still has the properties of that material. This smallest piece is called an *atom.*

Atoms are extremely small: a human hair has a width of about 100,000 atoms! Not all atoms are the same size. For example, an aluminium atom is larger than a helium atom. But even the largest atoms are far too small to see with your eyes.

## What Are Atoms Made Of?

As atoms are so small, you might suppose they are the smallest things in the universe. Not really. An atom is simply the smallest part of a material that retains any property of that material. But atoms themselves are composed of even smaller things!

All atoms, whether helium or aluminium or hydrogen or oxygen, are composed of tiny particles called *protons*, *neutrons* and *electrons*. Protons and neutrons are tightly packed in the centre of the atom, called the nucleus. Electrons are found on the outside of the atom. Protons have positive electric charge (shown by the symbol +), electrons have negative electric charge (−) and neutrons have no charge at all. Just as the north pole of one magnet repels the north pole of another magnet, positive electric charges repel each other. Negative electric charges also repel each other. But, just as the north pole of one magnet will attract the south pole of another magnet, positive and negative electric charges attract each other.

> We learnt about magnetic attraction in Year 3.

## Drawing an Atom

Maybe you're wondering what all these parts look like. It would be helpful if we could draw a scientifically accurate picture of atoms. Unfortunately, it is impossible to draw a completely accurate picture of an atom. Any picture we try to draw of an atom shows some characteristics correctly but shows other characteristics incorrectly.

This is one possible way to draw a hydrogen atom.

Some things about this drawing are accurate. For example, it shows the proton at the centre and the electron on the outside. But scientists now realise that some things about this picture are incorrect. They have learnt that the electron is more like a fuzzy cloud of negative charge that surrounds the nucleus. It does not really move around and around the proton, and it does not just exist at one particular distance from the proton. It can exist at a lot of different distances at the same time – so drawing it like a planet orbiting a sun is misleading. Maybe we should draw a hydrogen atom more like this.

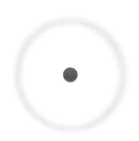

Do you see the trouble we are having? Scientists know that the electron is more like a fuzzy cloud, but they also know that it stays away from the nucleus. In a sense, the electron cloud spins. But how do we draw that?

Pictures are still very helpful, though. For the purposes of this chapter, we will use the simple, not-quite-right picture of electrons in orbit around a nucleus. At least this kind of drawing helps us keep track of the number of particles contained in the atom.

## Larger Atoms

Hydrogen is the smallest atom. The second smallest atom is helium. Helium has two electrons, one more than hydrogen has. How many protons do you think a helium atom has? If you said two, you are correct! This is because all atoms are electrically neutral – which is a way of saying that there are equal numbers of positive and negative charges, and they cancel each other out, just as positive two plus negative two equals zero. Since a helium atom has two electrons (negative charges), it must also have two protons (positive charges) to make all the charges exactly cancel out or equal zero.

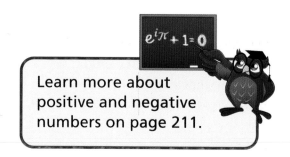

Learn more about positive and negative numbers on page 211.

The next question is: how many neutrons does a helium atom have? It is not possible to guess how many neutrons an atom has, because neutrons have no electrical charge. But through careful experiments, scientists have determined that most (but not all) helium atoms have two neutrons. About one out of every million helium atoms has only one neutron. But *all* helium atoms have two electrons and two protons.

There are different types of atoms, such as hydrogen and helium, but there are not different types of electrons, protons and neutrons (which are like ingredients that make different atoms). Scientists strongly believe that all electrons are exactly the same. It doesn't matter whether they come from hydrogen, helium or any other atom or from atoms on the Earth, Mars or a star in a faraway galaxy. All electrons are identical. And the same is true for protons and neutrons.

Because of this, all atoms of a given type are identical. For example, all 'regular' helium atoms (the ones with two neutrons) are identical.

## Can We Break Open an Electron?

You might be saying to yourself: 'I thought atoms were the smallest thing. But it turns out that they can be broken into electrons, protons and neutrons. Can these particles be broken into pieces, too?'

That's a good question. At present, scientists believe that electrons cannot be broken into anything smaller, but they think that protons and neutrons can be broken into smaller particles called 'quarks'.

Can quarks be broken into still smaller particles? Scientists don't know. Scientists make discoveries all the time and we don't have all the answers yet.

## Different Kinds of Atoms

Remember our definition of an atom as 'the smallest particle of a material that retains any property of that material'? In fact, that definition only applies to a material containing only one kind of atom. A collection of identical atoms is called an *element*.

This word may be new to you, but the idea isn't. When you see a piece of aluminium foil and ask what it is made of, the answer is 'aluminium'. Aluminium is an element. Do you know what a drinks can is made of? Aluminium. Aluminium foil and aluminium cans are made of the same element. Atoms are labelled as elements according to the number of electrons they contain, which is also the same number of protons they contain. The diagram below shows a single atom of each of the first six elements. Notice how each atom has one electron more than the previous atom?

These are only the first six elements. Scientists have discovered more than one hundred elements. After carbon, the next two are nitrogen (N) and oxygen (O). Other elements you may know about are copper, silver, gold, silicon and uranium.

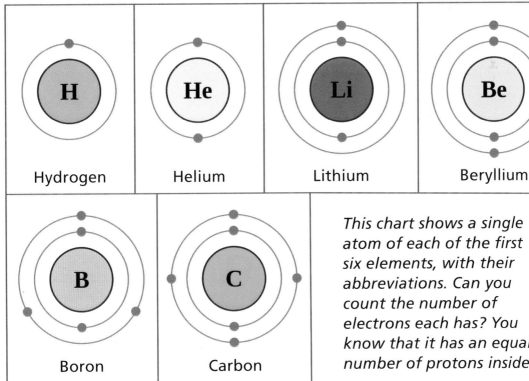

| Hydrogen | Helium | Lithium | Beryllium |
| Boron | Carbon |

*This chart shows a single atom of each of the first six elements, with their abbreviations. Can you count the number of electrons each has? You know that it has an equal number of protons inside.*

Atoms seldom stay on their own. Atoms stick together or *bond* in small patterns, called 'molecules'.

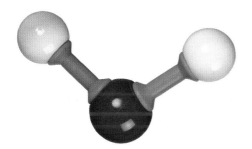

*Here's a simple way of drawing a water molecule. Water is made of two hydrogen (H) atoms and one oxygen (O) atom, so we also call it $H_2O$.*

Few things are made of only one element. Many are a combination of two or more. For example, the smallest particle of water is made of two hydrogen atoms and one oxygen atom. Because it is made of three atoms – two of one element and one of another – we can't call water either an 'atom' or an 'element'. This smallest unit of water is a 'molecule', which means atoms that combine to make up a particle of something new.

There are millions of other substances made of molecules, rather than single elements, such as sugar, salt, alcohol and petrol. Even odours consist of molecules. When you smell perfume, some of the molecules of the perfume are travelling through the air and into your nose. That's how you smell things! Many substances – like milk, paint and concrete – are mixtures of different kinds of molecules.

Living things are the most complicated of all. Trees, flowers, fish, dogs and human beings are made up of many different kinds of molecules. And, in living beings, these molecules don't always stay in the same configuration, or order. The molecules in you or in your dog are constantly breaking apart, moving around and recombining to form new molecules.

Yet everything we have been talking about here is composed of electrons, protons and neutrons. Take those three basic units and combine them many, many, many different ways, and you get the huge variety of stuff that makes up the universe.

## Measuring That Stuff

To measure the amount of a substance, scientists use the term *mass*. In the metric system, mass is measured in kilograms. For example, one pint of milk has a

$$e^{i\pi} + 1 = 0$$

Learn more about measuring mass in metric and imperial units on page 260.

mass of about 0.59 kilograms. An object's mass is the same everywhere in the universe, as long as it doesn't lose any molecules or pick up any extra ones.

At first, *mass* might sound like weight, the number you get when you stand on a scale to find out how heavy you are. But *weight* depends on how much gravity there is, and mass is the same no matter what the gravity. For example, the pint of milk will weigh

We learnt about gravity in Year 4.

less on the Moon than on the Earth, because there is much less gravity on the Moon. But the mass of the pint of milk is the same at either location.

There is another measurement scientists make to describe the things they're studying. They ask how much space an object occupies, and they call their answer *volume*. In the metric system, volume is often measured in litres. There are two ways to measure volume. You can calculate it with geometry or you can determine it through a process called *water displacement*. With geometry, you can measure the height and the area of the base of your milk container and use those numbers to calculate its volume. (We will be learning more about this in Year 6.) Or, using water displacement, you can submerge the milk container in water and see how much it makes the level of the water rise. Both methods will show you the volume of the container of milk.

*This container of milk displaces its own volume of water, which you can measure by reading the markings on the jug. You may have to use your finger to keep it completely submerged!*

*In Year 3 we learnt how Archimedes measured the volume of the king's crown using water displacement in his bath.*

Eureka!

If we know both the mass and the volume of an object, we can calculate another measurement important to scientists: *density*. Density is mass divided by volume. Objects with more density have more mass packed into the same space. For example, pour out the milk from your container and fill it with sand. Now the milk container has the same volume but higher mass, and therefore higher density.

Because water is so common on Earth, it is used as the basis of the metric system. Cold water has a density of exactly one kilogram per litre. But which do you think is more dense, water or ice? If you said water, you are correct. When water freezes, the molecules move apart slightly. The mass stays the same, but the volume increases. Since density is mass divided by volume, freezing water makes its density decrease. Ice is a little bit less dense than water. This is why ice cubes float in a glass of water.

Can there be a volume, or space, in which there is no matter at all, not even air? Yes. It is called a *vacuum* (no, we're not talking about a vacuum *cleaner* like a Hoover!). You can imagine a vacuum in your mind, but it is rare to find a perfect vacuum in the real world. Even in outer space, a few atoms float around. When a certain space contains many fewer atoms than normal, we can call it a *partial vacuum*.

Here is an experiment that will show you the effect of a partial vacuum. Ask an adult to help you try it. Find an old empty plastic bottle and put it somewhere where it does not matter if it gets a bit wet. Remove the cap, boil a kettle and – being very careful – pour in some boiling water, enough to cover the bottom. Notice that the inside of the bottle goes misty. It is now full of water and water vapour, which pushes the air out of the bottle. Screw the cap back on tightly and wait for about thirty minutes. What do you think will happen?

*A small amount of boiling water was poured into both of these bottles. The bottle on the left had its top left off so that air could get back in to replace the water vapour as it turned back into water. The bottle on the right had its top screwed on tightly.*

As the water vapour turns back to water, a partial vacuum is created. Air cannot get back in to your closed bottle, but it can push on the bottle so that the sides go in. If you had a metal container with stronger sides, it could hold the partial vacuum without collapsing but you would find it hard to get the top off again and it might break.

## Solutions

You may have noticed that oil and water don't mix very well. Try pouring a little oil and water into a bottle and shaking it. You will see that they separate again when you put the bottle down. One way of explaining this is to say that water molecules stick to each other really well, but they don't stick to oil molecules very well.

But what if you put a spoonful of sugar into a glass of warm water and stir it up? If you stir long enough, the sugar seems to disappear. Unlike oil, sugar molecules blend well with water molecules. Sugar is one of a certain kind of molecule that attracts water molecules well, pulls them apart and manages to mingle in between those water molecules.

*Try dissolving sugar in water at home.*

When this happens, we say the sugar has *dissolved* in water. We call the water the *solvent* and the sugar the *solute*. The sugar is still there, even though you can't see it!

Of course, you can't go on adding sugar to the solution forever. A solvent (in this case water) can only dissolve a certain amount of a solute (in this case sugar). When the maximum amount of a solute is dissolved in a solvent, we say that the solution is *saturated*.

# Electricity

## Zap!

Someone knocks at the door. You shuffle across the carpet to open it. But when you touch the doorknob, you feel a zap on your fingertip. What's going on? While unloading the tumble dryer, your sister's socks keep sticking to your pyjamas. After blowing up a balloon and rubbing it on your sleeve, it can stick to the wall. Why is that? You're in your bedroom in the dark and, when you take off your sweater, you see tiny sparks. Where did they come from?

The answer to each of these questions lies in the movement of tiny electrons.

## Static Electricity

*This boy's hair is standing on end because of static electricity.*

Electrons, as you remember, are the subatomic particles that zip around the nucleus of an atom. Electrons have a negative electrical charge, while protons in the nucleus have a positive electrical charge. Attraction between opposite charges keeps electrons from flying free of the atom, but it doesn't hold them very tightly. When objects rub together, electrons can get knocked loose and go off on their own.

For instance, as clothes tumble together in a dryer, electrons from atoms in some pieces of clothing rub off onto other pieces. Your sister's fuzzy socks might lose electrons while your pyjamas pick them up. The socks end up with more protons than electrons, and thus more positive electrical charge than negative electrical charge. The pyjamas, on the other hand, end up with more electrons than protons: they become negatively charged. That means that the socks and pyjamas develop opposite charges – and, as you've learnt already, opposite charges attract each other. That's why the socks and the pyjamas cling together in the dryer.

When rubbing, or friction, makes an electrical charge build up, that charge is called static electricity. As you take off your sweater, it rubs against your shirt, picks up extra electrons, and builds up a charge. The sparks you see in the darkness are electrons flowing away in a sudden discharge of static electricity.

The zap you felt from the doorknob is discharged static electricity, too. As you rubbed your feet against the carpet, your body picked up extra electrons, which flowed to the doorknob when you reached for it.

## Making Light out of Electricity

When you turn on a light, you are starting up a flow of electrons through an electric circuit. This is called an electric *current*. It all happens with just the flick of a light switch. Let's see what is really happening at the level of electrons.

Here is an example of a simple circuit, consisting of four parts:

1. a circular copper wire
2. a light bulb of the old kind, such as you might find in a car, cooker or fridge
3. a battery
4. a switch

The battery is the source of energy. It has a positive and a negative pole. When the switch is turned on, electrons travel through the wire, making the full circuit from the negative pole of the battery, through the switch and the light bulb, and back to the positive pole of the battery. This is called a *closed circuit*, because the electrons complete a full loop.

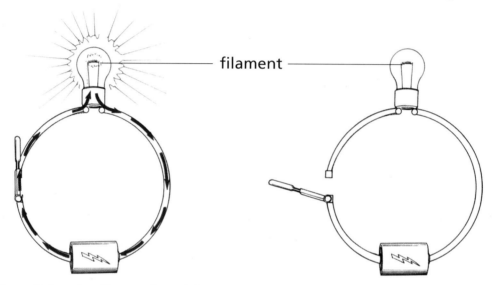

filament

A closed circuit allows electricity to flow around the circuit.

An open circuit stops the flow of electricity.

When the switch is turned off, the circuit is broken and the flow of electrons stops. This is called an *open circuit*, because there is a gap in the circuit, so the electrons cannot complete a full loop.

Take a look at an ordinary, older-style clear light bulb. Do you see the two wires sticking up? Stretched between them is a very fine wire called a *filament*. When you turn on the switch and create a closed circuit, electrons travel around the circuit and through the light bulb. However, compared with the rest of the circuit, the filament is a much narrower passageway for the electrons. It's as if traffic moving in eight lanes has had to merge onto a one-lane bridge, and the result is a traffic jam which backs up all the way around the circuit.

This electrical traffic jam is called *resistance* – the narrow filament *resists* the fast flow of electrons. And it is this resistance in the filament which causes heat to be produced. As the electrons squeeze and jostle their way through the narrow filament, they collide with the atoms in it causing them to vibrate, get hot and even glow! Thanks to resistance, light bulbs can turn electricity into light.

*This LED lightbulb is more energy-efficient than the old filament bulbs.*

Perhaps you have noticed how hot a filament bulb gets when it's on? In the past, many fingers were burned by impatient people who tried to change the lightbulb before it had cooled down. Nowadays we don't see many filament-type lightbulbs around. That's because we have found more efficient ways of producing light from electricity. Light-emitting diodes (LEDs) and fluorescent bulbs are much colder when they're on, so less electrical energy is wasted as heat. All the better for impatient fingers too!

## Conductors and Insulators

Most household wires that carry electrical current are made of copper, the same metal that gives pennies their red-brown colour. Electrons move readily between the atoms in copper, so electricity flows well through copper. That makes copper a good conductor of electrical current. Other metals make good conductors, too.

Some materials do not conduct electrical current very well at all (in other words, electricity will not flow through them). These materials are called *insulators*.

You see examples of conductors and insulators every day. Anything that you plug into a wall socket for electricity uses a cable made of both a conducting and an insulating material. The wire inside is probably copper, but the part that you see on the outside is made of plastic or rubber. The copper conducts the electricity, but the plastic or rubber insulates it from your hands. Thanks to the insulation, you don't get a shock when you touch the cable.

The last thing you want to do is to become part of an electrical circuit! Respecting the power of electrons could save your life. Your body makes tiny amounts of its own electricity but that is different. Electricity from the mains or a big battery can do a lot of damage. Avoid fiddling around inside electrical appliances, especially when they are plugged in. Water is a good conductor, so it is especially important not to touch light switches or appliances when your hands are wet or when you are in water. In other words, don't use your hair dryer while you are in the bath. The shock could kill you.

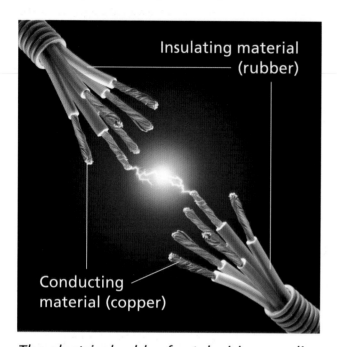

**Insulating material (rubber)**

**Conducting material (copper)**

*The electrical cables for televisions, radios and other electrical appliances contain insulating materials and conducting materials. If conducting materials are exposed, they can be dangerous!*

Insulation also prevents bare wires from touching each other. When bare wires touch, current can flow between them and take a shortcut instead of completing the full circuit. This shortcut means that the current can avoid any resistance inside the device being powered (remember the narrow one-lane bridge of the filament in a bulb?). Immediately, the electric traffic jam is cleared and the electrons can race through the thick wires easily. This is called a *short circuit*.

In a short circuit the device won't work – after all, what electron would choose a traffic jam over a fast moving motorway? But worse still, the speeding electrons will collide violently with the atoms in the wires, making them hotter and hotter. The situation can get dangerous, because the wires can become hot enough to start a fire.

Some good safety measures include replacing frayed cables, keeping pets from nibbling wires and keeping cords away from heaters and places where they can be rubbed or pinched.

Overloading a circuit by plugging in too many appliances can cause wires behind the walls to heat up, too. Safety devices such as fuses and circuit-breakers are designed to interrupt the circuit if too much current threatens to heat up the wiring. A fuse is a tiny ceramic tube surrounding a thin metal strip. If too much current runs through the fuse, the metal strip melts, breaking the circuit and stopping the flow of electricity before the wires get too hot.

## Electromagnets

Electric current can be switched on and off by opening and closing a circuit. Some magnets can be turned off and on in the same way. They are called *electromagnets*.

If you were to take an iron nail and wrap an insulated electrical wire around it about ten times, then connect it to a circuit, you would be making a very simple electromagnet. When you close the circuit (or turn the system 'on'), the current flows through the wire coiled around the nail. That movement of electricity creates a magnetic field that changes the ordinary nail into a magnet. The more times the wire is coiled around the nail, the stronger a magnet that nail becomes. Switch off the electric current, and the nail loses most of its magnetic force of attraction. It becomes an ordinary nail again.

Magnets that can be turned on and off are useful in many ways. Television receivers, loudspeakers, metal detectors as well as motors and brakes in some cars depend on electromagnets to work. Cranes move tons of steel using powerful electromagnets. They can use those magnets to pick up loads and, with a flick of the switch, drop those loads.

Electromagnets are also used in special trains called 'maglevs' (for 'magnetic levitation'). Instead of wheels that run on a track, maglev trains use electromagnets that run along a guide rail. Electric current flows through the electromagnets. The magnetic pole in the tracks attracts the pole of the

*This Chinese maglev train flies along its magnetic track at speeds of up to 300 miles per hour.*

train's magnets and pulls it along, but the magnetic field pushes it away so the train cars hover above the guide rail and glide smoothly along at high speed.

# Geology

## Layers of Planet Earth

Have you ever wondered what it would be like to journey down, down, down to the centre of the Earth? To get there, you would have to dig a hole 3,872 miles deep, through four different layers of the earth.

The top layer – the layer on which you live – is called the crust. The crust is about 25 miles deep, made of solid rock.

Once you dig through the crust, you reach a very hot second layer called the *mantle*. Here it is so hot that instead of hard rocks, the Earth's material flows like incredibly thick syrup. Geologists call the most runny parts of the mantle *magma*. In some places, the mantle can be 1,800 miles deep.

Continuing down towards the centre of the earth, you come next to the third layer – the outer core. This layer, made of searing hot liquid metal, is nearly as thick as the mantle.

Deeper still, you reach the inner core at the Earth's centre, estimated to be about the size of the Moon. Here at the inner core, the temperature is hotter than at the surface of the Sun! But the pressure from all the layers of Earth around the inner core keeps it from melting.

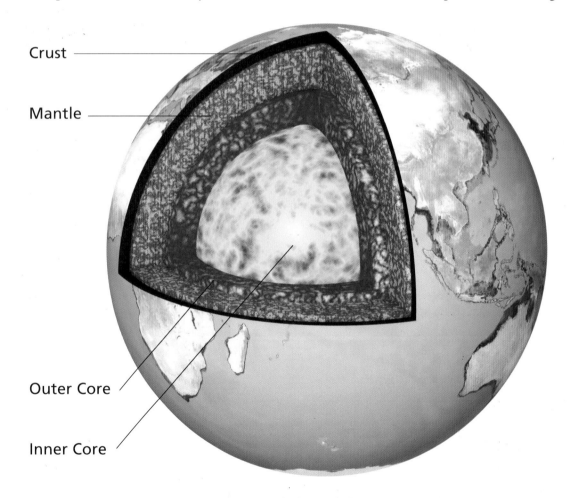

Crust

Mantle

Outer Core

Inner Core

*Layers of the Earth*

The word 'geology' comes from the Greek word gaia [guy-ah], which means 'Earth'. Geology is the study of the Earth, its matter and its history.

# Earthquakes

It was early morning on 18 April 1906, in the city of San Francisco, California. Eva Campbell was fast asleep when her bed began to lurch violently across the room. Her whole house was trembling: 'It rocked like a ship on a rough sea... Quiver after quiver followed... until it seemed as if the very heart of this old earth was broken and was throbbing and dying away slowly and gently.'

On that terrible morning, San Francisco was shaken by one of the most destructive earthquakes ever. Many people died, crushed by falling buildings or trapped in fires that started when gas lines broke.

More recently, devastating earthquakes destroyed many buildings in China's Sichuan Province in 2008 and again in 2013, as well as in Haiti in 2010. An earthquake is a sudden and violent shaking of the Earth's crust. Earthquakes can be strong enough to shake buildings and bridges off their foundations, to open cracks so big that cars fall into them, and to cause huge avalanches. On the other hand, some earthquakes can be so mild that people don't even notice them. In fact, an earthquake happens somewhere in the world every 30 seconds.

*Earthquakes destroyed many buildings in Sichuan Province in 2013.*

Geologists record the vibrations from earthquakes with machines called *seismographs.* Seismographs measure tremors underground and plot them like a graph. Normally, the ground is stable and the seismograph plots a fairly straight horizontal line but, during an earthquake, it measures and draws the size of the tremors like in this picture.

*This seismograph is measuring ground movement during an earthquake.*

To compare the *magnitude,* or strength, of different earthquakes, geologists often use a chart called the Richter [RIK-ter] scale. The Richter scale gives scientists a way to compare earthquakes. An earthquake measuring 2 on the Richter scale is 10 times stronger than an earthquake rated 1. No earthquake has ever measured greater than 9 – thank goodness, because when an earthquake measures 9 on the Richter scale, its magnitude is equal to an explosion of 200 million tons of dynamite!

## Earth's Moving Plates

The Earth's crust is something like a big, messy jigsaw puzzle, made of many pieces called *plates.* The line where two plates meet is called a plate boundary. Some plates are locked tightly together where they meet. Others move past each other. Some move apart, and can create deep cracks in the Earth's crust. Other plates will even overlap at their boundaries and lie on top of each other.

Wherever two plates move past each other, geologists say there is a *fault.* San Francisco sits right on a fault called the San Andreas Fault, which runs the length of California, and that is one reason why California experiences so many earthquakes. In Iceland, the European continental plate is moving away from the North American continental plate.

It feels as if the ground we stand on is solid and motionless, but in fact the plates that make up the Earth's crust move. They push, pull and rub against each other.

What makes the plates move? Like rafts on water, the Earth's plates float on the mantle. When the mantle moves, so do the plates. The mantle is always flowing. Hotter rock rises to the surface, cools, then sinks. These movements jostle the plates.

*There are deep fault lines between the continental plates in Iceland that move about one inch farther apart each year.*

The sliding of rock against rock in the Earth's crust can cause pressure to build up over time, until suddenly – CRACK! – the rock fractures, stored energy is released, and the ground trembles.

Sometimes, an earthquake happens on the ocean floor. Its energy pushes seawater into a giant wave called a *tsunami* [soo-NAH-mee]. A tsunami can travel more than 400 miles per hour. As it approaches shore, where the water is shallower, it grows taller and taller, pushed by the energy behind it. A tsunami can grow as tall as a ten-story building before the curling wall of water crashes down on land.

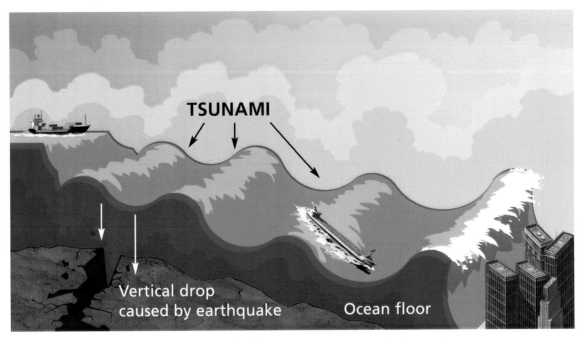

*Earthquakes beneath the ocean can send gigantic waves, called tsunamis, tumbling towards land.*

## Volcanoes

Volcanoes are like safety valves for the planet's furnace. They release built-up pressure from inside the Earth. Volcanoes form when hot magma from the mantle squeezes up through weak spots in the Earth's crust, usually where plates meet. The volcano erupts when that incredibly hot liquid comes gushing out of the Earth. Once it flows out of a volcano, magma is called *lava*. A volcanic eruption can keep going for hours, days, even months. Ash and hunks of fiery rock spew from the opening in the Earth, and over time they pile up and harden into a mountain.

*Stromboli is one of the most active volcanoes on Earth.*

Sometimes volcanoes erupt quietly, without a lot of noise and explosions. Glowing-hot lava oozes out from the opening on top and runs down the sides of the volcano. Other times volcanoes erupt violently, flinging hot lava, gases and pieces of rock into the air. Volcanoes often erupt many times over the course of centuries, like Mount Stromboli in Italy. Sometimes they erupt quietly and sometimes explosively, building up a mountain of layers of hardened lava. Other times, volcanoes like Eyjafjallajokull in Iceland erupt, sending cinders and ash into the sky which we read about in Year 2.

## World-Famous Volcanoes

Mount Vesuvius, on the western coast of Italy, erupted in A.D. 79 and buried the ancient Roman cities of Pompeii and Herculaneum in ash and cinders. Twenty thousand people were killed. The tons of ash almost perfectly preserved Pompeii for centuries. Archaeologists digging in the area more than 1,500 years later unearthed the entire town, complete with houses, shops, restaurants, temples, signs and paintings. Even the bodies of people who had lived in Pompeii were well preserved, trapped and hardened by ash.

### Will it erupt?

An 'active' volcano is one that is erupting or is expected to erupt sometime in the future. 'Dormant' means a volcano has not erupted for a while, and no one knows for sure whether it will ever erupt again. 'Extinct' means the volcano has not erupted since humans have been recording history, and probably never will again.

Krakatoa, a volcano on an Indonesian island, erupted in 1883 with an explosion so powerful that it was heard almost 3,000 miles away. Volcanic ash shot 17 miles up into the Earth's atmosphere, darkening the skies for almost 20 hours. The force of the eruption created a 30-metre-high tsunami that took the lives of 36,000 people on the nearby islands of Java and Sumatra. The ash sent into the atmosphere by Krakatoa changed the colour of sunsets around the world for months after the eruption.

When Mount St Helens, in Washington state in the United States, erupted in 1980, 230 square miles of forest were blown down or burned. The winds from the blast were measured at more than 600 miles per hour, and trees were flattened for 15 miles around. Rocks as big as a hilltop tumbled down, filling up a valley 150 feet deep – the largest landslide in recorded history. Hot ash, a metre thick, blanketed the area nearest the volcano. Despite all this devastation, life has returned to Mount St Helens in the years following the eruption. Plants have sprouted through the ash. These plants have created a little bit of soil in which more seeds, brought by the wind, have taken root and begun to grow. Scientists predict that by 2200, a forest will cover Mount St Helens once again.

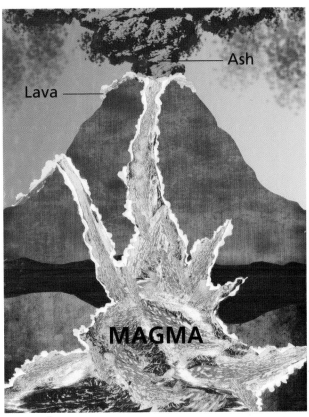

When a volcano erupts, hot magma forces its way through the cracks in the Earth's crust and erupts on the surface as lava.

When the lava erupting from this volcano cools, it will form a new layer of rock.

The top of Mount St Helens blew off during the eruption of the volcano in 1980, but plants are starting to grow back now.

# Hot Springs and Geysers

*Iceland not only has active volcanoes but also geysers, like this one.*

*Hot springs in Rotorua, New Zealand*

In some places in the world, a lot of volcanic activity is going on under the Earth's surface. Magma that is forcing its way up through the crust heats up water that has seeped down through cracks. Sometimes the hot water bubbles up to the surface and forms steamy ponds called hot springs. Sometimes the Earth's underground shape makes that hot water shoot up into the air, creating *geysers*. Geysers form when water collects in underground caves and chambers. The water gets hotter and hotter, until finally it boils and turns to steam. Just like the steam pressure that makes a kettle on the hob whistle, the force of this underground steam blasts through the cracks in the Earth's crust.

Some areas of the Earth have famous geysers and hot springs. In Iceland, the Strokkur geyser erupts regularly about every four to eight minutes, and sometimes the water can go up to 40 metres high. The Yellowstone National Park, in the United States, sits on a hot spot of underground volcanic activity. One famous geyser at Yellowstone erupts so regularly that it is called Old Faithful. In New Zealand, Rotorua is known for its hot springs, bubbling mud and geysers.

Learn more about New Zealand on page 100.

# Drifting Continents

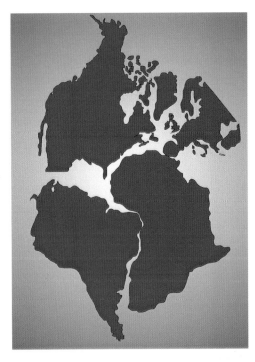

If you could go back in time 300 million years – before the time of the dinosaurs – and look down from space, the Earth would look very different. Geologists believe that, back then, the continents we know today were crowded together in one giant land mass. They have named that land mass 'Pangaea' [pan-JEE-uh] a word made up from the Greek for 'all the Earth'. Over 100 million years, the super-continent of Pangaea gradually broke into pieces. Oceans flowed in between the newly-formed continents. Even though the continents only drifted a few inches apart each year, a few inches per year for millions of years adds up to a lot of changes. Geologists call those changes *continental drift*.

*Can you recognise the shapes of any of today's continents in Pangaea?*
*It drifted apart over millions of years.*

# Building Mountains Over Time

From space the Earth looks like a smooth blue and white marble. But down here on the planet, we know its surface is anything but smooth. The land is wrinkled and bumpy. Mountains poke up from every continent and from the ocean floor. Scientists divide mountains into several categories based on how they were formed.

## Dome-shaped mountains

Volcanoes can build mountains by spitting out piles of lava, cinders and ash, like we saw on page 314. Volcanic mountains can also form without an eruption. Magma beneath the surface swells and pushes up a mountain-sized bump. Before it finds a vent, the magma cools and hardens into dome-shaped mountains. Ben Nevis, Britain's highest mountain, is a dome mountain.

*Do you see the snow on top of Ben Nevis's dome?*

317

## Folded mountains

Imagine a tea towel, spread on the table. Now picture what happens when you push the edges toward the centre. The more you push, the more the towel wrinkles and crumples into folds. The same kind of thing has happened to the crust of the Earth in different places, making formations called *folded mountains*.

*Mt Everest is the tallest mountain in the world.*
*It is in the Himalayas, which are folded mountains.*

The Earth's tallest mountains, the Himalayas, formed 45 million years ago when two crustal plates collided deep beneath an ancient ocean. The tremendous force of the impact made the ocean floor between the plates bend and fold into mountains and valleys. You may have a hard time believing that the Himalayas were once part of an ocean floor, but fossils of sea creatures can still be found embedded in the rock on the mountains' peaks! The Alps in Europe are folded mountains, too.

## Fault-block mountains

*The Vosges are fault-block mountains.*

Sometimes, when plates meet on a fault line, the rock is brittle. Then the crust cracks into huge blocks. Sometimes when plates push against each other one side gets slowly tilted into a ridge. One side is steep, the other gently sloping. If the plates are stretching apart, a block in the middle can move downwards like a giant ditch and the blocks on either side get slowly lifted. These are all called *fault-block mountains*. On either side of the river Rhine are areas of fault-block mountains, called the Vosges in France and the Black Forest in Germany.

# Making Rocks

Mountains are made of rocks, but what are rocks made of? Rocks are made of chemicals called *minerals*. There are over 2,000 kinds of minerals on Earth. Some rocks are made of a single mineral, and others are combinations. To classify a given rock, geologists consider how it was formed.

We first looked at different kinds of minerals in Year 2.

Rocks that were made from cooling magma or lava are called *igneous* [IG-neeus] rocks. The name comes from *ignis*, the Latin word for 'fire'. Heavy, speckled granite; light, powdery pumice; black, glassy obsidian – even though they all look different, these are all igneous rocks. They started as hot magma and cooled into rock.

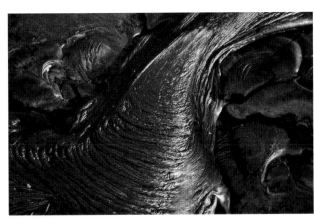

*When this lava flow from a volcano in Hawaii cools and hardens, the rocks will be igneous rocks.*

Rocks that were made when layer upon layer of sand and debris settled down together are called *sedimentary* rocks. Their name comes from the Latin word *sedo*, which means 'settle down'. Over millions of years, layers of sediment pressed down in the bottom of ancient oceans and rivers. The pressure cemented tiny grains together into rock. Limestone is a sedimentary rock, made mostly of the compressed bones and shells of millions of tiny sea creatures. Sandstone is another sedimentary rock.

The last family of rocks is called *metamorphic* [met-uh-MORE-fick] rock. This family gets its name from the Greek word *metamorphosis*, which means a transformation or change of shape, because metamorphic rocks are

*The Falkenstein in Germany is a sandstone peak. Can you make out the layers of sand that have build up over the years?*

*Marble is often sculpted into beautiful artwork. We saw some examples from ancient Greece in Year 3.*

rocks that have changed form. Some metamorphic rocks have changed through heat. When magma collects underground, it heats the surrounding rock to such high temperatures that the minerals become cooked. They change into new minerals, and the rocks containing them change form. Others have changed through pressure. Immense weight, like the weight of a mountain, can press down and change minerals. Marble, for example, used for its beauty in sculpture and buildings since the time of the ancient Greeks, is a metamorphic rock. Heat and pressure underground turn limestone into the rock we know as marble.

## From Boulder to Rock to Pebble to Soil

While plate movement is building mountains up, other forces are wearing them down. Wind, water, ice and plant roots crack and crumble rock over time, taking huge boulders and turning them into fist-sized rocks, then pebbles, then sand and finally into tiny particles that contribute to the Earth's soil. This process is called *weathering*.

Imagine a boulder on a mountainside. After a million years a little crack appears in its surface. When it rains, water trickles into the crack. On chilly nights – and there are many chilly nights on the top of a mountain – the water in the crack freezes and expands. Like a wedge, that ice pushes the sides of the crack in the boulder wider and wider apart. The processes of freezing, thawing and freezing again work on the crack until it becomes a network of cracks. Particles of dust and dirt carried by wind and water settle into those cracks. Seeds blown by the wind land in the soil collected in the cracks. The seeds sprout, and small plants' roots push against the sides of the cracks and make them wider still. Then one sunny day, a jagged piece of the boulder cracks off and somersaults down the side of the mountain, crashing into other boulders in its path and chipping pieces off them. That's the first step in the boulder's crumbling journey from big rock to future soil.

How long does it take for an entire mountain to crumble away? Geologists have calculated that a mountain gets approximately 7.5 cm shorter every 1,000 years.

The ocean weathers rocks as well. Have you ever noticed that most of the pebbles on a beach are round and smooth? Rocks and sand tumble together in the surf, grinding off all the rough edges. Over time, the action of the waves turns rocks into pebbles and then into sand.

Water and wind, plants and ice, all cause *physical weathering*. But rock also gets weathered by chemicals that occur naturally in the Earth. When water mixes with certain gases from the atmosphere, for example, it sometimes results in a weak acid called 'acid rain', which can eat away at the surface of rocks. Some plants also produce weak acids which seep into the Earth and affect the rock around them. These are examples of *chemical weathering*.

*The face of this gargoyle has been worn away by physical weathering and acid rain.*

## Erosion

Weathering is just one way that the surface of the Earth changes. Another way has to do with gravity. Because of gravity, water, soil and rocks are constantly tumbling down Earth's slopes, hills and mountains. This process is what we call *erosion*, another important way that the surface of the Earth changes.

We learnt about coastal erosion in South West England in Year 4.

Suppose a small pebble slides down a mountain slope, and heavy rains wash it into a stream. The pebble is carried by rushing water over a waterfall and down the mountain, where the stream empties into a river. The pebble falls to the river bottom and is pushed along by the current. It tumbles among other pebbles, rocks, sand and soil. Gradually it becomes a rounder, smoother and smaller pebble than it was when it began its journey, its sharp edges worn away by the constant rubbing against other pebbles and sand on the riverbed. As the pebble approaches the sea, it may be deposited on one of the islands at the river's delta, or swept out to sea.

Every day, this process of erosion is happening on Earth. Streams and rivers carry millions of tons of sediment – rocks, pebbles, sand and soil – from land to ocean daily. Why don't the oceans fill up with sediment? The answer is: because nature recycles.

Over millions of years, layers of sediment are squeezed into sedimentary rock on the ocean floor, which has as many mountains and valleys as the surface of the Earth above water. The deepest undersea valleys are places where the Earth's plates meet. There, sedimentary rock is pressed down into the mantle, where it melts into magma. The magma circulates under the Earth's crust and, when it finds weak spots, it shoots up lava which builds up new mountains – and the cycle begins again.

Wind can also change rock and soil on the surface of the Earth. Windblown sand, especially in desert areas, works like a sand-blaster over time, smoothing sharp rock edges or carving away softer rock on cliffs and mountainsides. Wind can carve unusual rock formations, creating caves, towers and arches.

Ice is a rock carver, too. Huge masses of ice and snow called glaciers [GLAY-see-ers] form on high mountains and in very cold regions. Glaciers are like rivers of ice that are hundreds or even thousands of years old. Even though they seem frozen solid and motionless, glaciers creep slowly downhill. Stones trapped by glaciers scrape the ground beneath them and carve grooves in the rock. Large glaciers carve out the landscape.

*Can you spot the tiny red dots to the left of the Briksdal Glacier in Norway? Those are people!*

About 10,000 years ago, the Earth emerged from an Ice Age, a period of more than a million-and-a-half years when colossal glaciers, nearly two miles thick, moved over much of what is now North America, northern Europe and northern Asia. The glaciers gouged out huge areas as they advanced and grew. At the end of the Ice Age, when the glaciers melted, the holes gouged out by the glaciers filled up with water. Today we call some of those water-filled, glacier-made holes in the north-west of England the Lake District!

## Layer upon Layer

If you were to dig a hole in the ground, going down a metre, you would see several layers of different colours of soil.

The top layer, probably darker than the rest, is the *topsoil*. Topsoil contains tiny pieces of weathered rock mixed with *humus* [HYOO-mus], or decaying matter from plants and animals. Air and water move through the tiny spaces between grains of topsoil. Plants spread broad networks of roots in the topsoil, and their roots help hold the soil down and prevent erosion. As plants die, they decay and add to the humus, which will feed future plants – another one of nature's many recycling projects.

Beneath the topsoil, the next layer down is called the *subsoil*. It is made mostly of weathered rock and clay, with very little humus. While topsoil replenishes itself every year, it takes hundreds of thousands of years for the subsoil to form. Some tree roots grow long enough to reach the subsoil.

*Can you see the roots of the grass in the topsoil, and four different colours of subsoil that are exposed?*

Under the subsoil is a layer made of solid rock, called the *bedrock*. Bedrock is far enough underground to be well protected from wind, water and freezing, and so it has not weathered into soil.

# Meteorology

## The Fascinating World of Weather

The sky darkens with threatening storm clouds. Suddenly, there's a brilliant flash – crackle – ka-BOOM! Thunder rumbles around and rattles the windows. 'It must be the angels' bowling night,' someone says, or 'That's Thor, the Viking god, in his big boots clomping across the sky.' All around the world, all through history, human beings have made up stories to explain the powerful forces that we witness as weather.

Human beings have also spent centuries making a scientific study of the weather. The study of weather is called *meteorology*, coming from a Greek word *meteoros*, meaning 'high in the air' and the suffix -ology, meaning 'study of'. The people who study weather are called *meteorologists*.

# Layers of Air

Exosphere >400 km

Thermosphere 50-400 km

Mesosphere 30-50 km

Stratosphere 10-30 km

Troposphere 0-10 km

Weather happens because our planet is wrapped in layers of air, called the Earth's atmosphere, and because the Sun is constantly bombarding the Earth with energy. Without an atmosphere, Earth would look like the Moon – a waterless, lifeless hunk of rock. Our atmosphere is constantly absorbing energy from the Sun, and that energy moves around from place to place, creating weather.

*The Earth's main atmospheric layers.*

Earth's atmosphere is made of five main layers of air: the outermost layer, the exosphere [EX-oh-sfeer]; the thermosphere [THURM-oh-sfeer]; the mesosphere [MEZ-oh-sfeer]; the stratosphere [STRAT-oh-sfeer]; and the lowest layer, which touches the surface of the Earth, the troposphere [TROH-poh-sfeer].

## The Ozone Layer

Ozone in the stratosphere absorbs ultraviolet radiation from the Sun, which in high quantities can be very harmful, even deadly, to many creatures on Earth. In the twentieth century, scientists discovered that a hole had developed in the ozone layer over Antarctica. This allowed even more unhealthy amounts of ultraviolet radiation to reach Earth. These changes mainly affected people living in the Southern Hemisphere. The further south you go, the greater the amount of harmful ultraviolet radiation you may encounter. This hole in the ozone layer was caused by some chemicals produced by humans, such as chemicals in old fridges and spray cans. In 1987 those chemicals were banned in 197 countries (the largest international agreement in history!) and since then the ozone layer has been recovering. Scientists are keeping a close eye on it and predict that it will have fully repaired itself within 50 or so years.

When you breathe, you are inhaling air from the troposphere. But clouds are also in the troposphere. Most of Earth's weather happens in the troposphere.

The stratosphere, from about 10 to 30 kilometres above the Earth, contains a tiny amount of a gas called ozone, which protects us from ultraviolet radiation, part of the energy that comes from the Sun.

The mesosphere, from 30 to 50 km above the Earth, acts as a protective shield in another way. Perhaps you have seen shooting stars streaking across the night sky. These are meteors, hunks of rock streaking through space at incredible speeds. Sometimes they come so close to Earth that they enter the atmosphere. But when they rub against air in the mesosphere, all but the largest meteors heat up so intensely that they burn to cinders before reaching Earth.

The ionosphere, the thermosphere and exosphere are the outer layers of the atmosphere. They are constantly showered by X-rays, ultraviolet radiation and electrons sent towards Earth by the Sun. So much energy from the Sun reaches these layers that temperatures climb over 2,200 degrees Celsius! That's like the inside of a furnace.

Have you ever climbed into a car that has been all closed up on a hot, sunny day? Then you know what it's like when the Sun's energy shines into a place and gets trapped inside. It gets hot!

In much the same way, the Sun's energy shines into the Earth's atmosphere. Sunlight passes through the layers of the atmosphere and warms up the land and the oceans. Some of the sunlight bounces back into the atmosphere and heats up gases in the air. The gases absorb the heat energy, holding it in the Earth's atmosphere rather than allowing it to return to space. Thanks to that process, the Earth is a comfortable place for life instead of a freezing cold planet.

## Uneven Heating

When you look at the weather maps in the newspaper or watch the weather report on TV, you can see that weather isn't the same everywhere on Earth – it isn't even the same in different cities and towns across the UK! From warm breezes and gentle rains to hurricanes, blizzards and ice storms, weather is always changing. It changes because the Earth is heated unevenly, and because heat energy moves around in the Earth's atmosphere.

The Sun doesn't shine with the same intensity on every region of Earth. It shines on the area near the Equator the most directly of all, so the air around the Equator heats up the most. It shines the least directly at the North and South Poles, so the air at the poles stays the coldest. These differences in temperature make the air in the atmosphere move around.

*Weather reporters watch high and low pressure areas to predict tomorrow's weather.*

Have you ever noticed that when you open an oven, hot air rises up on your face, but when you open a refrigerator, cold air spills down on your feet? Hot air rises and cold air sinks. As air is heated, its molecules spread out. It becomes less dense. It is lighter and puts less pressure on the Earth. When we talk about a mass of warmer, less dense air in the atmosphere, we call it a *low-pressure* air system. Cooler air contains molecules that are more densely packed together, or closer together. It puts more pressure on the Earth, and we call it a *high-pressure* air system.

Nearer to the Equator, warm, low-pressure air systems can rise, spread apart and move towards the Earth's poles. At the same time further away from the Equator, cooler, high-pressure air systems may sink and move towards the Equator in order to fill the spaces left by the rising low-pressure system. Before long, the intense heat of the Sun nearer to the Equator heats up these high-pressure systems. They in turn become the next warm, low-pressure system to rise and move away, and so the cycle continues. Cycling currents of air such as this, known as *cells*, operate at many different latitudes around the globe. This continual exchange of warm and cool air creates *wind*.

## Winds

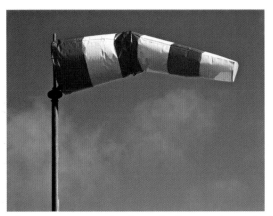

A famous poem asks, 'who has seen the wind?' No one, of course. But we certainly see what wind can do. Meteorologists have developed ways to describe wind by measuring its speed and direction. For instance, a north wind at 20 miles per hour is a wind coming from the north and moving at miles per hour.

*If you see a wind sock fluttering, it is probably a breezy day. If it is blown straight out like this one, the wind is strong and it might be a gale.*

A wind that blows 10 or 20 miles per hour is called a *breeze*. If the wind gusts up to 40 or 50 miles per hour, it is called a *gale*. If it travels 75 miles per hour or faster, it qualifies as a *hurricane*.

To measure wind speed, meteorologists use an instrument called an *anemometer*, with three arms and a cup at the end of each arm. Wind blows into the cups and makes the arms spin. By counting its spins during a certain time period, meteorologists can measure the speed of the wind.

*An anemometer measures wind speed. The faster the wind, the faster it spins.*

## Weather Patterns

Some wind patterns continue their movements almost all the time and in the same general direction. These winds are called the Earth's *prevailing winds*. They are our strongest, most persistent winds, and they shape big weather patterns. Different parts of the globe experience

We learnt about temperate and alpine climates in Year 3.

different prevailing winds. During the Age of Exploration, Christopher Columbus and other explorers and traders used the prevailing winds, also known as trade winds, to carry them back and forth across the Atlantic Ocean.

There are many other weather patterns that remain generally constant in certain areas of the world. Average temperatures, the amount of rainfall or snowfall and the average amount of moisture in the air (that is, the *humidity*), all determine the climate of every region in the world. *Climate* is the average weather pattern for a region.

Climate is influenced not only by weather patterns but also by geological patterns, such as whether the region is a large land mass or a group of islands, whether it is flat or mountainous and whether it is near a body of water. The world has many different climates. Each climate supports a different group of plants and animals and a particular kind of human community.

Tropical climates occur in places near the Equator. Temperatures stay hot and day length changes little throughout the year. Polar climates occur in places near the North and South Pole. Temperatures stay cold, even below freezing, and there is extreme variation in day length between seasons. Imagine how different the animals, plants and human habitations must be in these two climates.

*What sorts of differences would you find in a tropical climate and a polar climate?*

## Cloud Families

Clouds can look like big gingerbread men or two-headed, fire-breathing dragons or your Aunt Louise. No two clouds look just the same, but we first learnt in Year 3 that scientists sort clouds into categories, according to their shape. Identifying clouds can help you understand – and even predict – the weather.

*Cirrus* [SIH-rus] clouds ride highest in the troposphere, where the air is coldest. Made of ice crystals, they look thin and wispy.

*Cumulus* [KYOOM-yuh-lus] clouds form on sunny days when updrafts of warm, wet air rise to a cooler level. Cumulus clouds are big and puffy, and they usually mean fair weather.

*Which two different kinds of clouds can you see in this picture? At the top are feathery cirrus clouds and, down below, are big, puffy cumulus clouds.*

*Stratus* clouds look like flat sheets that can stretch out to the horizons, blocking out sunshine. One thick type of stratus cloud, called *nimbo-stratus*, often carries a lot of rain.

See pictures of each of these categories of clouds in the Year 3 book.

## When Push Comes to Shove

Air masses with different levels of humidity and different temperatures are moving constantly above the surface of the Earth. They don't always mix. Often they collide. As you can imagine, a lot of things can happen when wet, low-pressure air meets dry, high-pressure air. The boundary where one air mass meets another is called a *front*.

Sometimes a cold air mass wedges itself under a warm air mass. The boundary between them is called a *cold front*. The cold air below forces the warm air to rise swiftly. The warm air cools rapidly and its water vapour forms heavy clouds, full of precipitation. These conditions result in thunder, lightning and rainstorms, followed by bright, clear weather.

Sometimes a warm air mass overtakes a cold air mass. The boundary between them is called a *warm front*. The low-pressure mass of warm air rides up on top of the cold air and slowly pushes it out of the way. These conditions result in stratus clouds and a long, steady rain.

## Lightning and Thunder

◀ Dark, massive clouds signal the approach of one of nature's loudest and most dazzling sound and light shows: a thunderstorm. As a cold front moves through an area, especially during spring and summer, it pushes up warm, humid air. The moist air piles up higher and higher into towering, miles-high, flat-topped clouds called *cumulonimbus*.

In cumulonimbus clouds, condensed droplets quickly cool into ice crystals. Strong air currents jiggle the ice crystals up and down inside the cloud. As the ice crystals crash, bump and rub against each other, electrons loosen and jostle around as static electricity, just as they do when your socks and pyjamas tumble against each other in the clothes dryer.

*Lightning strikes over Stonehenge.*

Electrons that have been bumped loose collect in the bottom of the cloud, giving it a negative charge. That negative charge is attracted to the positive charge of the Earth that is in the ground under the cloud. Crackle! Zap! A huge amount of stored energy is released as the negative electrons rush down towards the positively-charged ground. The brilliant white flash of lightning that we see is a powerful electrical current flowing through the air.

A lightning bolt heats up the air around it so that it is five times hotter than the surface of the sun. That air expands quickly, and it violently vibrates the air all around it. Those vibrations reach our ears when we hear the thunder that so often accompanies lightning.

Light travels much faster than sound. The flash of a bolt of lightning travels to our eyes at 186,000 miles per second (which, you may remember from Year 4, is the speed of light). Sound from the same event – the clap of thunder accompanying the lightning bolt – travels only one-fifth of a mile per second.

You can use this information to make a rough estimate of how far away lightning has struck. As soon as you see a flash of lightning, count the seconds until you hear the thunder. Divide the number you reached by five, and you have the distance in miles between you and the bolt of lightning.

And yes, lightning can strike twice in the same place, especially when a building has a lightning conductor to carry the electricity safely to the ground.

## Tornadoes

The most dangerous thunderstorms are the ones that create tornadoes – whirling, funnel-shaped clouds that reach down to the surface of the Earth and suck things up. Tornadoes can be so powerful that they pick up freight trains and toss them around.

*Tornadoes are violently turning spirals of wind that are extremely dangerous.*

Meteorologists think that tornadoes are caused by the interaction of warm, humid updrafts (or swift winds moving from the Earth upwards) and cool downdrafts (swift winds moving from the sky down to Earth). They do not know exactly why the air begins to spin around and forms the funnel cloud. To find out, scientists track tornadoes and post measuring instruments in their paths. Big tornadoes are rare in Britain but they still occur.

*A tornado caused this damage in Birmingham in 2005.*

## Hurricanes

Hurricanes form over tropical oceans in areas of low pressure. Warm, moist air rises rapidly from the warm water and forms clouds. More warm, moist air rushes in to replace it. Air gets sucked up faster and faster, creating storm clouds and a tall, spiralling column of wind.

331

*During a hurricane, it is not safe to go outside. There are extremely strong winds and heavy rain that can seriously damage buildings.*

The column of wind pulls more and more moisture from the ocean, growing larger and picking up speed. The *eye* of the hurricane is the hole in the storm at the centre of the spiral. In the

*From above, a hurricane looks like a spiral of clouds, with the eye in the centre.*

eye, the air pressure is very low and the winds are, for the moment, calm.

To track hurricanes and learn more about them, meteorologists fly airborne laboratories directly into the storm. They fly in jets equipped with instruments designed to photograph and measure the storm from high above.

## Forecasting the Weather

When you wake up in the morning, do you sometimes wonder what you ought to wear – long trousers or shorts, a raincoat or a sunhat? How do you decide? Chances are, you listen to the weather forecast. It tells you how hot the day is predicted to be, whether it may rain and how low the temperature will drop after the sun goes down in the evening.

How do people forecast the weather? To predict the weather, people need both a general knowledge of weather patterns and specific information about what's happening at the present moment. A complicated network of instruments, placed all over the world – and above the world – create pictures of air masses as they move in the Earth's atmosphere. Weather balloons carry instruments high into the atmosphere. Radar equipment sends out signals that bounce off rain and ice crystals inside clouds to create pictures of clouds and measure how fast they are moving.

At least every hour, 200 weather stations around the UK record temperature, humidity, air pressure, wind speed and wind direction. Each station sends those data to the Meteorological Office, where all this information is combined into a big picture of current weather conditions. They have a scheme allowing schools to set up weather stations and join in.

Even with all this information, meteorologists can never be certain exactly what the weather will bring tomorrow. They are usually very close and thousands of people are watching to tell them when they get it wrong.

Air moves from areas of high pressure into areas of low pressure and, as it moves, the weather changes. The gauge on a *barometer* (seen here) tells whether the air where you are has high or low pressure. When the barometer is falling, it means that air pressure is getting lower. Clouds will probably move in and rain or snow may fall. When the barometer is rising, it means that air pressure is getting higher, and you can expect clear skies and less humidity.

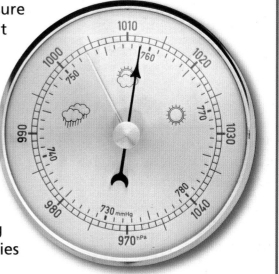

*This barometer is falling, showing that it is fair weather now but it may rain later.*

# Evolution

Do you have a pet? A hamster, a cat or a guinea pig? Maybe a dog? Does your pet have a name? Do people ever comment that your pet thinks it is human or that it takes after its owner?

Obviously, pets are different animal species and are not humans. In Year 3 we learnt how animals' babies, or *offspring*, often look a lot like their two parents, but they are not exactly alike. Each baby is unique with its own hair colour, eye colour, height and build. These are all *characteristics*. What other characteristics can you think of? There are many characteristics that a baby may share with one parent, or the other parent, or both. These can be characteristics that you see (such as the ones we mentioned) or others that you can't see, such as intelligence or speed.

When animals have offspring – like kittens, lambs or puppies – the parents and the young are from different *generations*. Grandparents, parents and children are three different generations. In Year 4 we learnt about the classification of different animals. Cats like the ones

*This cat's offspring shares many of her characteristics, but not all of them.*

you see as pets are not only mammals – they are also cats; lions are also mammals and a different type of cat. We say they are a different *species* of cat. Many, many generations and years back, these domestic cats and these lions shared a common parent. What characteristics do they share, and which characteristics are different? And where do these differences come from?

In the wild, every living thing, or *organism*, has to compete to live. Not every organism lives, and not every one has the chance to have offspring. If grandparent lions had offspring and one was able to run a lot faster than the other, that one would have better chances of outrunning its prey so that it would have more to eat. This lion would live longer than its sibling because of its characteristic of being a speedy runner. This means that this lion would probably have more offspring of its own.

The speedy lion might have offspring that inherit its characteristic of being speedy, and the offspring might also have the characteristic of having a large, strong build like their other parent. These baby lions have characteristics that would help them survive better than other lions, such as their cousins who can't run as quickly and are perhaps smaller and not as strong. The characteristics that help our lions survive will make it more likely for them to have their own offspring and pass on these characteristics to their own babies. The animals with characteristics that are not as helpful for survival will eventually, after many generations, die out. An animal that is better adapted to its habitat has more chance of survival.

Where do those characteristics come from? They happen by accident as organisms reproduce. The scientific term is *genetic mutations*. Parents pass their *genes* to their offspring,

which help determine the characteristics of the offspring. Because each young animal is slightly different from each of its parents, the make-up of its genes is a bit different. A baby lion can have fur that is the lighter colour of the mother, the darker colour of the father or a colour in between with patterns that are different – a mutation. If it helps the offspring to avoid death, then that mutation becomes more common in the next generation too. As animals *reproduce*, or have offspring, the babies become more different from their parents, and even more different from their grandparents because they share fewer genes with them.

The world is full of different species of plants and animals that have adapted to their surroundings. It takes a long time. Changes that happen by accident will only occasionally be helpful. But the world is old. The moa in New Zealand was a large, flightless bird. It had no need to fly because it was big enough to fight off anything that might kill it or steal its eggs. Mutations that prevented offspring from flying did the Moa no harm. Then people arrived in New Zealand and found a bird that was good to eat and could not fly away. They ate so many that the species died out. Moas are now extinct. There was not enough time for newer generations to evolve a means of escape.

You can see a moa in the map on page 100.

Evolution means gradual change. In biology, it is the idea that all forms of life today are descended from earlier forms. By the process of *natural selection*, changes or mutations are passed on more often if they help an organism survive better in its habitat, so it can live longer and pass the change on to more offspring. Most varieties with harmful mutations, or without the adaptations that give a real advantage, eventually die out. The enormous variety of species we see today – think of cats and lions – results from the great variety of habitats and *selection pressures* that shape the evolution of a species. As small changes happen over many generations, the differences multiply, so that living things descended from the same parents can end up being very different from each other.

# The Lives of Famous Scientists

## Charles Darwin (1809–1882)

*Charles Darwin*

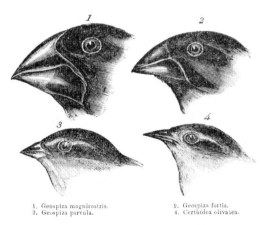

1. Geospiza magnirostris.   2. Geospiza fortis.
3. Geospiza parvula.          4. Certhidea olivaæa.

*Darwin sketched the different shapes of the finches he saw on the Galapagos Islands.*

Charles Darwin was born in Shrewsbury, where his father was a doctor. When he studied at Cambridge, he became interested in all of the different species of plants and animals that we see in nature. He wanted to understand why such variety of life existed. Aged 22, he was invited to sail to South America, working as a naturalist on the ship *HMS Beagle*. For five years he sailed the world and collected samples of rocks and animals, just as he had loved collecting shells when he was a little boy. He found many rocks containing fossils of things that had lived millions of years ago but had become extinct.

Out in the Pacific Ocean, far from the South American coast, the *Beagle* reached the Galapagos Islands. Darwin found finches and tortoises there. There were six species of finches, similar except for their beaks. Some birds had big, powerful beaks and others were thinner and sharper, but with gradual steps from thinnest to thickest like half-sizes in a shoe shop. Darwin considered whether one species from long ago had gradually separated into several different forms. He discovered that different species, each with its own characteristics, had evolved from a shared ancestor. Now they are called Darwin's finches.

Darwin explored the different islands of the Galapagos, and he found that the tortoises were gigantic, but they were not all the same. On some hot islands they had long necks for feeding on tall, spiky cactus plants. The tortoises even had a notch in their shells that let them stretch higher. On cooler islands, there was plenty of grass to eat at ground level and the tortoises had short necks. It suggested to Darwin that the tortoises had slowly adapted to suit the islands' different habitats. The different species of giant tortoises of the Galapagos all shared a common parent many generations back, but this original species of tortoise evolved to have different characteristics in the different habitats of the different islands.

When he came home, Darwin spent several years sorting out his ideas. Only when another scientist, Alfred Russel Wallace, described some similar ideas did Darwin publish his great book *On the Origin of Species by Means of Natural Selection*. 'Natural selection' was his term for the idea that animals and plants best suited to their environment are more likely to survive and reproduce. Other people call it 'survival of the fittest'. The book is central to our understanding of the theory of evolution. It took many years for people to accept the idea. Some did not like the thought that we shared common ancestors with apes.

With so many facts to support it, Darwin's theory was gradually accepted. He joined the Royal Society and was eventually honoured with a burial in Westminster Abbey, very near to Isaac Newton. *On the Origin of Species* is his most famous work but he never stopped writing, even in old age.

## Michael Faraday (1791–1867)

Many questions start out beginning with 'What would happen if...' One of the greatest 'what if' question-askers ever was Michael Faraday. This man's curiosity led him to discoveries about electricity that changed the world.

Faraday was the son of a poor English blacksmith, someone who made things from metal. Because the family was poor, Faraday didn't go to school. At age thirteen he was sent off to work as an apprentice to a bookbinder, to learn how to put books together. For years Faraday made the most of his job by reading all the books that came into the shop to be bound. He also went to

*Michael Faraday*

public lectures, where scientists would tell people about their discoveries. Whilst he did this, Faraday kept a journal of his thoughts.

At one series of lectures by the famous scientist Sir Humphry Davy, Faraday wrote down everything the speaker said and bound it up to make it into a beautiful book for Davy. Not long after, Davy injured his eyes and was temporarily blinded by an explosion in his laboratory. He needed someone to help him so he sent for Faraday and asked if he would help with experiments. In return, Faraday would be allowed to use the laboratory and equipment for his own experiments. Faraday made the most of this opportunity. This would be his lab for the next 50 years.

Faraday's most famous experiments had to do with electricity and magnetism. A Danish scientist called Øersted had found out that a magnetic compass needle would move when an electric current was sent through a nearby wire. This gave Faraday an idea. If the current could move the magnet, then maybe the magnet could move the current. He wondered, 'What if electricity and magnetism are really two examples of the same force and can be converted back and forth?'

To test this idea, Faraday set up an experiment to see if the movement of a magnet could produce an electric current. He made a coil of wire and attached it to a current detector. When he moved a magnet in and out of the coil, a current was produced. Next he attached a copper disc to wires and spun the disc between the two poles of a horseshoe magnet. This made a steady current through the wires. Faraday had built the first electrical generator, a machine that makes electricity.

*Faraday's first electrical generator*

Faraday is remembered as one of the greatest scientists ever. His discoveries gave other scientists and inventors the knowledge they needed to invent electric motors, generators, the telegraph, the telephone and just about every other electrical device we use today.

*Faraday gave many lectures to share scientific knowledge and experiments with lots of different people.*

Faraday was also one of the first scientists to think that it is important to share scientific experiments with everyone, not just other scientists. He started up the Christmas lectures for children at the Royal Institution in order to show them his experiments. Sometimes his experiments did not go as expected. Then he would say, 'The failures are just as important as the successes.' Michael Faraday was always learning, even from his failures.

Faraday's work enabled Alexander Graham Bell to invent the telephone, which we learnt about in Year 4.

## Florence Nightingale (1820–1910)

Florence Nightingale was born in 1820 into a wealthy family. So it was clear what she was expected to do when she grew up: she should marry a rich gentleman and bring up a wealthy family.

But Florence had other ideas. She loved to use her mind. She was fascinated by mathematics. When a young man asked her to marry him, she thought long and hard, and then said no. She believed that she was destined to lead another sort of life.

When she told her family that she wanted to work as a nurse in a hospital, they were shocked.

*Florence Nightingale worked tirelessly to help wounded soldiers.*

In those days, hospitals were dirty, dreary places. Wealthy people paid doctors to come to their homes to take care of anyone who was ill. Only people with little money stayed in hospitals. And that often made things worse, since most hospitals were so filthy that diseases spread faster there than anywhere else. But Florence Nightingale understood that hospitals could, and should, be kept clean. She had visited a hospital in Germany where women took excellent care of patients. The place was clean and people often became well there. She decided to devote her life to improving medical care in Britain.

In 1854, Britain went to war in a part of Eastern Europe called the Crimea (which is now part of the Ukraine). The Government asked Florence Nightingale to go with 40 other nurses and run the hospital for British soldiers. She found the hospital dirty and full of diseases, and the soldiers cold, starving and badly wounded.

Florence Nightingale worked as hard as she could to keep British soldiers from dying. She was called 'the lady with the lamp', because she worked through the night, carrying a lamp to light her way. She became famous around the world for the good work she was doing. After the war, Florence Nightingale wrote many reports with careful facts and figures to show that fewer people would die if hospitals were cleaner.

The hospitals began to do what she said they should. She also helped start a nursing school in London. She spoke out for the poor, saying that they deserved good, clean medical care. Thanks to her work and ideas, nursing is a respected profession today.

## Elizabeth Garrett Anderson (1836–1917)

Like Florence Nightingale, Elizabeth Garrett was a very determined woman who followed her dreams, even if it meant going against what was expected of women at that time. Garrett was a clever child, and her determination to become a doctor, the first female doctor to qualify in England, is what makes her stand out. Garrett paved the way for women to be able to go to university and study the same medical degrees as men.

Garrett grew up in a large family in East London and had eleven brothers and sisters. Her family wasn't very well off but her father became a prosperous businessman and sent her to a good school. She was also influenced by two very successful women.

One of these was Emily Davies, who campaigned for women to be allowed to go to school and also to university. Nowadays everyone in this country receives an education but, when Garrett was young, not

*Elizabeth Garrett Anderson*

many girls went to school. Even if they were lucky enough to go to school, young women were not allowed to go to university. Davies helped to change this, and worked to open the first college in England for women – Girton College at Cambridge University, which opened in 1869. Like Davies, Garrett wanted women to gain rights in society, and they worked together to campaign for women to be able to receive university education, to have access to more jobs and to vote for the politicians they wanted.

Elizabeth Garrett also met Elizabeth Blackwell, who was the first woman to receive a medical degree and become a doctor in the United States. Inspired by both Emily Davies and Elizabeth Blackwell, she decided that she would delay getting married and become a doctor. Only men were doctors then and Garrett's decision surprised many people. Some people were angry because they didn't think women should (or could!) become doctors.

It was very difficult for Garrett to become a doctor. Medical schools wouldn't accept women at that time, and all of her applications were rejected. She decided to go to a nursing school where she went to classes for doctors instead of the ones for nurses. However, women weren't supposed to join these classes and, when some of the male students complained, she was forced to leave the school. When Garrett learnt that the Society of Apothecaries didn't officially say in their rules that women weren't allowed, she studied hard and eventually earned a certificate allowing her to become a doctor in 1865.

Garrett then set up her first medical practice and, later, she founded St Mary's Dispensary for Women and Children in Marylebone. (A dispensary is a place that can give out medicine prescribed by a doctor.) Here she treated women and children who wanted to see a female doctor. Garrett's dispensary did very well and people thought she was a very good doctor. She became a visiting doctor at the East London Hospital, which is also where she met her future husband James Anderson.

Although Elizabeth Garrett Anderson had become a successful doctor with her medical certificate, she still wanted to earn a medical degree as male doctors did. No university in Britain would allow her in to study, even though she was a good doctor already. She found out that she could study for a medical degree at the University of Paris, so she taught herself to speak and read French and then earned her medical degree in Paris.

Elizabeth Garrett Anderson went on to open the New Hospital for Women in London (which is now named after her), and at that time she let only women work there. By challenging the medical system and fighting for women's rights, she made it easier for other women to become doctors. In 1876 the Government decided to change the law and allow women to study medicine at university and, nowadays, lots of women are doctors. She fought tirelessly for women's rights throughout her life and in 1908 became the first female mayor in England, of a town called Aldeburgh on the Suffolk coast.

# Charles Drew (1904–1950)

Charles Drew was born in Washington DC in 1904. When Drew was fifteen, his sister died of tuberculosis. As he watched her condition deteriorate, Drew wished he could do something to help. It was then that he first thought about the possibility of becoming a doctor.

There was only one problem with this idea: Drew was an African-American. In those days, much of American society was segregated, or separated, on racial lines: black people and white people went to different schools and could not sit together in restaurants or on buses. Only a handful of universities would accept African-American students – and medical school would be another hurdle beyond university. But Charles Drew managed to succeed against the odds.

In secondary school, Drew was a strong student and an outstanding athlete. Eventually he was offered a scholarship to a university called Amherst College. At Amherst, Drew was a star athlete who played American football. He could probably have become a professional athlete, but he remained interested in science and medicine. In 1928, he entered a medical school in Canada and began his lifelong study of blood.

*Charles Drew*

Earlier in this chapter you learned a little about blood and the various substances it contains. But much of what we know today was not known in the 1930s and '40s, when Charles Drew was studying blood. Doctors did know that people who lost a lot of blood could be given new blood in a procedure called a blood transfusion, but it wasn't easy to get a blood transfusion in 1940. There was no way to keep blood fresh or take it where people might need it. Charles Drew discovered that if he removed the solid cells (like red blood cells) in blood, and kept only the liquid part, called plasma, the blood could be stored for a long time. It could then be used in transfusions whenever and wherever it was needed. After making this discovery, Drew set up the first blood bank in New York City.

When the Second World War started in 1939, many people were wounded and needed blood transfusions. Charles Drew suggested sending plasma instead of whole blood. He started collecting blood, separating the plasma and shipping it safely to injured people. His work saved thousands of lives.

When America joined Britain in fighting the war, Charles Drew became the first director of the blood bank of the American Red Cross. He led efforts to collect blood for American soldiers and sailors. But the Army told the Red Cross to keep blood donated by African-American people separate from blood donated by white people. Some white people disliked black people so much that they did not want to get any 'black' blood, even if it might save their lives. Charles Drew explained that this was not right: there is no such thing as 'black' and 'white' blood: blood is blood. But no one listened. This made Drew very angry. To make his point, Drew resigned from the Red Cross in protest. The Red Cross continued to segregate blood on racial grounds throughout the Second World War, but civil rights reformers eventually persuaded the organisation to stop this racist practice.

After resigning from the Red Cross, Drew returned to Washington DC, where he taught medicine at Howard University and became famous as a surgeon. He died in 1950, after a tragic car accident.

By using his talents to help other people, Charles Drew set an example for people of all races. He proved that it is what you achieve in life, not the colour of your skin, that shows your true worth as a person.

# Suggested Resources

## Books

### General

*Ultimate Book of Science* (Oxford Children's) 2010

### Human Body

*Human Body: A Children's Encyclopedia* (Dorling Kindersley) 2012

*Little Brainwaves Investigate the Human Body* by Caroline Bingham (Dorling Kindersley) 2010

*Picture This: Human Body* by Margaret Hynes (Kingfisher) 2013

*Controlling the Blood* by Penny Preston (Franklin Watts) 2010

*Body: An Amazing Tour of Human Anatomy* by Robert Winston (Dorling Kindersley) 2005

## Geology

*Investigating Rocks* by Will Hurd (Raintree) 2009

*My Tourist Guide to the Centre of the Earth* by Lizzie Munsey (Dorling Kindersley) 2013

*Sweeping Tsunamis* by Louise Spilsbury (Raintree) 2010

*Shattering Earthquakes* by Louise Spilsbury (Raintree) 2010

## Meteorology

*Our Earth in Action: Weather* by Chris Oxlade (Franklin Watts) 2009

*The Science Behind Weather* by Darlene Stille (Raintree) 2012

## Online Resources

At-Bristol Science Centre: www.at-bristol.org.uk

Discovery Museum, Newcastle: www.twmuseums.org.uk/discovery

Glasgow Science Centre: www.glasgowsciencecentre.org

Met Office Education: http://www.metoffice.gov.uk/education

Museum of the History of Science, Oxford: www.mhs.ox.ac.uk

Natural History Museum London: www.nhm.ac.uk

Royal Institution Christmas lectures: www.richannel.org/christmas-lectures

'Invigorate, bringing science to life' at the Royal Society invigorate.royalsociety.org

Science Museum, London: www.sciencemuseum.org.uk

ThinkTank, Birmingham Science Museum: www.thinktank.ac

# Illustration and Photo Credits

Mark Beech: **2**, **3 (all)**, **7**, **8**, **47**, **48 (a, b)**, **50 (a-c)**, **52**, **56**, **57**, **59**, **60**, **61**, **62**, **63**, **64**, **65**, **66**, **67**, **68**, **195 (b)**, **196**, **197**, **200**, **201**, **202**, **302 (c)**

Jack Baumgartner: **170 (b)**

British Museum Images, © The Trustees of the British Museum: **164 (c)**, **169**

Antoine-François Callet (1741–1823), *Portrait of Louis XVI*, 1788 (oil on canvas), Musée National des Châteaux de Versailles et de Trianon / Wikimedia Commons: **136**

Thomas Chippendale, ribbon-backed chair, Victoria & Albert Museum, bequeathed by Mr C. B. O. Clarke: **155**

Paul Collicutt: **73 (a, b)**, **113**, **301**, **313**, **315 (a)**, **324**

Paul Collicutt/Gail McIntosh: **14**, **15**, **18**, **21**

John Closterman (1660-1711), *Portrait of Queen Anne (1665-1714)*, 1702 (oil on canvas), National Portrait Gallery, London, UK: **117 (b)**

John Constable (1776-1837), *The Hay Wain*, 1821 (oil on canvas), National Gallery, London, UK / The Bridgeman Art Library: **85 (c)**

Nathaniel Dance-Holland (1735–1811), *Portrait of James Cook (1728-1779)*, 1775 (oil on canvas), National Maritime Museum / Wikimedia Commons: 103

Jacques-Louis David (1748–1825), *Napoleon Crossing the Alps at Grand-Saint-Bernard*, 1800 (oil on canvas), Kunsthistorisches Museum / Wikimedia Commons: **137 (b)**

Howard Davie (1914-1944), *Illustration for Robinson Crusoe*, Private Collection, © Look and Learn / The Bridgeman Art Library: **31**

Disney Enterprises, Inc. 'Baloo, Disguised as an Ape, Dancing with King Louie' from *The Jungle Book*. © 1967 Disney: **205**

Disney Enterprises, Inc. 'Mowgli and Baloo Dancing' from *The Jungle Book*. © 1967 Disney: **203**

Ed Dovey: **116**

English Heritage: **79 (b)**

English School (20th century), *The Boston Tea Party*, Private Collection / © Look and Learn / The Bridgeman Art Library: **133 (b)**

Jean Leon Gerome Ferris (1863–1930), *Capture of the Pirate, Blackbeard, 1718*, 1920, Wikimedia Commons: **148**

Glyn Genin: **188**

Benjamin Haydon (1786–1846), *The Anti-Slavery Society Convention, 1840*, 1841 (oil on canvas), National Portrait Gallery: **142**

Robert Alexander Hillingford (1825-1904), *The Duke of Marlborough (1650-1722) Signing the Dispatch at Blenheim* (oil on canvas), Private Collection / Photo © Bonhams, London, UK / The Bridgeman Art Library: **120 (b)**

Luke Jefford: **297 (a, b)**

Luke Jefford & iStockphoto: **30**

Sir Godfrey Kneller, Bt, *John Churchill, 1st Duke of Marlborough*, National Portrait Gallery: **120 (a)**

Emma Lennard and Nigel Williams: **185**

Emanuel Leutze (1816–1868), *Washington Crossing the Delaware*, 1851 (oil on canvas), Metropolitan

Stanislaus Walery (1890-1920), *Elizabeth Garrett Anderson (1836-1917)*, Private Collection / The Stapleton Collection / The Bridgeman Art Library: **340**

John William Waterhouse (1849 - 1917), *The Lady of Shalott*, 1888 (oil on canvas), Tate. © Tate, London 2013: **10**

Antoine Watteau (1684 - 1721), *Pilgrimage to Cythera*, 1717 (oil on canvas), Louvre Museum / Wikimedia Commons: **154**

Benjamin West (1738-1820), *The Death of General Wolfe (1727-59)*, c.1771 (oil on panel), Private Collection / Phillips, Fine Art Auctioneers, New York, USA / The Bridgeman Art Library: **128**

Robert Whelan, Emma Lennard: **302 (a, b)**, **303 (a, b)**

Wikimedia Commons: **58 (a)** (photo by Ester Inbar), **58 (b)** (photo by Jan Derk), **74** (photo by Andres Rueda), **78 (a)**, **81**, **82 (b)** (photo by Martin St-Amant, CC-BY-SA-3.0), **83 (a)** (photo by Jan van der Crabben), **83 (b)** (photo by National Park Service), **83 (c)** (photo by M. Disdero), **85 (a)** (photo by Jonathan Billinger), **85 (b)**, **87 (a)** (photo by Andrew Dunn), **87 (c)** (photo by Harold John Phillips), **88 (b)** (photo by Highways Agency), **88 (c)**, **90** (photo by John Phillips), **93 (a)** (photo by Steve F. E. Cameron), **93 (b)** (photo by Michael Beckwith), **96 (a)** (photo by Johannes Püller), **96 (b)** (photo by Thomas Schoch), **97**, **98 (a)**, **98 (b)** (photo by Jacques Grießmayer), **99 (a)** (photo by David Iliff, CC-BY-SA 3.0), **99 (b)** (photo by Stefan Kraft), **101 (a)** (photo by Sonya & Jason Hills), **101 (b)**, **102 (a)** (photo by Jon-Eric Melsæter), **105** (illustration by François Godefroy), **107** (photo by Muhammad Mahdi Karim), **109** (photo by Ahmed Al Badawy), **112**, **113** (photo by Michal Osmenda), **115** (painting by Said Tahsine), **117 (a)**, **119 (b)**, **121**, **122** (painting by Sir Godfrey Kneller), **124** (painting by John Pettie), **125** (painting by David Morier), **126 (a)**, **129**, **130**, **131**, **132** (photo by Steve Evans), **133 (a)** (engraved and printed by Paul Revere), **137 (a)** (painting by William Hamilton), **141** (courtesy of the British Museum), **143**, **144** (from the British Cartoon Collection), **145**, **146** (engraving and print by William Hogarth / Samuel Davenport), **152 (a)** (photo by Bernard Gagnon), **156 (a, b)**, **158** (designed by Marcel Breuer), **163 (a, b)**, **164 (b)**, **165** (photo by Andreas Praefcke), **166** (photo by Kevin Eng), **167 (all)**, **168 (a)** (from Jacques Hnizdovsky), **168 (b)** (photo by Stephanie Chan), **170 (a)**, **171 (b)** (engraved by William Hogarth), **172** (engraved by William Hogarth), **173** (etched by Rembrandt), **174** (woodblock print by Katsushika Hokusai), **175** (print by Henri de Toulouse-Lautrec), **187 (a)** (photo by The City of Vancouver), **190**, **191 (a)**, **195 (a)**, **243**, **256**, **265**, **289 (a)**, **290 (c)**, **294 (b)** (photo by Patrick J. Lynch), **294 (c)**, **295** (from the National Cancer Institute), **299 (a-f)**, **305** (photo by Ken Bosma), **307**, **316 (b)**, **317 (a)** (image by Gunnar Ries), **318 (b)** (photo by Samuel Wernain), **319 (b)** (photo by T. Ermer), **320** (photo by Luis Miguel Bugallo Sánchez), **321** (photo by Nino Barbieri), **322**, **323**, **328 (a)** (photo by Robert Young), **329**, **331 (b)**, **332 (b)**, **336 (a)** (painting by George Richmond), **336 (b)** (illustration by John Gould), **338 (a)**, **342** (from the U.S. National Archives and Records Administration)

John Wootton (1682–1764), *King George II at the Battle of Dettingen, with the Duke of Cumberland and Robert, 4th Earl of Holderness, 27 June 1743* (oil on canvas), National Army Museum / Wikimedia Commons: **123 (b)**

# Text Credits and Sources

## Poems

'The Rhinoceros' by Ogden Nash. Used with permission from Carlton Books.

'Dreams' from Collected Poems of Langston Hughes (Vintage) by Langston Huges. © The Estate of Langston Hughes. Used with permission from David Higham Associates.

# Index